THE ART OF ENGLISH

General Editor A. Dora Gough, B.A. (Hons.)

A General Course for Secondary Schools
by
ROGER MANSFIELD

4

There is an art of reading as well as an
art of thinking and an art of writing,
Isaac D'Israeli

Illustrated by Tom Wanless

SCHOFIELD & SIMS LTD HUDDERSFIELD

First printed 1967
Reprinted 1968
Reprinted 1969
Reprinted (Twice) 1970
Revised and Reprinted 1971
Reprinted (Twice) 1972
Reprinted 1973
Reprinted 1974
Reprinted 1975
Reprinted 1976

Printed in England by Netherwood Dalton & Co. Ltd.

Bound in Scotland

ACKNOWLEDGMENTS

The author and publishers wish to thank the following for permission to include the copyright material listed below:

Routledge & Kegan Paul Ltd., for an extract from *Grandad with Snails* by Michael Baldwin.

The Literary Executors of the Dylan Thomas Estate and J. M. Dent & Sons Ltd., for the poem *Schoolmaster* from *Quite Early One Morning* by Dylan Thomas and an extract from *A Visit to Grandpa's* from *Portrait of the Artist as a Young Dog* by Dylan Thomas.

The London Association for the Teaching of English for the poems *Crazes* by Maureen Fallon, *And When You are Young* by Elizabeth Read, *The Oldest Member of My Family* by P. R. Edwards, *Watching Television* by Jacqueline Archer, and *The Closing of the Forge* by Charles Fyson, from *And When You are Young, Prose and Verse by Young Writers, 5-18*.

The Guardian, for an extract from *The N.S.P.C.C. in Need* by Terry Colman.

David Higham Associates Ltd., for extracts from *The Day of the Triffids* by John Wyndham, and *There is a Happy Land* by Keith Waterhouse, Michael Joseph, and for the poems *Aunts Watching Television* from *Collected Poems of John Pudney*, Putnam, and *My Friend Malony* by Charles Causley from *Johnny Hallelujah*, Rupert Hart-Davis.

Curtis Brown Ltd. and Michael Joseph Ltd., for an extract from *Brothers In Law* by Henry Cecil.

Scorpion Press, for the poem *Bedtime Story* from *The Broken Places* by George MacBeth.

Damon Runyon Jr., for an extract from *A Piece of Pie* by Damon Runyon.

The Hogarth Press Ltd., for an extract from *The Wall* from *Fireman Flower* by William Sansom.

Christopher Logue, c/o Peter Janson-Smith Ltd., for his poem *Good Taste*.

The poem *The Horse* by Christine Arscott is taken from 1st *Poets in the Classroom*, and *Dreams* by Jacqueline Dewar, *Loneliness* by Photini Tryforos, *All the Fun of the Fair* by Janet Hughes and *The Blacksmith* by Lindsay Flaxman from 2nd *Poets in the Classroom*, both books edited by Laza Sheridan. The books are anthologies of poems written by London School children for the Broadsheet-London Schools' Drama Association, Poetry Writing Projects. The first book, now out of print, was published by the London Schools' Drama Association, the 2nd *Poets in the Classroom* is published by the Premier Press Ltd., 30 Osborn Street, London, E.1.

William Heinemann Ltd., for an extract from *The Long and the Short and the Tall* by Willis Hall.

Mr. Harold Owen and Chatto & Windus Ltd., for the poem *The Dead-Beat* from *The Collected Poems of Wilfred Owen*, edited by C. Day Lewis.

Hamish Hamilton, London, for fables from *Vintage Thurber* by James Thurber, copyright © 1963.

Gordon Gridley, for his poem *The Hero*.

The South-East Regional Examinations Board for the Certificate of Secondary Education, for extracts from an oral examination paper.

Her Majesty's Stationery Office, for material from *The Annual Abstract of Statistics No. 103*, 1966, and *Britain: An Official Handbook*, 1966. Also for permission to reproduce *Poster P.E.5, Parliamentary Election—Directions for the Guidance of the Voters in Voting*.

Laurence Pollinger Ltd., for extracts from *Shot Actress-Full Story* from *Twenty Tales* by H. E. Bates, Jonathan Cape, and *The Coldest Winter Since* 1854 by William Saroyan from *Little Children*, Faber.

Johathan Cape Ltd., for the poem *Headline History* from *Collected Poems* by William Plomer, and an extract from *The Kitchen* by Arnold Wesker.

Miss E. A. Wolf, for the poem *The British Journalist* from *The Uncelestial City* by Humbert Wolf, published by Gollancz.

ACKNOWLEDGMENTS

Chatto & Windlus Ltd., for an extract from *The Uses of Literacy* by Richard Hoggart.

Penguin Books Ltd., for extracts from *Thinking to Some Purpose* by Susan Stebbing, *Crime* in a *Changing Society* by Howard Jones, *The English Penal System* by Winifred Elkin, and *Hanged by the Neck* by Arthur Koestler and C. H. Rolph.

The Institute of Practitioners in Advertising, for material from their 1966 *National Readership Survey*.

Faber and Faber Ltd., for extracts from the play *A Resounding Tinkle* by N. F. Simpson.

Dobson Books Ltd., for the poem *Scorflufus* from *A Dustbin of Milligan* by Spike Milligan.

Harold Matson Company, Inc., for an extract from *The Prize of Peril* by Robert Sheckley, reprinted by permission. Copyright © 1958 by Mercury Press, Inc. Copyright assigned 1959 to Robert Sheckley.

City Lights Books, for the poem *Breakfast* by Jacques Prévert, translated by Lawrence Ferlinghetti, reprinted by permission. Copyright © 1947 by Les Editions du Point du Jour.

Imperial Chemical Industries Ltd., for part of an article originally published in the November 1955 issue of *ICI Magazine*.

Miss Sonia Brownell and Secker & Warburg Ltd., for an extract from *Animal Farm* by George Orwell.

W. H. Allen & Company, for an extract from *The Loneliness of the Long Distance Runner* by Alan Sillitoe.

Hutchinson & Co. (Publishers) Ltd., for an extract from *The Courage of His Convictions* by T. Parker and R. Allerton.

Wilfred De'Ath, for an extract from a BBC interview entitled *Just Me and Nobody Else*, printed in *The Listener*.

A. D. Peters & Co., for an extract from *The Pedestrian* from *The Golden Apples of the Sun* by Ray Bradbury.

The Essex Music Group for the poem *Little Boxes* by Malvina Reynolds.

Longmans, Green & Co. Ltd., for an extract from *The Hidden Persuaders* by Vance Packard.

J. M. Dent & Sons Ltd., for the poem *Lather as You Go* by Ogden Nash from *Collected Verse from 1929 On.*

H. J. Heinz Company Limited, for material from a television advertisement scenario.

The Marvell Press, for the poem *Toads* by Philip Larkin from *The Less Deceived*, reprinted by permission.

The Observer, London, for text and diagram material from *The Observer Weekend Review*.

University of Chicago Press, for the poem *The Picnic* from *Ghosts of the Heart* by John Logan, reproduced by permission. © 1960 by the University of Chicago.

And the following for permission to reproduce copyright photographs:
Radio Times Hulton Picture Library, pages 24, 105.
J. Allan Cash, page 61.
The Imperial War Museum, page 78.
Paul Popper Ltd., page 202.

AUTHOR'S NOTE

THE ART OF ENGLISH is a five year English series for secondary schools, comprising two complete but closely integrated courses. The "General English Course" is designed for the less academic pupils in comprehensive and modern schools. The "Certificate English Course" is suitable for those pupils in grammar, comprehensive and modern schools who aim at an Ordinary Level Certificate in English Language. The two courses are planned on a common basis, and the obvious similarities in topics and layout can be readily appreciated by pupils as well as teacher. Transfer from one course to another is greatly facilitated, and both courses cover work for the Certificate of Secondary Education, though the approaches naturally differ.

Although the "General Course" covers the requirements of the various Certificate of Secondary Education examinations, its main aim has been to present English not so much as a separate subject, but as a means of understanding and broadening experience. For this reason, the activities suggested are an integral part of the course, showing the relationship of English not only to other areas of the school curriculum but to many aspects of everyday life.

Together, the Certificate and the General English Courses form the basis for a complete English syllabus for secondary schools.

BOOKS FOUR AND FIVE

These two books follow the same general pattern as the first three in the series, but there are a number of modifications which make them particularly suitable for young people in their last years at school.

The work is still based upon extracts from good, modern books that pupils will enjoy reading in full at this stage; the fact that many of these books have since been chosen for C.S.E. reading lists is a reliable indication of their suitability, although, of course, there are extracts from other books which are well outside the scope of such examinations. Furthermore, the extracts themselves are now even longer and more effective as a stimulus to discussion, writing and further reading. There are also more poems, accompanied by questions, than in previous books. To enable the teacher to select for written work those questions that he feels are most appropriate to the needs of his particular class, the questions following the extracts are no longer divided into separate sections for discussion and for written answers.

The "Method Exercises" have been replaced by a "Techniques" section, which is divided into two parts. The first deals with the various uses of language and covers not only the techniques that are commonly examined—analysis of advertisements, comparison of reports, how authors gain their effects, comprehension, etc.—but many other aspects of the written and spoken word. The second part deals with the accepted conventions of correct English—vocabulary, punctuation, paragraphing, simple grammatical constructions, etc. Obviously this is not a rigid division, but it is hoped that the teacher will find it convenient when selecting the work that is most relevant for his pupils.

At this stage, the suggestions under "Oral Work" and "Activities and Research" not only link English work with other subjects and the outside world, but can also provide a basis for C.S.E. Orals and Projects.

Since senior pupils are less concerned with reading books of a certain type (e.g. ghost stories, war stories, Westerns, biographies, etc.) and are more aware of style and treatment, the "Further Reading" section at the end of each chapter now usually recommends other books by the author of the extract, rather than a variety of books by different authors on the chapter theme.

Roger Mansfield.

CONTENTS

The contents of each chapter are arranged in the following order.

1. Passage.
2. Appreciation and Discussion.
3. Poem
4. Discussing the Poem. } (when included)
5. Techniques.
6. Topics for Written Work and Pupil's Work.
7. Oral Work.
8. Activities and Research.
9. Further Reading.

Michael, aged seven, lives in his grandparents' house, the back garden of which has a wall at the bottom, leading to an alley.

CHAPTER 1 # Story from Childhood

One day I sat talking to myself in the garden. I had two armies, one in the pile of stones and one in the grass. I could see the army in the grass advancing, and my lips were booming the guns.

"Got any snails?" said a voice.

I looked up. A clean boy, with a jacket on, stood on top of the wall that was the edge of the town. He was very smart for the alley. Generally I did not answer people from there. But he looked all right. I was not supposed to speak to boys without jackets; nor to the family without shoes down the road.

"Snails?" I asked. Then, as he climbed over the wall, "Be careful of the rhubarb."

"Rhubarb! My father's got fifty cabbages!" He kicked round the plants. "Yes: I can see you've got plenty. Half a mo: I'll be back with my bucket." And he was gone again. I heard his footsteps slap down the alley.

I went back to my battle. There was smoke all over the garden.

"Where are they, then?"

I looked up, feeling cross. He was already climbing the wall, with a creaking bucket. He wore sandals. I had always wanted sandals.

"Haven't you got me any?"

I went on with my game.

After a time I grew intrigued to hear the bucket creaking round and round the garden. He kept on talking to himself too, saying things like: "Yes, I thought so . . . I thought so . . . there's another one . . . that's worth a pretty penny . . ." just like a grown-up.

I went and watched him. He had a pile of snails in the bucket. "That's stealing," I said.

"What—snails? People kill snails."

"That's what my dad does," I said. "And Boss, and Nan. And Aunt Rene!" And I killed one with a stone.

"Spoil sport," he said.

"Who's that, Michael?" asked my grandmother's voice from the back door.

The boy got ready to run.

"It's only Nan," I said. Fancy anyone being afraid of Nan. Everyone knew she was kind.

"Yeah!" he mocked.

"Only me, Nan," I called out. The garden was very quiet. It was my first big lie.

"Come on then," he said. "Let's go." And he went over the wall.

I caught at the big sharp flints and struggled after him. It was hard to get up; but the alley was near on the other side. Wully the cat was coming along with a dead bird in his mouth like a ripe plum. I always found myself seeing things. We ran down the alley.

The world was much larger, flint walls, and mud, and edges of grass, as we ran past all the back gardens in a row. We came out at the green-grocer's where Nan took me to buy vegetables. The boy ran across the road. "Come on," he called.

I had never crossed a road before, but I went, wondering which was the way home. He opened a gate by a shop and we ran down a path. "Here they are," he said.

There were two tea-chests in the garden, joined by pieces of wood. He lifted the lids of the tea-chests, and I saw them—hundreds of snails, hundreds, eyes on horns, eyes going into horns, bodies going into houses, shells of all sorts of colours, black, brown, grey, mottled ones and striped ones. They were sticking to the floor, the walls, the lid, and to one another, in great bunches like conkers. They were wonderful.

He put back the lids, and then took a snail from his pocket. It was snow-white. "Whitewash," he explained. Then he brought out a hand-ful of pink ones. I gasped. "The house," he said. I saw the house was painted pink, and that there were ladders and pots by the wall, and I understood him.

"You and me," he said.

"When?" I asked.

"Always," he said. Then he picked up the bucket and called out, "C'mon." We went carefully through his father's fifty cabbages, leaf by leaf. We turned wood by the wall; we kicked over bricks and stones. Everywhere we went there were snails. We talked to them, kissed their shells, and put them in the bucket.

"C'mon," he said again. And we went out of the gate.

Once more I crossed the road, and once more went up the alley, which was now full of people. They called their words, but we had things to do. Over the wall we went, and into the rhubarb. The garden was wet and smelled of elderberry and cat.

"Where've you been?" called Nan.

"Hiding," I lied.

She came out and hooded her eyes in the sun. It was too much for them and she went in. We were poachers and the great adventure of the snails went on.

It went on for weeks. We collected them and their babies by the bucketful. His father would kill them among the weeds, so they were our secret. We prowled around one anothers' houses with them in our hands and pushed them down the backs of chairs so they would be comfortable. Sometimes we put them in the salad for a laugh, so the women would scream, and we could eat all the family's lettuce. Sometimes we put them in our pockets and sat on them; but we tried to treat them kindly, because we loved them.

One day we raced our snails on the table where his father sold trousers. I had watched through a door while his father stood with a measure round his neck and chalk in his hands, talking to men with creases: I had watched the blinds drawn up and the cloth folded, and his father go in to tea. Then we pulled the table from the shop into the yard, and started our races. The table was leathery green and the snails moved along it unrolling silver slime. We raced them in twos and fours. A face stood at my shoulder.

Then another, breathing over my head.

Then another.

The *boys* had got in!

One put his hand on a snail and pulled it, plop, from the table. It was Beauty!

He held it high in the air while my partner grabbed at it. Then he bent down and scooped its shell in some sand. Beauty bubbled through the sand and the sand wriggled. We grabbed again. He held us off, and the shell snapped between his thumb and finger. He wiped it off on my partner's coat.

We started to cry.

They did not run in a hurry: they jeered until they heard footsteps. Then they walked through the gate and slammed it shut.

His mother stood beside us.

We went on crying—but all she saw was the table covered with lines and the box of snails.

I knew it was the end, even if his father did not find out. She had told us off before, about him wrapping snails in his handkerchief and spoiling the wash. Last night he had taken some to bed with him and rolled on them. It was our last chance.

He went on crying.

He was doing well. His mother was holding his head; and I was wiping the table. Then his dad came out.

She was on our side, but his dad told us off about pockets, and cabbages, and spoiling the garden. It was no use her winking. She did not stop him, even when he said, "At once!"

"Get rid of them, *at once*," he said. And they both went in.

My partner stopped crying the minute they went. He kicked at the table. Then he kicked a flowerpot smash against a wall.

"Upstairs," he said.

I looked at him, trying to know what he meant. With his red face I never knew. I did what he said because he seemed to know, to have done things before like my family had.

We picked up the smallest box and took it up through the shop, up the wooden stairs where his father kept shoes, with leather for laces, and bottles, and coloured ties.

Up in the attic we tipped them on to the dusty floor. The sticky ones we stuck on the walls.

"I'll know they're here," he said. He kissed one and wrapped it up in some cloth that had the white lines men wear for trousers.

We went downstairs for the other box.

His father's fifty cabbages stood like trees for a battle. We dropped all the snails into the slots of the cabbages and thought of them living there. We had one or two left.

"These are no good," he said.

So we killed them . . . .

When I went home I sat listening to stories, and wanted to say about the snails. But I couldn't. I wanted to do my own story, so I could nod, and hum, and look in the air, and cough by the fire, until they asked what my story was.

Then I should tell them.

(from *Grandad with Snails* by Michael Baldwin)

APPRECIATION AND DISCUSSION

(In Books 4 and 5 there will be no division of questions into those for discussion and those for written answers. Answer in writing, those questions selected by your teacher. Remember that your answers should normally be in complete sentences).

1. What sort of people frequented the alley?
2. Why was Michael "not supposed to speak to boys without jackets; nor to the family without shoes"? What, do you imagine, was Michael's home like?
3. Why would the boy's bucket have creaked?
4. Explain what the author meant by "the world (*outside the garden*) was much larger".
5. Did Michael have any reason for lying to Nan when she asked him who was in the garden and, later, where he had been?
6. What did the father of Michael's friend do for a living?
7. What can you deduce about the boys who spoilt the snail race? Were they older or younger than the two friends? Where might they have come from?
8. What did the narrator mean when he said that his friend "was doing well" when he cried in front of his mother?
9. "We tried to treat them kindly, because we loved them." Were the two boys genuinely concerned about the snails? Try to define how they would have felt about them, drawing upon evidence in the passage, from the memory of your own attitudes in childhood, and from your observation of young children.
10. Why did Michael feel that he couldn't tell his family about the snails? Why did he want to do so?
11. Did you, as a child, ever play games that would have seemed pointless or irritating to adults?
12. Because children's thoughts turn rapidly from one thing to another, this account includes details that appear to be irrelevant, or illogically placed. Can you find examples of this in the passage? Have you any other comments to make about the style in which the passage is written?

13

Schoolmaster

Oh yes, I remember him well, the boy you are searching for:
he looked like most boys, no better, brighter, or more respectful;
he cribbed, mitched, spilt ink, rattled his desk and
garbled his lessons with the worst of them;
he could smudge, hedge, smirk, wriggle, wince,
whimper, blarney, badger, blush, deceive, be
devious, stammer, improvise, assume
offended dignity or righteous indignation as though to the manner born;
sullenly and reluctantly he drilled, for some small
crime, under Sergeant Bird, so wittily nicknamed
Oiseau, on Wednesday half-holidays,
appeared regularly in detention classes,
hid in the cloakroom during algebra,
was, when a newcomer, thrown into the bushes of the
Lower Playground by bigger boys,
and threw newcomers into the bushes of the Lower
Playground when *he* was a bigger boy;
he scuffled at prayers,
he interpolated, smugly, the time-honoured wrong
irreverent words into the morning hymns,
he helped to damage the headmaster's rhubarb,
was thirty-third in trigonometry,
and, as might be expected, edited the School Magazine.

Dylan Thomas

DISCUSSING THE POEM

1. Who, do you think, was recalling these memories of the boy?
2. Explain what is meant by the verbs "cribbed", "mitched", "hedged", and "blarney".
3. In what sort of situations would the boy have assumed "offended dignity or righteous indignation"?
4. Why was Sergeant Bird nicknamed "Oiseau"? Do you think this was witty?

5. What did the older boys do to the younger boys when they first arrived at the school? How can you tell that this was something of a tradition? Are there any "traditions" similar to this at your school?
6. "While shepherds washed their socks by night" is one example of "wrong irreverent words" that can be sung to a hymn. (To which hymn would these words be sung?) Can you give any other examples of words and phrases that the boy might have interpolated?
7. What is implied by the phrase "as might be expected" before "edited the School Magazine" in the last line?
8. Pick out the alliteration in the poem. Can you find any examples of onomatopoeia?
9. How many of the comments about this boy could be applied to you?

TECHNIQUES

The Use of Language, and Style

1. *Sentence Structure.* Most of the extract from "Grandad With Snails" is written in short, jerky sentences and uses the simple vocabulary of a small boy, in order to evoke through its style, as well as its content, the atmosphere of childhood.

Do you think this technique has been successful?

Combine the short sentences in each of these groups into one well-constructed sentence. (Avoid the excessive use of "and", "but" and "then".)

e.g. Then we pulled the table from the shop into the yard, and started our races. The table was leathery green. The snails moved along it unrolling silver slime. We raced them in twos and fours.

The snails unrolled silver slime as we raced them, in twos and fours, along the leathery green table that we had pulled from the shop into the yard before starting our game.

(*a*) He opened the box and took out a marble. It was bright red.
(*b*) We finished our game. After that I went to the library. I wanted to borrow a book.
(*c*) The boy next door is my friend. He has been my friend for three years. He will be leaving school at the end of this term. He has not yet got a job.

15

(*d*) We walked through the wood. We walked until we reached a small stream. In this stream we saw several fish. We also saw an eel. It was a large eel.

(*e*) He was like most other boys. He cribbed his homework. He spilt ink. He rattled his desk. He garbled his lessons.

How many grammatically incomplete sentences can you find in the passage? Consider where they have been used and say what effect they give.

2. *Similes and Metaphors.* (i) Study this simile from the passage:
" . . . a dead bird in his mouth like a ripe plum".

What two things are being compared? In how many respects are these two things similar? Would the simile be clearer if the words were arranged in a different order? How many other similes can you find in the passage?

Complete the similes below by adding original comparisons.

(*a*) The setting sun was like ———.

(*b*) The silence was as soft and silky as ———.

(*c*) The jagged mountain peaks were like ———.

(*d*) My father's voice was as rough as ———.

(*e*) The slime left by the snail was like ———.

(ii) After considering the example from the passage, complete the sentences below as metaphors, by selecting the most vivid but exact word from those in brackets. Then use words of your own choice.

"the snails moved along *unrolling* silver slime"

(*a*) The aeroplane ——— a vapour-trail across the sky. (made smeared left)

(*b*) The words ——— slowly from his lips. (dripped came gushed)

(*c*) Small, bright ——— began to appear in the black sky. (stars holes bulbs)

(*d*) The ——— of light ——— through the darkness. (finger beam ray jabbed went shone)

(*e*) Gradually the twisting ——— of fog ——— the flickering lights. (clouds layers tentacles obscured strangled covered)

3. *Ambiguity.* "He kissed one and wrapped it up in some cloth that had the white lines men wear for trousers."

This sentence, taken from the passage, is ambiguous. One meaning it could have is quite nonsensical, since men do not wear white lines for trousers. (Do you think the author intentionally made this mistake and, if so, why?). Rewrite the sentence so that its proper meaning is quite clear.

Now correct the mistakes in the following sentences.

(*a*) Everybody will go into the school playground and pick up the rubbish, including the teachers.

(*b*) I collected the snails from the rhubarb patch where they lived on Sunday.

(*c*) Did you see that interesting programme about the snail on your television?

(*d*) Several birds used to nest in those trees but they were all killed by the hungry cats and boys from next door.

(*e*) The thrush picked up the snail and after breaking the shell on a large stone, consumed it.

4. *Paragraphing Direct Speech.* Study the way in which this extract has been paragraphed, particularly the direct speech. How would you re-arrange it to make it conform to the paragraphing plan that you have been taught for direct speech? (The extract from "The Day of the Triffids" in the next chapter follows these rules fairly closely.) What other alterations would you make?

5. *Plurals and Apostrophes.* (i) Give the plural form of the following words:

alley　　story　　box　　cloth　　handkerchief　　leaf　　child.

(ii) What is the difference between the italicised words in the sentences below?

(*a*) The *boys* were punished.

(*b*) The *boy's* to be punished.

(*c*) The *boy's* punishment was severe.

(*d*) The *boys'* punishment was severe.

(*e*) The *families* without any money are to leave.

(*f*) The *family's* without any money.

(*g*) The *family's* money has been stolen.

(*h*) The *families'* money has been stolen.

TOPICS FOR WRITTEN WORK

In Books 2 and 3 a distinction was made between two types of writing—
Objective (*Practical*) and **Emotive** (*Creative*). This, however, is a very
broad distinction; and there is a considerable overlap. Even within the
two categories there are many different styles, and for each piece of
writing it is necessary to select the style most appropriate to the subject
and the intention. For example, "A Piece of Pie" (Chapter 3) and "A Visit
to Grandpa's" (Chapter 7) may both be termed "creative" writing, but
the situations with which they are concerned are quite different, as are
their styles. Both "Visit to Grandpa's" and "There is a Happy Land"
(Chapter 11) are about childhood, but their styles are still very different,
because the authors wished to create different effects. Similar differences
exist within "objective" writing. Imagine working from a set of cake-mix
instructions expressed in similar terms to a legal document: "In order
that the purchaser of this product Patent No. 673129 and hereinafter
referred to as 'Fluffy Doh-Doh' may cause the said 'Fluffy Doh-Doh' to
be used in accordance with the intention of the manufacturers . . . "!

In Book 4 you will not usually be told whether the topics for written
work should be treated objectively or emotively. Decide for yourself
which approach is the more suitable and then try to adopt a style of
writing which helps to create the particular effect you want to achieve,
e.g. a "slangy", conversational style, or a rich, poetic style, etc.

1. "The memories of childhood have no order and no end" wrote Dylan
   Thomas. Delve into your own memories of early childhood and recall
   one adventure, one day, one pastime or one incident involving a
   particular friend around which you can build a short story.

Hints

Although the memory may be confused, try to give your account of it
some order and shape. Arrange it in paragraphs and search for an
interesting opening and conclusion. You could either try to imitate
Michael Baldwin's style and make it seem as though a child is telling the
story, or use a more formal, straightforward style such as an adult,
recalling his childhood, would employ. In any case, include similes,
metaphors and alliteration, and vary the length and structure of your
sentences.

2. Give an account of an average child's development up to the age of
   seven.

Hints

Use reference books, and also ask your mother for information about this subject. You could divide your essay by dealing with one year in each paragraph; or you could deal with one aspect of development, e.g. teeth, speech, movement, in each paragraph.

3. Describe in detail a number of children's games.

Hints

You may base your description either on personal experience, or use reference books such as "The Lore and Language of Schoolchildren", I. & P. Opie, (O.U.P.)

(See "Activities and Research" No. 1)

Pupils' Work

Crazes

"Salt, mustard, vinegar, pepper . . ." and the skipping season has started.

It is usually a sweltering afternoon. The sun beating mercilessly down upon her glistening brow, the stranger witnesses the start of the season. It is in such a clime that the skipping fanatics begin to chant their mournful dirge, first skipping and then running to take their place once more.

This infatuation goes on until the days grow shorter and bleaker. Then it is the knitting phase.

The ardent skippers sit in frozen huddles and gossip, their breath condensing in the December air. The stranger looks at them, their agile fingers blue with cold, and her cosy radiator and woolly clothing grow warmer.

When the snow begins to melt and the hoar frost to thaw, the knitters play "jacks". They are clad in the fruits of their winter's labour. These are, however, of little avail, for the cruel March winds play havoc with their hair and penetrate their woolly pullovers. The eyewitness sniffs and edges closer to the fire.

As the days grow warmer and spring buds appear on the trees, the leap-frog craze becomes evident. Exhilarated shrieks of excitement grow more intense as the width of "backs" to leap grows wider and the hurrying and scuffling of "Pass Ball" begins.

The onlooker relectantly emerges from her Winter hibernation and sits, still in gloves and muffler, to watch their sport in a sheltered alcove.

The mercury rises and the onlooker sheds her warmer garment. She sits, peaceful in the silence. Then, out of the summer's intense heat, she hears, uncertainly at first, but steadily increasing in volume, the familiar chant: "January, February, March . . . ."

Maureen Fallon

And When you are Young

. . . And when you are young you play. On the important morning when you can do all your buttons up and hold the spoon at breakfast, a new life begins. Run, run, run everywhere, push, and scream and pull and laugh and shout at your neighbour. It is hot—so hot that when you place your feet on the tiles they leave misty imprints and your knees smell salty when you hug them, and because it is summer you go to bed while it is still day and wear a cotton nightdress.

Summer, all the smells and sounds associated with the season, the hot crumbly earth in little ridges where the tractor has been; the clack-clack-clack of the cream machine; the buzzing of flies round the cattle; the bed of chrysanthemums in the back garden, and the sweet smell of the ripe fruit in the bowl on the dresser. Life is important and good, and each moment is lived for the next; the haystack is full of mice and the bruise on your leg has turned green—there is so much to do and yet so little time.

And the smell of the corn!—it is a dry, pungent smell which is everywhere, and as the tractor travels round the fields, the flying seeds become caught in your hair. "Evening supper" is mentioned again, above you, and one always stays up for this; when the harvest is gathered in, and the workers come over to the farm and play the piano and make speeches, and everyone is laughing. You simply must do a handstand against the wall, and another one, partly because the blood rushing to your cheeks adds to the excitement, and partly because a younger friend is in sight, and she cannot do handstands.

The new sense of quietness and peace accompanies the evening hours, and now the sky is a deep blue, while the clouds are mere wisps, tinged with pink, moving and twisting at the edges. People are running past, the tractor stopped hours ago, and is standing in the yard, with the steel framework shining in the light. Singing and music are throbbing in the air and in your head, and suddenly, you realize that harvest can only be like this and that this is a perfect sacrifice; and as you tremble at the surprising intensity of your feelings, you stare up unexpectedly at the sky, to see a flight of ducks silently streak across the sun and disappear gradually beyond the horizon.

Elizabeth Read

ORAL WORK

1. Practise reading aloud this extract from "The Guardian". (Imagine that you are making an appeal for donations to the N.S.P.C.C.) Vary your reading as much as possible: make the emotional parts of the passage really forceful; adopt a relaxed, "chatty" style for other parts; deal crisply and briefly with details that could otherwise become boring to a listener.

Last year (1965) the N.S.P.C.C. helped 120,805 children. It is a voluntary organisation and it is desperately short of money. It badly wants to open a new research department—last year it had to move from its old head-quarters in Leicester Square to new offices—and now it has an overdraft at the bank. So it is launching an appeal for £250,000 to put it on its feet.

The pity is that most of the society's work is unknown. Only the atrocious cases get in the papers. One reads about Patrick who was kept for five years in a hen coop, who when he was found at the age of seven could only jump about like a frog and imitate hen noises; about the girl whose body was so infested with sores that she had to be anaesthetised before she could be moved from her filthy bed; and about the 18-month-old child who was tied naked to a chair in a freezing cold room.

But the greater part of the society's work is not with such outright in-humanity. In a way the word cruelty in the title is misleading, and so is the traditional picture of the "cruelty" man rescuing maimed children from end-of-the-century slums. Children are still rescued, but of the 120,000 children helped last year only 9,632 had been assaulted. The rest had just been neglected . . . .

The public cannot be said to be entirely ignorant of this work, or alto-gether apathetic, but animals seem to attract more sympathy. In the last year for which there are figures the N.S.P.C.C. received £317,967 in legacies, a sum which is not quite half the £684,667 bequeathed in the same time to the R.S.P.C.A.

The R.S.P.C.A. are a bit unhappy when anyone makes this comparison, but it is no reflection on them that people prefer to leave their money to cats and dogs. Probably all it means is that most people think child cruelty is the State's business.

Relations between the two societies have always been friendly. Indeed the beginnings of the N.S.P.C.C. owe something to a legal fiction accepted by a New York court that a child was a young animal.

It happened like this. In the 1870's a missionary in New York came across a child called Mary Ellen who was cruelly beaten by her father. Police told her they could do nothing, that animals but not children were protected by the law.

So she went to the New York Society for the Prevention of Cruelty to Animals, whose inspectors rescued the child and carried her, wrapped in a horse blanket, before a judge, who jailed her parents.

A New York S.P.C.C. was formed, and in 1882, the first English S.P.C.C. was started in Liverpool, based on the American model.

Today there is no need to resort to legal fiction. But every now and again an N.S.P.C.C. inspector finds a child in distress, wraps it in a blanket, and takes it off to hospital. Child welfare may be the State's business, but it is also the business of anyone else who will help. There are some families who can never have too much help. (From *The Guardian*, Feb. 19th, 1966).

21

2. Each of these statements about the above extract is true, false, or un-known (i.e. one cannot deduce it for certain from the passage). Say which is correct in each case, and explain to the rest of the class how you arrive at your answer. When two people have different answers, which they both think are correct, open the question to class discussion.

(a) At the time of writing, the N.S.P.C.C. had not opened its new research department.

(b) The new offices of the Society are not in Leicester Square.

(c) The word "cruelty" in the Society's title is misleading because there are no longer any cases of cruelty.

(d) Less than 12% of the children helped by the N.S.P.C.C. in 1965 had been assaulted.

(e) Other children helped (not those assaulted) were all cases of neglect.

(f) The R.S.P.C.A. were left half as much again as the N.S.P.C.C. (in people's wills) in the last year for which figures were available.

(g) The writer was certain that most people assumed the State should deal with cruelty to children.

(h) The writer thought it likely that most people assumed cruelty to animals was not the State's business.

(i) In the 1870's, in New York, the law protected animals, but not children, from cruelty.

(j) The first society for preventing cruelty to children was started in New York.

(k) The first English society for the prevention of cruelty to children was not started for ten years after the New York society.

(l) A "legal fiction" (as used in the passage) is a story book that the law permits to be published.

(m) In Britain, at the time of writing, the government and local auth-orities undertake child welfare.

(n) The writer believed that State help meant there was no further need for the N.S.P.C.C.

3. Hold a class discussion on points raised by the extract and then go on to discuss the following topics:

(a) the amount of money given to child welfare and animal organisa-tions respectively;

(b) the way some children are neglected because both parents are out at work;

(c) parents today do not discipline their children enough;

(d) points on which parents often fail to understand their children as they grow up;

(*e*) the sort of recreational facilities that are most appropriate for children of various age groups.
4. Prepare a short talk on an organisation that helps children in need. (See "Activities and Research" No. 2.) Or give a talk on the childhood of a famous man or woman. (See "Activities and Research" No. 4.)

ACTIVITIES AND RESEARCH

1. Compile a book about children's games. Some of the essays which have been written could be included. You might like to extend the book to cover games played by children in other countries.
2. Find out about the work of an organisation that helps children in need. Collect facts, figures and case-histories. Articles or advertisements in the Press, and entries in reference books will provide information, or you could write a short business letter to the secretary at the head office of your chosen organisation, asking for information. Here are some possible societies for your research:
the N.S.P.C.C.; Dr. Barnado's Homes; U.N.I.C.E.F.; Save the Children Fund; the Children's Aid Society; the Shaftesbury Homes.
3. Invite an old-age pensioner to talk to your class about his or her childhood. Ask about social conditions, the school-leaving age, discipline, the interests of young people, fashions, the cost of living, etc., when he was young. Compare this picture with that of today.
4. Using sources such as "Who's Who", the "Dictionary of National Biography", the *Great Lives* volume of the "Oxford Junior Encyclopaedia" and other reference books or individual biographies, find out about the childhood of one or more well known men and women, past and present. Compare your findings. For instance, how many of the men and women showed early promise and how many gave no sign of their talents until later in life?

23

FURTHER READING

Grandad with Snails by Michael Baldwin (Routledge and Kegan Paul; Hutchinson Unicorn edition).

This autobiographical story of childhood covers Michael's colourful career between the years of seven and nine. While living in Grandad's house he takes part in many delinquent escapades—he gathers snails, forms his own gang, ties up the neighbours' door-knockers, and so on. Then he is suddenly evacuated to the country, where "Silky" initiates him into the delights of poaching, catching bad-tempered goats, and growing whiskers. One day, after Michael has returned home, Grandad dies, and the boy realises, with a shock, that he has grown up.

In Step with a Goat (Hodder and Stoughton).

This is an autobiographical account of the author's years in the Territorial Army. It is interesting to compare his obvious love of army life with the sentiments expressed in his poem *After the Bang* (from *Death on a Live Wire*, published by Longmans). The book is very lively and humorous and, although difficult in parts, certainly worth trying.

It is probably better if you wait a year or so before trying Michael Baldwin's other books, which, at this stage, you will almost certainly find too difficult. But keep the following two titles in mind for later reading.

Sebastian and Other Voices (Secker and Warburg).

One critic describes this collection of stories as "beefiness and beeriness, soldiering on an upset stomach". The backgrounds to the stories and their unsavoury characters include bomb sites and demolition areas, holiday beaches, a sectarian hall, and the "school treat".

Miraclejack (Secker and Warburg).

Bertram Swale, failed novelist and unreformed drunk, becomes deeply involved with Sym, the Miraclejack, a man who can scale the outside of any building with almost miraculous ease. It is a violent, fast moving, and complex novel.

CHAPTER 2

If . . . . .

A sudden disaster has blinded almost the entire population of the world. One night Bill Masen and Josella Playton, two survivors in London, see a light on top of the University Tower. The following morning, on going to investigate, they find outside the gates a large crowd of blind people whose sighted leader is shouting to a man inside.

He spat with contempt, and raised a long, oratorical arm.
"Out there," he said, waving his hand towards London at large, "—out there there are thousands of poor devils only wanting someone to show them how to get the food that's there for the taking—. And you could do it. All you've got to do is *show* them. But do you? Do you? No, what you do is shut yourselves in here and let them bloody well starve when each one of you could keep hundreds alive by doing no more than coming out and *showing* the poor devils where to get the grub. God almighty, aren't you people human?"

The man's voice was violent. He had a case to put, and he was putting it passionately. I felt Josella's hand unconsciously clutching my arm, and I put my hands over hers. The man on the far side of the gate said something that was inaudible where we stood.

"How long?" shouted the man on our side. "How in hell would I know how long the food's going to last? What I do know is that if bastards like you don't muck in and help, there ain't going to be many left alive by the time they come to clear this bloody mess up." He stood glaring for a moment. "Fact of it is, you're scared—scared to show 'em where the food is. And why? Because the more these poor devils get to eat, the less there's going to be for your lot. That's the way of it, isn't it? That's the truth—if you had the guts to admit it."

Again we failed to hear the answer of the other man, but, whatever it was, it did nothing to mollify the speaker. He stared back grimly through the bars for a moment. Then he said: "All right—if that's the way you want it!"

He made a lightning snatch between the bars, and caught the other's arm. In one swift movement he dragged it through, and twisted it. He grabbed the hand of a blind man standing beside him, and clamped it on the arm.

"Hang on there, mate," he said, and jumped towards the main fastening of the gates.

The man inside recovered from his first surprise. He struck wildly through the bars behind him with his other hand. A chance swipe took the blind man in the face. It made him give a yell, and tighten his grip. The leader of the crowd was wrenching at the gate fastening. At that moment a rifle cracked. The bullet pinged against the railings, and whirred off on a ricochet. The leader checked suddenly, undecided. Behind him there was an outbreak of curses, and a scream or two. The crowd swayed back and forth as though uncertain whether to run or to charge the gates. The decision was made for them by those in the courtyard. I saw a youngish-looking man tuck something under his arm, and I dropped down, pulling Josella with me as the clatter of a sub-machine-gun began.

It was obvious that the shooting was deliberately high; nevertheless, the rattle of it and the whizz of glancing bullets was alarming. One short burst was enough to settle the matter. When we raised our heads the crowd had lost entity and its components were groping their ways to safer parts in all three possible directions. The leader paused only to shout something unintelligible, then he turned away, too. He made his way northwards up Malet Street, doing his best to rally his following behind him.

I sat where we were, and looked at Josella. She looked thoughtfully back at me, and then down at the ground before her. It was some minutes before either of us spoke.

"Well?" I asked, at last.

She raised her head to look across the road, and then at the last stragglers from the crowd pathetically fumbling their ways.

"He was right," she said. "You know he was right, don't you?"

I nodded.

"Yes, he was right . . . And yet he was quite wrong, too. You see, there is no 'they' to come to clear up this mess—I'm quite sure of that now. It won't be cleared up. We could do as he says. We *could* show some, though only some, of these people where there is food. We could do that for a few days, maybe for a few weeks, but after that—what?"

"It seems so awful, so callous . . ."

"If we face it squarely, there's a simple choice," I said. "Either we can set out to save what can be saved from the wreck—and that has to include ourselves: or we can devote ourselves to stretching the lives of

27

these people a little longer. That is the most objective view I can take." ...

She nodded slowly.

"Put like that, there doesn't seem to be much choice, does there? And even if we could save a few, which are we going to choose?—and who are *we* to choose?—and how long could we do it, anyway?"

"There's nothing easy about this," I said. "I've no idea what proportion of semi-disabled persons it may be possible for us to support when we come to the end of handy supplies, but I don't imagine it could be very high."

"You've made up your mind," she said, glancing at me.

There might or might not have been a tinge of disapproval in her voice.

"My dear," I said. "I don't like this any more than you do. I've put the alternatives baldly before you. Do we help those who have survived the catastrophe to rebuild some kind of life?—or do we make a moral gesture which, on the face of it, can scarcely be more than a gesture? The people across the road there evidently intend to survive."

(from *The Day of the Triffids* by John Wyndham)

APPRECIATION AND DISCUSSION

1. What were the main arguments for and against helping all the people who had been blinded?
2. What was the major flaw, the false assumption, in the argument put forward by the leader of the blind mob?
3. Do you think the people in the University building refused to help the blind mob find food because they were afraid there would then be less for themselves?
4. How would the blind people have felt (*a*) as they listened to their leader arguing with the man behind the gate (*b*) when those in the courtyard opened fire on them (*c*) after the incident?
5. Was the leader of the blind mob justified in using force to try and make those in the University building do as he wanted?
6. Would the people in the University building have been justified in shooting to kill, had the blind mob not been dispersed by the first few rounds which were aimed high?
7. What would you have done if you had been one of the few sighted people left after the disaster? Would you have tried to look after a group of blind people or would you have joined a sighted group

such as the one in the University building? What would your reasons be for taking this course of action?

8. What would you have done if you had been blinded?

9. Assuming that you and other sighted people set to work to organise a community that would survive and develop despite the catastrophe, what sort of site would you choose and what sort of supplies and equipment would you take? Consider the dangers that would have to be faced, and give reasons for the choice you make.

10. What proportion of blind people could be included in such a community? What sort of blind people would you recruit (or would you not discriminate)? What jobs could they do?

11. Remembering that social needs and conditions would be very different from those in our present society, say what changes might have to take place in the laws relating to marriage, crime, education, government and the distribution of wealth.

12. "The Day of the Triffids" is set in the early 21st century and one of the developments that have taken place is the breeding of "triffids" (grotesque, walking plants with a lethal sting). These were easily controlled while humans were able to see, but after the catastrophe they became a great menace.

What aspects of present-day life could become very dangerous if people lost their sense of (a) hearing (b) smell (c) touch (d) taste? Consider not only the immediate dangers but those that would arise indirectly. What changes would have to be made?

Long long ago when the world was a wild place
Planted with bushes and peopled by apes, our
Mission Brigade was at work in the jungle.
      Hard by the Congo

Once, when a foraging detail was active
Scouting for green-fly, it came on a grey man, the
Last living man, in the branch of a baobab
      Stalking a monkey.

Earlier men had disposed of, for pleasure,
Creatures whose names we scarcely remember—
Zebra, rhinoceros, elephants, wart-hog,
      Lion, rats, deer. But

After the wars had extinguished the cities
Only the wild ones were left, half-naked
Near the Equator: and here was the last one,
      Starved for a monkey.

By then the Mission Brigade had encountered
Hundreds of such men: and their procedure,
History tells us, was only to feed them:
      Find them and feed them;

Those were the orders. And this was the last one.
Nobody knew that he was, but he was. Mud
Caked on his flat grey flanks. He was crouched, half-
      Armed with a shaved spear

Glinting beneath broad leaves. When their jaws cut
Swathes through the bark and he saw fine teeth shine,
Round eyes roll round and forked arms waver
      Huge as the rough trunks

Over his head, he was frightened. Our workers
Marched through the Congo before he was born, but
This was the first time perhaps that he'd seen one.
      Staring in hot still

Silence, he crouched there: then jumped. With a long swing
Down from his branch, he had angled his spear too
Quickly, before they could hold him, and hurled it
      Hard at the soldier

Leading the detail. How could he know Queen's
Orders were only to help him? The soldier
Winced when the tipped spear pricked him. Unsheathing his
        Sting was a reflex.

Later the Queen was informed. There were no more
Men. An impetuous soldier had killed off,
Purely by chance, the penultimate primate.
        When she was certain,

Squadrons of workers were fanned through the Congo
Detailed to bring back the man's picked bones to be
Sealed in the archives in amber. I'm quite sure
        Nobody found them

After the most industrious search, though.
Where had the bones gone? Over the earth, dear,
Ground by the teeth of the termites, blown by the
        Wind, like the dodo's.

George MacBeth.

DISCUSSING THE POEM

1. This poem is set in the future, when termites have taken over the world from men. A giant ant is telling a "bedtime story" to its young. What details in the poem would have enabled you to deduce these points?
2. The ant said that the world in the past (i.e., as we know it now) was "planted with bushes". What do you surmise, from this phrase, about the plant life of the ants' world?
3. Who was the giant ant referring to when it said that the world had been "peopled by apes"?
4. What is a baobab?
5. How had Man been destroyed? Why were the few remaining humans to be found near the Equator?
6. How did the ants regard Man's past activities? What was their attitude to the few remaining humans?
7. Do the ants seem in any way more civilized than we are at present? For what reasons might the ant have referred to the world in the past as "a wild place"? (After all, our civilization is very advanced.)

31

TECHNIQUES

The Use of Language, and Style

1. *Logical Thinking.* Facts: Since they are blind, most people will never be able to fend for themselves. They can be supported for only a short time by the few who have survived the disaster. No outside assistance is available.

Deduction: To attempt to save the majority of the population would be a waste of valuable resources (supplies, manpower, etc.). Those fitted to survive should therefore concentrate all their energies upon saving themselves, otherwise nobody is likely to survive.

Accepting that the original information is correct, the above is an example of logical thinking. Comment on the logic and accuracy of the following deductions.

(a) Facts: I have two pieces of metal which I intend to bolt together. In each of them I have drilled a hole 4 mm in diameter. The only bolt I have is 5 mm in diameter.

Deduction: The bolt is too large for the holes and to solve the problem I must get a smaller bolt.

(b) Facts: Two years ago a Space Age Washing Machine cost £100. One year ago the price was increased by 20%. This year the price has been reduced by 20%.

Deduction: One year ago the price rose to £120. Now, however, a Space Age Washing Machine costs the same as it did two years ago.

(c) Fact: The first question often asked by murderers when they are arrested is, "Will I be hanged?".

Deduction: Murderers are afraid of the death penalty. Capital punishment is therefore an effective deterrent.

(d) Facts: According to one superstition, walking under a ladder will bring bad luck. Twenty five out of the thirty people in my class walked around, instead of under, a builder's ladder propped against the school hall, which is being repaired.

Deduction: Most of the people in my class are superstitious, and would also believe in the superstition that if a black cat crosses your path, it will bring good luck.

(e) Facts: Road casualty figures for the town of Brumpool—deaths 25; serious injuries 120; minor injuries 510. 64% of the deaths, 65% of the serious injuries and 80% of the minor injuries occurred on roads where there was a speed limit of 50 km/h.'

Deduction: There is more chance of accidents occuring on roads where there is a 50 km/h speed limit. This speed limit is of no value and should be abolished.

Write out correct deductions for the above.

2. *Alliteration and Onomatopoeia.* (i) Pick out examples of alliteration in the poem. It is rarely extended, but is, nevertheless very effective.

e.g. "the world was a wild place"

Make up sentences, containing alliteration, to describe:

(*a*) cold, drizzling rain (*b*) fresh, glistening snow (*c*) the noise of a jet aircraft (*d*) a bulldozer at work (*e*) a boat on a stormy sea.

(ii) Consider these onomatopoeic words used by John Wyndham.

"a rifle *cracked*"

"The bullet *pinged* against the railings, and *whirred* off"

"the *clatter* of a sub-machine gun"

"the *rattle* of it and the *whizz* of glancing bullets"

How effective is his use of onomatopoeia in the above descriptions? Replace the italicised words with others of your own choice.

Make up sentences, containing onomatopoeia, to describe the items listed in part (i) of this exercise. If you wish, you may invent words to convey the sounds and impressions.

e.g. The *wishy* rain *splittered* unceasingly against the window.

Correct English, and Vocabulary

3. *Dictionary Work and Parts of Speech.* (i) Give the dictionary definition of each italicised word, as it is used in the passage. To help you, the part of speech for each word, when used in this sense, has also been given in italics.

the food's going to *last* v.i.	(ii) (a.)
one *swift* movement a.	(n.)
a *blind* man a.	(n.)
on the *arm* n. from O.E.	(v.t. Latin derivation)
tighten his *grip* n.	(v.t.)
one short *burst* n.	(v.t. or v.i.)
he was *right* a.	(v.t. or v.i.)
if we *face* it v.t.	(n.)
the most *objective* view a.	(n.)
a *moral* gesture a.	(n.)

(ii) Now give the dictionary definition of each of the above words when it is used as the part of speech given in brackets. Use five of the words, with these meanings, in complete sentences.

4. *Etymology.* An etymological dictionary gives the origins of words as well as their meanings.

e.g. bicycle *n*. vehicle with two wheels, propelled by the rider (Latin *bi*-, two, and Greek *kyklos*, wheel).

The main part of the word, *kyklos,* to which the prefix *bi*— is added, is called the root. When new words are added to the English language, they are frequently still made from Latin or Greek root-words.

(*a*) Four other names suggested for the triffids when they were first discovered were:

trichots   tricusps   tridentates   tripeds.

The prefix, *tri*—, (from the Latin *tres*, or Greek *treis*, three) was used in each case because the plants moved along on an "active, three-pronged root".

Find out the root-word in each of the four names given above. (Look up: dichotomy; cusp; dental; biped.)

(*b*) The language derivations of words are normally abbreviated.

e.g.   L = Latin   G = Greek

What abbreviations does your dictionary give for the following languages?

Arabic   Celtic   Danish   Dutch   German   Hebrew
Italian   Old English (Anglo-Saxon)   Persian   Spanish

Use your dictionary to find three English words derived from each of the above sources.

(*c*) Give the meaning of the following Latin and Greek prefixes, all of which have frequently been used to build up English words. For each one, find three English words that incorporate it.

Latin		Greek	
ex-	trans-	anti-	micro-
extra-	sub-	auto-	poly-
inter-	super-	hypo-	tele-

(*d*) From what Latin or Greek root-words have these recent additions to the English language been made?

cosmonaut   aerosol   automation   stereophonic   megaton

(*e*) Other words are often formed by combining or adapting existing English words.

e.g.   hovercraft   panel-game   to tape

Find five more words of this kind.

(*f*) Some words enter the language first as slang, and then become permanent, accepted additions.

e.g.   Second World War terms — blitz   quisling   spiv
Post-war terms — beatnik   brainwashing   teenager

List terms that have been coined recently, discuss how likely these are to become permanent parts of our language, and attempt dictionary definitions of some of them.

5. *Paragraphing and Punctuation of Direct Speech.* This passage follows fairly closely the rules you have been given for paragraphing and punctuating direct speech. When you have written out correctly the two shortened extracts below, check them with the original. (Cuts are indicated thus . . .)

(*a*) Paragraph, and insert quotation marks.

He spoke with contempt and raised a long oratorical arm. Out there, he said,—out there there are thousands of poor devils only wanting someone to show them how to get the food that's there for the taking . . .   God almighty, aren't you people human? The man's voice was violent. He had a case to put, and he was putting it passionately.

(*b*) Paragraph, and insert quotation marks and capital letters.

i sat where we were, and looked at josella . . . it was some minutes before either of us spoke. well? i asked, at last. she raised her head to look across the road, and then at the last stragglers from the crowd pathetically fumbling their ways. he was right, she said. you know he was right, don't you? I nodded.

TOPICS FOR WRITTEN WORK

1. Choose any one of the possibilities listed under "Oral Work" No. 1, and use it as the basis for a science fiction short story.

Hints

Jot down all the points that arose from class discussion of the possibility you have chosen, and work out your plot bearing these in mind. Who will you have as your central characters? Will the story be narrated by one of these, as in "The Day of the Triffids"? What would be the most effective stage at which to begin your story: before the possibility had become a reality; with the emergence of the problem; or after the problem had been in existence for some time? Do not forget to include in your story the changes brought about within society, e.g. the way in which government, marriage, crime, etc., would be affected. See how some of these points have been treated in the short story "The Demonstrators" in the "Pupils' Work" section.

2. Write a poem about the world as you imagine it would be if mankind were to be destroyed.

Hints

What could have destroyed mankind? Which form of life, do you think, would take over the world? Would it be plants or animals? How might human civilization be remembered by the new, dominant life-form? How would other animals and plants be affected? Study the construction of "Bedtime Story", and the techniques used by George MacBeth, before you begin your poem. Where appropriate, use alliteration and onomatopoeia, and invent words.

3. Combine your answers to Questions 9, 10, 11 in the "Appreciation and Discussion" section into an essay.

Hints

Do not make this into a story. Set out under headings all the points you are considering, e.g. Site, Supplies, Size of Community. After stating your views, give logical reasons to support them.

ORAL WORK

1. Discuss how mankind in general, and our society in particular, would be affected *IF*:
   (*a*) all the world's seas rose by 50 metres
   (*b*) we could be kept alive for ever, although old and infirm
   (*c*) we could be kept permanently young
   (*d*) we learnt to communicate telepathically
   (*e*) machines could be organised to do all the work for us
   (*f*) we reached an uninhabited planet that could support human life
   (*g*) the world became seriously overpopulated
   (*h*) some terrible plant disease destroyed nearly all our crops
   (*i*) all forms of animal life, except humans, were destroyed.

The above points could all be discussed by the class as a whole, or the class could divide into nine groups, each taking one point, and report its conclusions through a spokesman.

2. What major scientific advances, do you think, will be made in the next twenty years? Wherever possible quote recent investigations and discoveries reported in newspapers and magazines. For example, one newspaper reported that in 1966 "a Professor Suda in Japan successfully reanimated a cat's brain after it had been kept for six months in a deep freezer". This could indicate that we are approaching the stage where humans can be kept alive for an indefinite period; someone could be put in a deep freezer and brought back to life fifty years later, without having aged at all.

3. Act or mime the way in which different people would have reacted when they woke up to find that they were blind. What would they have said? Where would they have gone? What would they have done when they finally realised that there was nobody to look after them or cure them?

4. Read aloud the extract from "The Day of the Triffids". This could be done either by one person, or by groups of three (one person taking the part of the narrator, another the leader of the blind mob, and the third the part of Josella). Make your reading as dramatic as you can. Others in the class can provide background noises, such as the shouting of the crowd and the noise of the machine gun.

5. Through class discussion, distinguish between dead and living languages. Give examples of dead languages, consider how important they are in the world today, and say whether you think they should still be studied at school and university. Can a knowledge of Ancient Greek, for example, help one to understand English more easily? Why are plants and animals given Latin names? Discuss also some of the additions made to the English language in the last ten years and consider their significance.

Pupil's Work

The following short story investigates how society might be affected if people no longer had to work.

The Demonstrators

To a stranger from the previous century, particularly the depression years of the 1930's and 1970's, a crowd of people, such as these, marching with their posters, would not have been an uncommon sight. If he had glanced at the posters they would have seemed very familiar. These people were marching on London over the shortage of work. Posters like "Strike Now—More Work", "Reintroduction of Overtime" or "Longer Hours" were dotted amongst the crowd like boats on a sea. But there was a vast difference between this and past workers' demonstrations. Ever since the Revolution of Automation, seventeen years before, working hours for men and women had been cut more and more. The Revolution had begun officially in the South, when the giant computer X32L was completed, and had spread its tentacles over the country in a matter of months. London had become the nucleus of automation, with its moving pavements, and roads, lifts and all types of independent automatic machines in the shops and offices. By 2035 the old face of London had almost completely disappeared; only Big Ben, St. Paul's and the Houses of Parliament remained. London had become a gigantic area of automated sky-scrapers and towering office-blocks, every one of which completely overshadowed the decaying G.P.O. building built in the 1960's.

At first, people had been delighted to do less work for the same money, but gradually their three-day week had become a two, then a one-day week. When work was abolished completely, people began to realise that the machines, hideous, efficient and blank, were not only taking over their jobs but ruling their whole lives. They began to go back to work in order to preserve their self-respect and their sanity. Having to create jobs for people caused difficulties, and so the Government charged a fee for the privilege of going to work. Rates soon became exorbitant. People neglected their homes and families, mortgaged their houses and pawned their clothes in order to find enough money to buy a job.

When the Employment Societies decided to increase their interest rates to 29%, it was the last straw for many people. A crowd formed in a street in Newcastle and quite spontaneously marched, angrily determined, towards London. Even a small mob cannot march without being noticed, of course. Reports were flashed to London. First they were thought to be exaggerated but later reports showed that, if anything, the earlier ones had been understatements. As soon as it became clear that the mob meant business, desperate attempts to turn them back were made. All moving pavements and other forms of transport were immobilized. It made no difference. Traffic control machines and alien blockade units were adapted and sent to deal with the crowd. These were overcome easily and the now vicious crowd moved on to the outskirts of London.

It was on the seventh day of their march that the mob reached North London. Desperate attempts were made to pacify them, but the now near-frienzied mob paid little heed. As the crowd moved, so they smashed and destroyed, burnt and plundered. All attempts to stop them proved futile as they moved on to the heart of London. They were determined to get what they had come for—the abolition of automation and free work for all. At long last the head of the mob came to Westminster. The Houses of Parliament were surrounded by a thick belt of tranquilizer gas. The crowd halted for a moment and the Prime Minister appeared overhead in a magnetic hovercraft, amid a chorus of jeers and boos. After a while they stopped and listened. The P.M. refused to *ban* automation, but he said he would cut down the amount of it. The crowd began to listen more closely.

He went on to say that free work would be reintroduced. The crowd began to calm. He had won them over.

Most of the crowd went to Battersea Park and burnt all their posters in a gigantic bonfire, and quietly began the march home. They had won. They had got what they came for. They were happy.

But the Prime Minister was not at all satisfied. He wrote in his diary that night: "Where will today's concessions end? There is only one logical outcome. The people will demand to be *paid* for working. The economy of the country will be ruined."

Alan Hinton

1. Find out about blind people and the organisations that exist to help them. What is braille? What is involved in training a guide dog? What sort of jobs can blind people do? Is there any way in which you could assist an organisation that is concerned with the blind? What are the causes of blindness? Can any forms of blindness be cured?
2. Many modern science fiction writers, such as John Wyndham, are concerned with the question of what society *might* be like under new circumstances. A number of older works of literature have also explored the same idea. Find out about Sir Thomas More's "Utopia" and Samuel Butler's "Erewhon". (The "Oxford Companion to English Literature" will give you quite a lot of useful information.) Decide whether books like "Robinson Crusoe" and "The Swiss Family Robinson" also come into the same category.
3. A film has been made of "The Day of the Triffids". See it if you have the chance, and compare it with the book.

FURTHER READING

The Day of the Triffids by John Wyndham (Michael Joseph; Penguin).
Although always exciting, John Wyndham's science fiction novels are much more than straightforward adventure stories, for they also analyse attitudes and customs to be found in society today. The normal situation is in some way disturbed—in this case, by a disaster which blinds all but a few people, and by the presence of the triffids, dangerous walking plants. We are then shown how well conventional values stand up to the stresses imposed by the new situation.
The Kraken Wakes (Michael Joseph; Penguin).
This is a story of conflict between Mankind and an alien form of life living in the deepest parts of the world's oceans. The almost imperceptible beginnings of the conflict, and the terrifying consequences demonstrate how easily misunderstanding and fear can lead to extreme violence. Although you may find parts of the story, which is told by a script writer, a little slow, the detail is always convincing.
The Midwich Cuckoos and *The Crysalids*
Two more science fiction novels by John Wyndham which are also very exciting and interesting.

CHAPTER 3 **A Curious Contest**

*When Nicely-Nicely Jones is unable to take part in the
great eating contest, arranged for him by his friends on
Broadway, against Joel Duffle from Boston, his place is
taken by a Miss Violette Shumberger.*

T his Joel Duffle suggests that the contest consist of twelve courses
of strictly American food, each side to be allowed to pick six
dishes, doing the picking in rotation, and specifying the weight
and quantity of the course selected to any amount the contestant making
the pick desires, and each course is to be divided for eating exactly in
half, and after Miss Violette Shumberger and Nicely-Nicely whisper
together a while, they say the terms are quite satisfactory . . . .

Well, Mindy is the official starter, and at 8-30 p.m. sharp, when there
is still much betting among the spectators, he outs with his watch, and
says like this:

"Are you ready, Boston? Are you ready, New York?"

Miss Violette Shumberger and Joel Duffle both nod their heads, and
Mindy says commence, and the contest is on, with Joel Duffle getting the
jump at once on the celery and olives and nuts.

It is apparent that this Joel Duffle is one of these rough-and-tumble
eaters that you can hear quite a distance off, especially on clams and
soups. He is also an eyebrow eater, an eater whose eyebrows go up as
high as the part in his hair as he eats, and this type of eater is undoubtedly
very efficient.

In fact, the way Joel Duffle goes through the groceries down to the
turkey causes the Broadway spectators some uneasiness, and they are
whispering to each other that they only wish the old Nicely-Nicely is in
there. But personally, I like the way Miss Violette Shumberger eats
without undue excitement, and with great zest. She cannot keep close
to Joel Duffle in the matter of speed in the early stages of the contest, as
she seems to enjoy chewing her food, but I observe that as it goes along
she pulls up on him, and I figure this is not because she is stepping up
her pace, but because he is slowing down.

When the turkey finally comes on, and is split in two halves right down
the middle, Miss Violette Shumberger looks greatly disappointed, and
she speaks for the first time as follows:

40

"Why," she says, "where is the stuffing?"

Well, it seems that nobody mentions any stuffing for the turkey to the chef, so he does not make any stuffing, and Miss Violette Shumberger's disappointment is so plain to be seen that the confidence of the Boston characters is somewhat shaken. They can see that a Judy who can pack away as much fodder as Miss Violette Shumberger has to date, and then beef for stuffing, is really quite an eater.

In fact, Joel Duffle looks quite startled when he observes Miss Violette Shumberger's disappointment, and he gazes at her with great respect as she disposes of her share of the turkey, and the mashed potatoes, and one thing and another in such a manner that she moves up on the pumpkin pie on dead even terms with him. In fact, there is little to choose between them at this point, although the judge from Baltimore is calling the attention of other judges to a turkey leg that claims Miss Violette Shumberger does not clean as neatly as Joel Duffle does his, but the other judges dismiss this as a technicality.

Then the waiters bring on the pumpkin pie, and it is without doubt quite a large pie, and in fact it is about the size of a manhole cover, and I can see that Joel Duffle is observing this pie with a strange expression on his face, although to tell the truth I do not care for the expression on Miss Violette Shumberger's face either.

Well, the pie is cut in two dead centre, and one half is placed before Miss Violette Shumberger and the other half before Joel Duffle, and he does not take more than two bites before I see him loosen his waistband and take a big swig of water, and thinks I to myself, he is now down to a slow walk, and the pie will decide the whole heat, and I am only wishing I am able to wager a little more dough on Miss Violette Shumberger. But about this moment, and before she as much as touches her pie, all of a sudden Violette turns her head and motions to Nicely-Nicely to approach her, and as he approaches, she whispers in his ear.

Now at this, the Boston character by the name of Conway jumps up and claims a foul and several other Boston characters join him in this claim, and so does Joel Duffle, although afterwards even the Boston characters admit that Joel Duffle is no gentleman to make such a claim against a lady.

Well, there is some confusion over this, and the judges hold a conference, and they rule that there is certainly no foul in the actual eating that they can see, because Miss Violette Shumberger does not touch her pie so far.

But they say that whether it is a foul otherwise all depends on whether

Miss Violette Shumberger is requesting advice on the contest from Nicely-Nicely and the judge from Providence, R.I., wishes to know if Nicely-Nicely will kindly relate what passes between him and Violette so they may make a decision.

"Why," Nicely-Nicely says, "all she asks me is can I get her another piece of pie when she finishes the one in front of her."

Now at this, Joel Duffle throws down his knife, and pushes back his plate with all but two bites of his pie left on it, and says to the Boston characters like this:

"Gentlemen," he says, "I am licked. I cannot eat another mouthful. You must admit I put up a game battle, but," he says, "it is useless for me to go on against this Judy who is asking for more pie before she even starts on what is before her. I am almost dying as it is, and I do not wish to destroy myself in a hopeless effort. Gentlemen," he says, "she is not human." ...

Well, in the meantime, after the excitement subsides, and wagers are settled, we take Miss Violette Shumberger to the main floor in Mindy's for a midnight snack, and when she speaks of her wonderful triumph, she is disposed to give much credit to Nicely-Nicely Jones.

"You see," Violette says, "what I really whisper to him is that I am a goner. I whisper to him that I cannot possibly take one bite of the pie if my life depends on it, and if he has any bets down to try and hedge them off as quickly as possible.

"I fear," she says, "that Nicely-Nicely will be greatly disappointed in my showing, but I have a confession to make to him when he gets out of the hospital. I forget about the contest," Violette says, "and eat my regular dinner of pig's knuckles and sauerkraut an hour before the contest starts and," she says, "I have no doubt this tends to affect my form somewhat. So," she says, "I owe everything to Nicely-Nicely's quick thinking."

(from *A Piece of Pie* by Damon Runyon)

APPRECIATION AND DISCUSSION

1. Broadway is a street in which American city?
2. What is meant by "strictly American food"? Why was this limitation imposed?
3. What did the first course consist of? What other foods are mentioned in the passage?
4. Plan a meal for an eating contest, consisting of twelve courses of typically British food. What rules would you devise for such a contest?
5. An eating contest is an unusual sort of competition. Can you (*a*) name any unusual contests or feats that have actually taken place (*b*) invent some odd contests?
6. Joel Duffle was a "rough-and-tumble" eater, and also an "eyebrow eater". What mannerisms have you noticed people displaying while they eat?
7. Explain the following words and phrases in more conventional English:

    "getting the jump"   "dough"
    "stepping up her pace"   "I am licked"
    "a Judy"   "a goner"
    "to beef"   "hedge them off".

8. Pick out examples of the unusual phrasing Damon Runyon has used to help convey the dialect of Broadway. (e.g., "he says like this:" is not a typical English construction).
9. What sort of sentences has Damon Runyon used to emphasise this manner of speaking, and to make his narrative seem casual and spontaneous?
10. Can you name any habits of speech peculiar to your area of the country? Have you noticed any peculiarities in the speech of people from other regions or other countries?
11. In what tense has this story been written? What effect does this create? Compare the style of this extract with that of "Grandad with Snails". What differences are there?
12. "It is wrong to present this sort of literature ('A Piece of Pie') to young people still at school. It encourages bad speech habits and has a detrimental effect upon their writing. They should only be given examples of good English prose to read and emulate." Discuss this statement with your teacher.

The Budding Bronx

Der spring is sprung,
Der grass is riz,
I wonder where dem boidies is.

Der little boids is on der wing,
Ain't dat absoid?
Der little wings is on der boid!

Anonymous

Epitaph on a "marf"

Wot a marf 'e'd got,
Wot a marf.
When 'e wos a kid
Goo' Lor' luv'll
'Is pore old muvver
Must'a' fed 'im wiv a shuvvle.

Wot a gap 'e'd got
Pore chap,
'E'd never been known to larf,
'Cos if 'e did
It's a penny to a quid
'E'd 'a' split 'is face in 'arf.

Traditional

DISCUSSING THE POEMS

1. What is meant by the expression "the birds were on the wing"? How has its meaning been taken in the first poem?
2. How does the pronunciation of words in the first poem differ from standard spoken English?
3. Of which American city is the Bronx a part?
4. Try reading part of the extract from "A Piece of Pie" in a Bronx accent. Does it seem appropriate?
5. In which part of Britain would you expect to hear words pronounced as they are spelt in the second poem?
6. How does the pronunciation, in the second poem, differ from standard spoken English? Can you differentiate between the pronunciation of "wot" and "what", "poor and pore", "shuvvle" and "shovel", "wos" and "was"?
7. How much importance, do you think, is attached to accent? How important do you consider it to be?

44

TECHNIQUES

The Use of Language and Style

1. *Accents.* (i) English is the "first" language (and, for the most part, the only language) of about 250 million people; another 100 million or so have a working knowledge of it as a foreign language. Naturally there are many variations in the way English is spoken by this vast number of people. There are, for example, differences in pronunciation.

Read aloud and compare the two poems on page 44, in which the accents are indicated by the spelling of the words. Read them again, with the "correct" pronunciation. What effect does this have?

Would "A Piece of Pie" have been funnier if Damon Runyon had attempted to reproduce by his spelling the accent of Broadway?

Indicate by different spellings the way in which you imagine the phrase "thirty thousand feathers on a thrush" would be pronounced by (*a*) a cockney (*b*) an inhabitant of the Bronx (*c*) a Scotsman (*d*) someone with an affected, "refined" accent (*e*) any other people with distinctive accents that you can reproduce in writing.

Rewrite "Epitaph on a 'marf'," in correct English.

(ii) The pace at which people speak also differs.

Can a general distinction of this sort be made between city dwellers and country folk? If so, can you give possible reasons for this difference?

Give examples of regions where people speak quickly, and regions where they drawl their words.

2. *Idioms and Dialect Words.* (i) Certain words and expressions used in speech are confined to particular countries, regions, or groups. These are known as dialect words (where they are confined to a region), and idioms.

Are there any words or expressions in the passage which are largely confined to America? (See Question 7).

Find out what the following Australian idioms and dialect words mean, and give their English equivalents.

(*a*) He's *done his dash* this time.

(*b*) It's a *bonzer* day today.

(*c*) I'm tired of listening to your *magging*.

(*d*) Both contestants were *shickered* at the end of the drinking contest, and both felt *real crook* the next day.

(*e*) Tell me, is that *fair dinkum*?

(ii) There are also variations in the construction and phrasing of spoken sentences. (Refer to the examples you picked out in answer to Appreciation and Discussion Question 8.)

These variations may be slight but they are very much a part of the characteristic speech of any country, region or group.

> e.g. Are you going to the shops?
>
> Is it to the shops you're going?
>
> It's to the shops you're going, are you?

Are you aware of any forms of phrasing which are peculiar to the region in which you live? If so, discuss with your teacher how they differ from standard constructions, and constructions used in other parts of the country.

3. *Sentence Structure.* In order to help convey the Broadway dialect, Damon Runyon used long "badly constructed" sentences. Which "joining word" (or conjunction) does he use excessively?

Rewrite each of the sentences indicated below, as either a series of shorter, balanced sentences, or one well-constructed sentence.

(*a*) This Joel Duffle suggests that the contest . . . (paragraph 1)

(*b*) Then the waiters bring on the pumpkin pie, . . . (paragraph 10)

(*c*) Well, the pie is cut in two dead centre, . . . (paragraph 11)

(*d*) Now at this, the Boston character . . . (paragraph 12)

4. *Exaggeration and Understatement.* (i) Which is the least effective of these four exaggerations? Why is it so weak?

(*a*) Nicely-Nicely can outeat anything that walks on two legs. In fact, he can probably outeat anything that walks on four legs, except perhaps an elephant, and even then the contest would be a photo-finish.

(*b*) When he was a baby, his mouth was so big his mother must have had to feed him with a shovel.

(*c*) I cannot take another bite, even if my life depends on it.

(*d*) When he smiled, his face split into two halves.

Make up original exaggerations to describe:

> an extremely fat man
>
> a man with a completely bald head
>
> an ugly man
>
> a man with a loud voice
>
> a very tough man
>
> an excessively mean man.

The literary term for exaggeration is hyperbole.

(ii) The opposite technique to exaggeration is understatement (or litotes). This can be just as effective, when it is original. Such understatements as "he is no fool" or "he is not exactly pleased" no longer have any force, however, because they have become so hackneyed, i.e. they are now clichés.

How effective is this understatement from the passage?

"even the Boston characters admit that Joel Duffle is no gentleman."

Consider the following example and then compose comic understatements that might be made in the dramatic situations given below.

"We're having a little trouble with the men," the manager told the Chairman of the Board, as the workers set fire to the factory.

(a) aboard a sinking ship

(b) stranded in the middle of the Sahara Desert

(c) trapped down a coalmine

(d) after being presented with a cheque for £100 000

(e) travelling in a jet aircraft at 1500 km/h

Correct English and Vocabulary,

5. *Business Letter.* Set out and punctuate correctly the following business letter.

wendle sports club 22 eastern road wendleton surrey wd 43 tx 1st november 19— the secretary allcomers sports club 5 nosuch avenue wimbledon london s.w. 19 3au dear sir we have recently added peanut pushing to our list of sporting activities and are anxious to arrange fixtures for the coming season although formed only this year our team contains several experienced nosers including our captain bert brunwin who has regularly represented great britain in international peanut pushing matches if you can give us a match any saturday in november or december would be convenient the match could be held here if you wish since we have recently installed in our gymnasium a highly polished pinewood floor for sprint races we also have an outdoor course covered with gravel splintered glass and pigmy stinging nettles for endurance races our supply of peanuts and nose-guards however is limited and we would have to ask you to bring your own after the contest we would of course provide nose liniment nose-plasters and refreshments i look forward to hearing from you yours faithfully albert dustwood hon sec

6. *Tenses.* In order to become familiar with different tense forms, each member of the class can take part of the extract from "A Piece of Pie" and change it from the present to the past tense, either verbally or in writing.

TOPICS FOR WRITTEN WORK

1. Invent and describe a curious contest or game.
Hints

How many people participate in the contest? Where would it be held? What equipment is needed? What is the object of the game? What are the rules? What name will you give to the game or contest that you have invented? (Use this as the title of your essay). Since nobody but you will know anything about the game or contest, your explanation must be very carefully planned and clearly expressed. You may draw diagrams where these will assist your explanation.

2. (a) Imagine that you have the task of explaining to a visitor from another part of the country, some of the dialect words and idioms of your district. (b) If you cannot find enough local words and phrases, imagine that you have to explain to a visitor from another country, some of the idioms used in Britain, particularly those which a foreigner would find strange.

Hints

Write your account in the form of a conversation. You could begin (b), for example, like this:

"I think we had better wait here for a while," I said after looking outside the station. "It's raining cats and dogs outside."

"What!" he exclaimed, looking startled, and then puzzled. "Where do these poor animals come from?"

You could also try to indicate the accent of your foreign visitor by spelling certain words and phrases as he would pronounce them.

If you attempt (a), you could spell certain words and phrases as they would be pronounced in the accent of your district. This would add to the confusion of your visitor.

3. Describe what food and drink you would prepare if you were giving a party for your friends.

Hints

Imagine that it is to be an informal party, held in the evening, and that about twenty people will be present. Say what sorts of food you will provide and explain why you have chosen these dishes. Under the name of each dish, give detailed instructions for preparing it; if there are many ingredients, list these, and the quantities required, at the beginning, Do not write your recipes in note form. Explain what drinks you will provide, and how you will serve these and the food. Give, also, details of the cost involved.

ORAL WORK

1. Discuss the following questions.—What accents are usually considered to sound attractive? What accents are often disparaged? In what ways can a strong accent or dialect be a hindrance? Does someone with a "public school" voice generally stand a better chance of succeeding in an important interview than someone with, say, a strong cockney accent? What other factors, apart from geographical location, influence the way in which people speak? If it were possible, would it be a good thing to teach everybody in Britain to speak with the same accent?

2. Each member of the class could choose a different accent, including those which many foreigners have, and demonstrate what it sounds like to the rest of the class.
3. Discuss the following argument.

"There are many variations in the pronunciation of any language, yet anyone speaking a particular language has little difficulty in communicating with others who also speak that tongue. This is a strong argument in favour of an international language. True, there might be wide variation in pronunciation, but it is easier to understand a different accent than it is to understand a completely different language. It would be a great step towards solving many world problems if a universal language such as Esperanto were taught in all schools throughout the world". (See also "Activities and Research" No. 3.)

ACTIVITIES AND RESEARCH

1. Using sources such as the "Guinness Book of Records", collect information about curious contests, feats and records. If you see any reports, in newspapers and magazines, of curious activities, cut out the articles and pin them on the notice board in your classroom, or stick them in an exercise book kept for this purpose. (You could call the book "A Collection of Curious Facts".)
2. Collect together all the words and phrases that, as far as you know, are confined to your area. Make a list of them and add to it whenever you discover new expressions.
3. Find out about Esperanto, and other "universal languages". If you then think you might be interested in learning Esperanto, there is a book in the *Teach Yourself* series (published by English Universities Press) which provides a simple introduction to the language.
4. Many simple stories can, in fact, be told by a series of pictures or still photographs. The great eating contest in "A Piece of Pie" is an ideal subject for such treatment. Discuss how this story could be told in, say, sixteen photographs. Try to work out shots that are interesting and effective, and that contrast with one another, or follow on smoothly; e.g. (*a*) a photograph from a distance, showing the two contestants sitting on either side of a table piled high with food (*b*) a close-up shot of Violette Shumberger's face as she stuffs in a mouthful of food (*c*) a close-up shot of Joel Duffle, chewing ferociously.

50

If members of the class could bring to school, cameras and some black and white film, groups could actually take a series of photographs to tell a simple story. Choose an incident that might occur in any school—a quarrel in the playground, an accident in which something is broken, a chase, or the scoring of a goal. Work out in advance how many shots will be required to explain the situation and the characters involved. Try to keep the number of shots required to one reel of film. The resulting series of photographs could then be mounted in order, with some brief captions to accompany them if you think this is necessary.

If a film camera is available, groups can try the further experiment of filming each of the still photographs for two or three seconds. You will find that such a film is often surprisingly effective.

FURTHER READING

A Piece of Pie from *Guys and Dolls* by Damon Runyon (Penguin).

This selection of twenty stories was compiled from a number of Damon Runyon's books. Although not a great author in the accepted literary sense, his anecdotes about the Broadway spivs and the small-town dwellers of the Middle West that he knew so well, gained him a place as one of the most popular and entertaining short story writers that America has produced. He died in 1946.

All This and That (Constable).

The thirty nine stories in this representative collection of Damon Runyon's work are all written in the dialect of Broadway and usually in the present tense, as in the extract from *A Piece of Pie*. It is this technique of narration that is the most distinctive feature of Runyon's work; it is a quality that is unique.

Runyon on Broadway (Constable).

Nearly twice the length of the above collection, this omnibus of 720 pages contains all the stories from *More Than Somewhat, Furthermore,* and *Take it Away*. There is an introduction by E. C. Bentley, and portrait and illustrations by Nicholas Bentley.

CHAPTER 4 **Time Stood Still**

*This story reflects very clearly the author's experiences
in the Fire Service during the London blitzes.*

It was our third job that night.
Until this thing happened, work had been without incident. There
had been shrapnel, a few enquiring bombs, and some huge fires: but
these were unremarkable and have since merged without identity into the
neutral maze of fire and noise and water and night, without date and without
hour, with neither time nor form, that lowers mistily at the back of my
mind as a picture of the air-raid season.

I suppose we were worn down and shivering. Three a.m. is a mean-
spirited hour. I suppose we were drenched, with the cold hose water
trickling in at our collars and settling down at the tails of our shirts.
Without doubt the heavy brass couplings felt moulded from metal-ice.
Probably the open roar of the pumps drowned the petulant buzz of the
raiders above, and certainly the ubiquitous fire-glow made an orange
stage-set of the streets. Black water would have puddled the City alleys
and I suppose our hands and our faces were black as the water. Black
with hacking about among the burnt up rafters. These things were an
every-night nonentity. They happened and they were not forgotten
because they were never even remembered.

But I do remember it was our third job. And there we were—Len,
Lofty, Verno and myself, playing a fifty-foot jet up the face of a tall city
warehouse and thinking of nothing at all. You don't think of anything
after the first few hours. You just watch the white pole of water lose
itself in the fire and you think of nothing. Sometimes you move the jet
over to another window. Sometimes the orange dims to black—but you
only ease your grip on the ice-cold nozzle and continue pouring careless
gallons through the window. You know the fire will fester for hours
yet. However, that night the blank, indefinite hours of waiting were
sharply interrupted—by an unusual sound. Very suddenly a long rattling
crack of bursting brick and mortar perforated the moment. And then
the upper half of that five-storey building heaved over towards us. It
hung there, poised for a timeless second before rumbling down at us. I
was thinking of nothing at all and then I was thinking of everything in
the world.

53

In that simple second my brain digested every detail of the scene. New eyes opened at the sides of my head so that, from within, I photographed a hemispherical panorama bounded by the huge length of the building in front of me and the narrow lane on either side.

Blocking us on the left was the squat trailer pump, roaring and quivering with effort. Water throbbed from its overflow valves and from leakages in the hose and couplings. A ceaseless stream spewed down its grey sides into the gutter. But nevertheless a fat iron exhaust pipe glowed red-hot in the middle of the wet engine. I had to look past Lofty's face. Lofty was staring at the controls, hands tucked into his armpits for warmth. Lofty was thinking of nothing. He had a black diamond of soot over one eye, like the White-eyed Kaffir in negative.

To the other side of me was a free run up the alley. Overhead swung a sign—"Catto and Henley". I wondered what in hell they sold. Old stamps? The alley was quite free. A couple of lengths of dead, deflated hose wound over the darkly glistening pavement. Charred flotsam dammed up one of the gutters. A needle of water fountained from a hole in a live hoselength. Beneath a blue shelter light lay a shattered coping stone. The next shop along was a tobacconist's, windowless, with fake display cartons torn open for anybody to see. The alley was quite free.

Behind me, Len and Verno shared the weight of the hose. They heaved up against the strong backward drag of water-pressure. All I had to do was yell, "Drop it"—and then run. We could risk the live hosing snaking up at us. We could run to the right down the free alley—Len, Verno and me. But I never moved. I never said, "Drop it" or anything else. That long second held me hypnotised, rubber boots cemented to the pavement. Ton upon ton of red-hot brick hovering in the air above us numbed all initiative. I could only think. I couldn't move.

Six yards in front stood the blazing building. A minute before I would never have distinguished it from any other drab Victorian atrocity happily on fire. Now I was immediately certain of every minute detail. The building was five storeys high. The top four storeys were fiercely alight. The rooms inside were alive with red fire. The black outside walls remained untouched. And thus, like the lighted carriages of a night express, there appeared alternating rectangles of black and red that emphasised vividly the extreme symmetry of the window spacing: each oblong window shape posed as a vermilion panel set in perfect order upon the dark face of the wall. There were ten windows to each floor, making forty windows in all. In rigid rows of ten, one row placed precisely above the other, with strong contrasts of black and red, the blazing windows stood to attention in strict formation. The oblong building, the oblong windows, the oblong spacing. Orange-red colour seemed to *bulge* from the black framework, assumed tactile value, like boiling jelly that expanded inside a thick black squared grill.

Three of the storeys, thirty blazing windows and their huge frame of black brick, a hundred solid tons of hard, deep Victorian wall, pivoted over towards us and hung flatly over the alley. Whether the descending wall actually paused in its fall I can never know. Probably it never did. Probably it only seemed to hang there. Probably my eyes digested its action at an early period of momentum, so that I saw it "off true" but before it had gathered speed.

The night grew darker as the great mass hung over us. Through smoke-fogged fireglow the moonlight had hitherto penetrated to the pit of our alley through declivities in the skyline. Now some of the moonlight was being shut out as the wall hung ever further over us. The wall shaded the moonlight like an inverted awning. Now the pathway of light above had been squeezed to a thin line. That was the only silver lining I ever believed in. It shone out—a ray of hope. But it was a declining hope, for although at this time the entire hemispherical scene appeared static, an imminence of movement could be sensed throughout—presumably because the scene was actually moving. Even the speed of the shutter which closed the photograph on my mind was powerless to exclude this motion from a deeper consciousness. The picture appeared static to the limited surface senses, the eyes and the material brain, but beyond that there was hidden movement.

The second was timeless. I had leisure to remark many things. For instance, that an iron derrick, slightly to the left, would not hit me. This derrick stuck out from the building and I could feel its sharpness and hardness as clearly as if I had run my body intimately over its contour. I had time to notice that it carried a footlong hook, a chain with three-inch rings, two girder supports, and a wheel more than twice as large as my head.

A wall will fall in many ways. It may sway over to the one side or the other. It may crumble at the very beginning of its fall. It may remain intact and fall flat. This wall fell as flat as a pancake. It clung to its shape through ninety degrees to the horizontal. Then it detached itself from the pivot and slammed down on top of us.

The last resistance of bricks and mortar at the pivot point cracked off like automatic gun fire. The violent sound both deafened us and brought us to our senses. We dropped the hose and crouched. Afterwards Verno said that I knelt slowly on one knee with bowed head, like a man about to be knighted. Well, I got my knighting. There was an incredible noise—a thunderclap condensed into the space of an eardrum—and then the bricks and the mortar came tearing and burning into the flesh of my face.

Lofty, away by the pump, was killed. Len, Verno and myself they dug out. There was very little brick on top of us. We had been lucky. We had been framed by one of those symmetrical, oblong window spaces.

(from *The Wall* from *Fireman Flower* by William Sansom)

APPRECIATION AND DISCUSSION

1. Which words and phrases tell you that this incident took place during war-time? What would have caused the fire?
2. Is there any evidence to indicate in which city the story is set?
3. Why does the author begin three sentences with "I suppose", when describing the time before the "third job"? (e.g., "I suppose we were worn down and shivering.")
4. How many firemen were working with the author? What were their names? What jobs were they doing?
5. Describe in your own words the layout of the area in which the firemen were working.
6. What was the author's state of mind before the burning building began to fall?
7. How did the author's thoughts change when he saw the wall about to fall? What did he mean by: "New eyes opened at the sides of my head"? How did he react physically?
8. What was the only risk the firemen would have run had they dropped the hose and escaped up the alley?
9. What was the author's predominant impression of the burning building?
10. What finally brought the firemen to their senses?
11. How many firemen survived? What saved them? Who was killed and why?
12. How does William Sansom's style differ from that used by Michael Baldwin in "Grandad With Snails", and that used by Damon Runyon in "A Piece of Pie"?

Good Taste

Travelling, a man met a tiger, so . . .
He ran. The tiger ran after him
Thinking: How fast I run: . . . But

The road thought: How long I am . . . Then,
They came to a cliff, yes, the man
Grabbed at an ash root and swung down

Over its edge. Above his knuckles, the tiger.,
At the foot of the cliff, its mate. Two mice,
One black, one white, began to gnaw the root.

And by the traveller's head grew one
Juicy strawberry, so . . . hugging the root
The man reached out and plucked the fruit.
How sweet it tasted!

Christopher Logue

DISCUSSING THE POEM

1. How would the poem be altered, in meaning or effect, if it were not arranged in these lines, but was printed like ordinary prose? Read it aloud by lines, and then by the punctuation marks only. Which words and phrases carry extra emphasis in the verse lines?
2. Do you think that one's senses become more alert when one is threatened with danger? If you were told that very shortly you were to die, would experiences become more intense for you? Compare the ways in which William Sansom and Christopher Logue have dealt with this idea of heightened sensibility. Which approach — the extract or the poem—did you find the more forceful?
3. What qualities and details in the poem are reminiscent of a fable or a fairy story?
4. Has the poem any sort of moral or "message"?
5. If we say that someone has "good taste", we mean that he appreciates beauty and that he can discriminate between what is good and what is bad. Is there any connection between this meaning of the term and the title of the poem?

TECHNIQUES

The Use of Language, and Style

1. *Vivid Description.* (i) William Sansom used very vivid and evocative words to describe his experience—words that immediately evoke a response in the reader.

- (*a*) From the list below, select the words that you find evocative and explain what you associate with these words. What feelings do they arouse in you and what pictures do they conjure up?

   mistily shirts fire-glow job jet white hours fester however unusual heaved squat spewed but middle diamond free snake anything hypnotised atrocity walls jelly moonlight silver pancake gun tearing then flesh

- (*b*) To you, "hear", "see", and "food" are probably not very evocative words. To what sort of people might they be evocative? What associations would they have for these people?

- (*c*) Make a list of evocative phrases that conjure up really vivid pictures, e.g. "rats' feet over broken glass" (T. S. Eliot).

(ii) After discussing how they create their effects, replace the italicised words and phrases in these sentences with equally vivid ones of your own.

- (*a*) Three a.m. is a *mean-spirited* hour.
- (*b*) You watch the *white pole* of water *lose* itself in the fire.
- (*c*) You know the fire will *fester* for hours yet.
- (*d*) On the left was the *squat* trailer pump, *roaring* and *quivering*; water *throbbed* from its overflow valves and a *ceaseless* stream *spewed* down its grey sides.
- (*e*) A *needle* of water *fountained* from a hole in the *live* hose pipe.
- (*f*) My rubber boots were *cemented* to the pavement.
- (*g*) *Orange-red colour* seemed to *bulge* from the black framework, *like boiling jelly that expanded inside a thick black squared grill.*
- (*h*) The *pathway* of light above had been *squeezed* to a *thin line.*

2. *Summarising.* (i) Imagine that you are the narrator in "The Wall" and that you have been asked to submit an official report of the incident. Summarise the events of the story. Eliminate all emotive description: select the relevant facts and express these in a simple, objective style. Make notes first.

(ii) Do you think this story contains too much description? If so, which parts would you eliminate in order to increase its pace?

3. *Tenses.* Most of the passage is written in the past tense, but at one point William Sansom switches to the present tense (and introduces

58

the pronoun "you"). Where does he do this, and why does he do so?

In order to assess the effect that tense can create, each member of the class can read part of the passage aloud, changing it from past to present tense. Make any other alterations that are necessary, e.g. "that night" to "tonight"; omit sentences that cannot be changed satisfactorily. Does the change of tense improve the story? Does it, for example, involve the reader more? Or does the carefully considered and often difficult vocabulary clash with the more spontaneous feeling created by the use of the present tense?

Correct English, and Vocabulary

4. *The Hyphen.* (i) The hyphen is used most commonly to form new words by joining two (or more) words together. Here, for example, are some of the compound words commonly formed from "low".

low-grade	low-necked	low-priced
low-slung	low-level	low-spirited
low-pressure	low-lying	low-pitched

Form as many compounds as you can from:

soft   long   hand   ship   turn.

If a compound word is used frequently, the hyphen is often omitted after a time.

It is often effective to make up new compound words for use in a description or poem. Which of these compound words from "The Wall" are conventional combinations and which have been created by William Sansom for use in this particular story, i.e. are original combinations?

air-raid	ice-cold	mean-spirited
five-storey	metal-ice	red-hot
fire-glow	water-pressure	stage-set
every-night	smoke-fogged	orange-red

(ii) The hyphen also has the following uses.

It is used to break a word at the end of a line of writing. When you use it for this purpose, always do so at a natural break between syllables.

e.g.   wonderful   wonder-ful *or* won-derful

Choose any words of more than two syllables that occur in the passage, and say where they could be broken.

It is also used when it would otherwise be difficult to recognise the addition of a prefix.

e.g.   co-operate   pre-eminent   re-address

How might the three words above be pronounced if the hyphen were omitted? List other words that need a hyphen for this reason.

Sometimes the hyphen is necessary to avoid ambiguity.

Explain the difference in meaning between the sentences in each of these pairs.

(a) I intend to reform the gang.
I intend to re-form the gang.

(b) My fingers almost froze on the cold water-tap.
My fingers almost froze on the cold-water tap.

(c) We have taken a cross-section of the population.
We have taken a cross section of the population.

(d) My uncle is a grand-piano dealer.
My uncle is a grand piano-dealer.

(e) This is the second hand-pump I have bought.
This is the second-hand pump I have bought.

5. *The Dash.* You must be careful not to confuse the hyphen with the dash, which is used to separate an extra remark from the rest of the sentence.

The remark may occur in the middle of a sentence.

e.g. "There was an incredible noise—a thunderclap condensed into the space of an eardrum—and then the bricks and mortar came tearing and burning into the flesh of my face."

In the above case, the remark is like an aside, an interruption, and commas could have been used instead of dashes. Dashes, however, are stronger punctuation marks.

The remark may occur as an afterthought at the end of a sentence.

e.g. "It shone out—a ray of hope."

Sometimes the afterthought is capable of standing as a complete sentence and could be separated by a full stop or semicolon.

e.g. "Sometimes the orange dims to black—but you only ease your grip on the ice-cold nozzle and continue pouring careless gallons through the window."

When it is used between two punctuated sentences, the dash indicates a longer pause than the full stop alone would give.

Use dashes to punctuate these sentences. Make sure that you write your dashes clearly, so that they do not look like hyphens.

(a) I glanced up at the window an orange rectangle.

(b) The new fireman he was appointed last month remained by the pump.

(c) The fire died down but we had to remain on duty for another five hours.

(*d*) We were not cowards far from it but that fire terrified us all.

(*e*) Len his face covered in soot ran to the engine to switch on the pump or so we thought.

6. *Vocabulary.* Refer to your dictionary to find the meanings of the following words, as they are used in the passage. The words and their definitions can then be copied into a "Vocabulary Notebook".

Nouns	Adjectives	Verbs
nonentity	petulant	perforate
panorama	ubiquitous	emphasise
flotsam	hemispherical	pivot
symmetry	vermilion	exclude
declivities	tactile	condense

Use the words in sentences of your own. At this stage, use them in a literal context; do not attempt to use them metaphorically as William Sansom has sometimes done.

TOPICS FOR WRITTEN WORK

1. "Fire!" Write a story or a prose description with this as the title.
Hints
   Make your descriptions as vivid and emotive as you can. Consider the words and phrases used by William Sansom, some of which are listed in Exercise 1. Use the hyphen to make up evocative compound words. Decide whether you will use the past or the present tense. (If you think you can handle it correctly, you could try a change of tense to emphasise a particular section.) Experiment with words that you have seen in other stories, but have never used yourself. Check their meanings first but, even if you are not sure of these, still include the words. Use your senses to collect details of description; refer to the sort of details that Sansom has included. The photograph on page 61 may help to give you some more ideas. You may use the following as your opening paragraph if you wish.

> The fire engine swooped urgently along the street, bells screaming, lights pulsing. Cars joggled aside into the gutter. Pedestrians goggled and pointed.

2. "Time Stood Still". Write a poem about any occasion when, for a moment, time seemed to stand still.
Hints
   Study Christopher Logue's simple but evocative style in "Good Taste". You may use his poem as a model if you wish, but try, nevertheless, to create the content of your poem from a personal experience. Which aspect of your experience was the most intense? Which sensation or impression was captured in the moment when time stood still? What were you doing beforehand? What were you thinking about? What sort of day was it? Were you threatened by any danger? How did you feel when the danger occurred?

3. Write a report entitled "Facts about the Fire Service".
Hints
   Give a brief account of the history of the Fire Service. When was it founded, and what sort of equipment was used in the early days? How is the modern Fire Service organised? What equipment is used now? What does a fireman's job involve? Include one paragraph on the Fire Service as a career. Use reference books to collect your information, taking it down in note form.

Pupils' Work

The Frost has Struck

The frost has struck the trees dead
And now, a frigid parasite,
Clings to their petrified boughs.
It has bitten into spiky leaves
And brittle iron fences,
Attacking with a cancerous film of white,
Dead white, that means no life
Or movement lingers here.
The scene is still, as if
Time does not pass where the frost film is,
The trees are held as if arrested in
Some motion, and quickly frozen.
The leaves have whispered, then stopped.

                              Peter Bernard

The Horse

A golden brown coat, a long sleeky body, well groomed, he galloped over
    the moors toward me.
I, taken unawares, turned as if to run, but could not move,
For fright had taken over my power of movement.
Now he was close upon me,
And I could see the sun shimmering through his mane, tangled with thorns,
    swaying in the early morning breeze.
On my knees I fell as if to beg for mercy,
But my sudden movement frightened him as his appearance had frightened
    me, and he turned, and galloped,
His tail out straight behind him.
I watched until his shape I could no longer see on the horizon.

                              Christine Arscott

ORAL WORK

1. Make up impromptu commentaries about exciting and spectacular events, such as a fire, a bank robbery or a dramatic rescue. Get other members of the class to act as spectators or as some of the individuals involved in the incident, and interview them. Try to make the interviews run smoothly by prompting your interviewees with questions whenever necessary.
2. Individually, or in conjunction with other members of the class, give an illustrated talk on either the Great Fire of London ("Activities and Research" No. 1), or on one of the services listed in "Activities and Research" No. 3.
3. Prepare a talk on one particular aspect of time and time-telling. (See "Activities and Research" No. 2.)

ACTIVITIES AND RESEARCH

1. Find out all you can about the Great Fire of London. Look at "Pepys' Diary" for an eye-witness account of the Great Fire of 1666. The entries for September 2nd to the 7th are particularly relevant, and another fire in Whitehall is mentioned under November 9th.
2. Find out the answers to the following questions about time and time-telling.

    What kind of a clock is: an electric clock, a grandfather clock, a cuckoo clock, an alarm clock, an eight-day clock, a Dutch clock, a water clock? Explain briefly how each one works.

    What is: a chronometer, a half-hunter, a jewelled movement, a luminous dial?

    What is meant by the following terms: Greenwich Mean Time, International Date Line, Time Zone, Lunar month, Leap Year?

    How often does a Leap Year occur? Why is it necessary? For how long has the present calendar system been in existence? What other systems have been used, e.g., in Early Roman times? What other systems are being advocated today?

    If you were stranded on a desert island, by what means could you tell the time?

    What are the advantages and disadvantages of the twenty-four-hour system of time keeping?

64

3. Collect information about the following services:
   (*a*) the Fire Brigade (*b*) the Police Force (*c*) Refuse Disposal (*d*) Street Lighting and Cleaning (*e*) Drainage and Sewage (*f*) the R.A.F. and the W.R.A.F. (*g*) the Army and the W.R.A.C. (*h*) the Navy and the W.R.N.S. (*i*) the W.V.S.
4. In Chapter 3, "Activities and Research" No. 4, you were required to break down a story into a series of still photographs. Working out a film script is basically the same, although, of course, a cine camera can *move*, and you will take a great many more shots. Find out something about the basic language of film-making and try to work out how you would film the story of "The Wall". Reckon a shot to be any continuous period with your cine camera running, whether you move it to take different views or not. Take account of these possible variables when working out your scenario.
   Distance: The camera can take close-ups, medium, and long distance shots.
   Position: You can take a front view or a side view, etc.
   Angle: You can shoot from above, below, etc.
   Movement: In one shot you can "pan" from side to side, tilt up and down, and "track" (or "zoom") in closer or out further.
   You might start like this.
   1. Long distance shot, showing the firemen and the fire engine in silhouette against the burning building.
   2. Close-up of a fireman's face.
   3. Medium distance shot of the trailer pump. Pan down into the gutter and zoom slowly on to a small piece of wood still smoking in the water.
   4. Close-up of hands holding the nozzle of a hose.
   5. Shot from below looking up at "the white pole of water" losing itself in the burning building.
   At one or more points you might decide to "freeze" the picture to give the impression of time standing still. Watch for this technique in professionally made films. On what sort of occasions is it used?

FURTHER READING

The Wall from *Fireman Flower* by William Sansom (Chatto & Windus).

The Wall is one of William Sansom's best-known pieces and has been translated into several languages. During the Second World War, Sansom served as a London fireman, and he later insisted that "the Blitz taught me to write seriously. It impelled me to write down what I really thought rather than what I imagined people wanted". *Fireman Flower* was, in fact, the first of his books to be published; it contains "realistic" stories, such as the one printed in this chapter, modern fables, and pure fantasies.

The Stories of William Sansom (Hogarth Press).

For this collection, William Sansom has drawn upon eight previous volumes of his stories and selected thirty-three of the best, including *The Wall*. Although you may find many of the stories rather difficult at this stage, there is a wide range to choose from—humour (*Three Dogs of Siena*, and *A Contest of Ladies*), terror (*How Claeys Died*), what Elizabeth Bowen in her introduction describes as "hallucination stories" (*A Saving Grace*), and, of course, a wealth of scenic description. Sansom is an outstanding short story writer and it is certainly worthwhile searching through this collection of stories that appeal to you.

He has also written travel books, two children's stories, and a number of novels, one of the most recent of which is:

The Last Hours of Sandra Lee (Hogarth Press).

A light-hearted but searching comedy about office life and "the relationship of man and object".

CHAPTER 5

Conflict

The action of the play takes place in the Malayan Jungle early in 1942. *A British patrol, cut off by the Japanese advance on Singapore, has taken shelter in a deserted store hut. Shortly after arriving there, they capture a Japanese soldier.*

CAST: *Sgt. Mitchem   Pte. Evans*
       Cpl. Johnstone   Pte. Bamforth
       L/Cpl. Macleish   A Japanese soldier

(*MITCHEM, MACLEISH, and JOHNSTONE turn and look at the Prisoner*).

EVANS (*crossing and joining the group*): What's the matter, Jock? What's happened?

MACLEISH: It's him. It's bright boy there. He's carrying a load of British issue fags.

EVANS: How did he get hold of them?

JOHNSTONE: How do you think? You can have three guesses. The thieving Nip!

MITCHEM (*drops the cigarette and grinds it beneath his heel*): If there's one thing gets my hump it's knocking off—it's looting.

JOHNSTONE (*holding out the cigarette to Macleish*): Well, come on, Jock, you'd better finish it. You're the one he gave it to. You reckon you're his mate.

MACLEISH (*snatching the cigarette*): I'll ram it down his rotten throat! I'll make him eat the rotten thing! (*He hesitates—for a moment we feel that he is about to carry out the threat—he hurls the cigarette across the room.*)

JOHNSTONE: You don't want to waste it, Jock. Not now you've started it. You never know how much that fag has cost. He's happen stuck his bayonet end in some poor Herb for that.

EVANS: There's some of them would kill their mothers for a drag.

MITCHEM (*to Macleish*): And you were telling me how they treat P.O.W.s.

EVANS: He wants a lesson, Sarge. He ought to have a lesson taught to him.

MACLEISH: I'll kill him!

MITCHEM: Will you? You swop sides quick. (*There is a pause as they turn to look at the PRISONER, who, uncertain of their attitude towards him, picks up the case, opens it, and offers a cigarette to Mitchem.*) Stick 'em! (*MITCHEM strikes the case from the prisoner's hand. The PRISONER raises his hands and places them on his head—on this occasion, however, the action is without humour.*) Thieving slob!

JOHNSTONE (*raising a fist*): Who goes in first?

MITCHEM: Hold it.

JOHNSTONE (*advancing threateningly on the prisoner*): Who gets first crack?

MITCHEM: Hold it a sec.

(*Johnstone checks himself.*)

MACLEISH (*almost to himself*): My brother's just nineteen. He's only been out here a couple of months. I haven't seen him since he docked. They whipped him straight up country. He's only just nineteen. (*A loud appeal to the patrol—as if in the hope of receiving a denial.*) For all I know he's dead!

MITCHEM: Jock—see'f he's lugging anything else he's lifted from our lads.

MACLEISH (*moving the prisoner*): Get up! Get on your feet! (*The PRISONER cowers on the form and MACLEISH jerks him savagely to his feet.*) Do as you're told! (*MACLEISH goes through the Prisoner's pocket and removes the wallet.*) There's this.

JOHNSTONE (*taking the wallet*): I'll have a look at what's in this. You carry on.

MACLEISH (*as the Prisoner reacts slightly at the loss of the wallet*): Stand still!

> MACLEISH goes through the Prisoner's trouser pockets and removes the usual miscellaneous assortment of articles: handkerchief, keys, loose change, etc. MACLEISH places these on the form. JOHNSTONE, slowly and carefully, tears the photographs into pieces and drops these and the wallet on the floor. The PRISONER starts forward and MACLEISH rises and strikes him across the face. BAMFORTH, who has just re-entered from the veranda, notices this incident.

MACLEISH: I said, stand still!

BAMFORTH: What's up? What's he done to ask for that?

EVANS: He's been looting, Bammo. From our lads.

BAMFORTH (*crossing to join the group around the Prisoner*): He's been what?

MACLEISH: We caught him with a fag-case stuffed with British army smokes!

BAMFORTH: You Scotch nit! You dim Scotch nit! I gave him them!

MITCHEM: You did?

BAMFORTH: I'm telling you. I gave him half a dozen snouts!

EVANS: You gave them him?

(*MACLEISH edges away from the Prisoner and BAMFORTH positions himself between the Prisoner and the members of the patrol.*)

BAMFORTH: What's the matter, Taff? Are your ears bad? I slipped him half a dozen nubs!

MACLEISH: I didn't know. I thought . . . I thought he'd knocked them off.

JOHNSTONE (*to Bamforth*): And who gave you permission?

BAMFORTH: I've had this out with you before. You show where it says I have to grease up to an N.C.O. before I hand out fags. What's mine's my own. I decide what I do with it.

MACLEISH: How was I to know? I . . . I've told you, boy, I thought he'd knocked them off.

BAMFORTH: You know what thought did.

MACLEISH (*searching for words*): How was I to know? . . . I mean, he gave one of them to me . . . I'd lit it up . . . I was having a drag . . . I was halfway down the lousy thing before I realized, you know—I mean, before I knew it was a Blighty fag . . . So how was I to feel? . . . What would you have done? . . . You tell me, Bammo . . . I could have choked, you know . . . I've got a brother who's up country.

BAMFORTH: If he's dropped in with a gang of Nips who think like you, God help the kiddie. God help him!

MACLEISH: I thought he'd looted them!

BAMFORTH: And so you pull the big brave hero bull. The raving highlander. Aren't you the boy? So what you waiting for? Well, come on, Jocko, finish off the job! (*BAMFORTH grabs the Prisoner, pinning his arms, and swings him round, holding him towards Macleish.*) Come on, come one! Come on, he's waiting for the hump. Let's see you slot him, Jock! Drop him one on! Let's see you do your stuff! Smash his face for him! Drop him one on!

MACLEISH: Lay off it, Bamforth.

MITCHEM: O.K., Bamforth, jack it in.

BAMFORTH: Haven't any of you got the guts to go the bundle? You were snapping at the leash when I walked in. What about you, Taff? You want to have a crack at him?

MITCHEM: I said drop it.

BAMFORTH (*loosing his hold on the Prisoner*): I didn't start it.
(*The PRISONER sits on form and returns the articles to his trouser pockets.*)

EVANS: It was a mistake, Bammo.

BAMFORTH: You bet it was.

EVANS: We thought he'd whipped them.

BAMFORTH (*stoops and picks up the wallet and a piece of the torn photographs*): You bastards. You even had to rip his pictures up. You couldn't leave him them even!

EVANS: I'll give you a hand to pick them up.

BAMFORTH: You couldn't even leave him them!

EVANS (*bends down and collects the torn pieces of the photographs.*): Happen he can stick them together again, Bammo. Here's a bit with a head on it. He could stick them together, easy enough, with a pot of paste and a brush. . . .

MACLEISH (*picks up the cigarette case from the floor and gives it to Bamforth*): He'd better have this back too. He'll . . . Maybe he'll be feeling in need of a smoke.

BAMFORTH: Yeh . . . Thanks, Jock. (*He crosses to return the cigarette case.*)

JOHNSTONE: Bamforth! Just a minute, lad.

BAMFORTH: Yeh!

JOHNSTONE: I'd like a look at that before you hand it on to him.

BAMFORTH: Ask him. Not me, It's his.

JOHNSTONE: He'll get it back. I only want it for a minute.

BAMFORTH (*hesitates, then crosses and hands the case to Johnstone*): He'd better get it back.

JOHNSTONE: He will. (*He inspects the case, slowly turning it over in his hands, then tosses it to Bamforth. BAMFORTH crosses to return it to the prisoner.*) Bamforth!

BAMFORTH (*turns*): You want something else?

JOHNSTONE: No, lad. Nothing. I was just wondering, that's all.

BAMFORTH: Well?

JOHNSTONE: Are you feeling in a generous mood today?

BAMFORTH: What's that supposed to signify?

JOHNSTONE: Did you give him the case as well?

BAMFORTH: I gave him half a dozen fags, that's all. I haven't got a case myself to give away. I gave him half a dozen snouts, I've told you half a dozen times. The case belongs to him.

70

JOHNSTONE: Does it?

BAMFORTH: The case is his.

JOHNSTONE: That's interesting. You'd better have another shufti at it then.

(*BAMFORTH inspects the case and is about to return it to the Prisoner.*)

MITCHEM: Pass it over, Bamforth.

BAMFORTH: What for? It's his.

MITCHEM: I'd like to once it over for myself.

BAMFORTH (*tosses the case to MITCHEM, who also examines it, then turns his glance upon the Prisoner*): All right! So it's a British case!

JOHNSTONE: Made in Birmingham.

BAMFORTH: So what? What's that supposed to prove?

MITCHEM: So tell us now how he got hold of it.

BAMFORTH: I don't know. Don't ask me.

JOHNSTONE: I bloody do! The way he got the snouts.

BAMFORTH: I gave him the fags.

JOHNSTONE: So you say.

BAMFORTH: I gave him the fags!

MITCHEM: And what about the case?

BAMFORTH: Look—I don't know. I've told you—I don't know.

EVANS: So he has been on the lifting lark? Half-inching from the boys up country.

MACLEISH: It begins to look that way.

(*MACLEISH and EVANS move menacingly towards the Prisoner.*)

(from *The Long and the Short and the Tall* by Willis Hall)

71

APPRECIATION AND DISCUSSION

1. What nicknames are used in this extract for Macleish, Bamforth, Evans and the Japanese prisoner?
2. Corporal Johnstone appears in the rest of the play as the most vicious member of the British party. Which actions and words of his in this extract contribute to this impression?
3. Can you guess why Macleish had been telling Mitchem how the Japanese treated prisoners of war?
4. Explain how Macleish's feelings about his brother influence his attitude to the prisoner. Consider his friendliness as well as his hostility. What kind of man is he basically?
5. Much of the conflict in this play is between Bamforth and Johnstone. Using the evidence in this extract as a guide, can you explain why their personalities might clash?
6. Examine Bamforth's use of sarcasm. Give examples and discuss whether they are effective.
7. Sergeant Mitchem carries responsibility for the patrol and their prisoner. Does this affect his words and actions here?
8. What kind of character is Evans? Notice his reactions when he first hears that the cigarettes are British, after Bamforth has revealed that he gave the cigarettes to the prisoner, and again when Johnstone points out that it is a British cigarette case.
9. Would either Johnstone or Macleish have been justified in killing or beating up the prisoner if he had stolen the cigarettes?
10. Since the prisoner might have endangered the lives of the British soldiers, whether they had taken him back to base with them or left him behind alive, should they have killed him?
11. This incident reveals several examples of hasty, irrational judgements. How justified was each member of the patrol in his attitude to the prisoner? If they sometimes had inadequate reasons, what other motives might have prompted their behaviour?
12. Can you think of any argument Bamforth could now use to defend the prisoner?

CREATIVE WRITING

72

The Dead-Beat

He dropped, — more sullenly than wearily,
Lay stupid like a cod, heavy like meat,
And none of us could kick him to his feet;
Just blinked at my revolver, blearily;
—Didn't appear to know a war was on,
Or see the blasted trench at which he stared.
"I'll do 'em in," he whined. "If this hand's spared,
I'll murder them, I will."

     A low voice said,
"It's Blighty, p'raps, he sees; his pluck's all gone,
Dreaming of all the valiant, that aren't dead:
Bold uncles, smiling ministerially;
Maybe his brave young wife, getting her fun
In some new home, improved materially.
It's not these stiffs have crazed him; nor the Hun."

We sent him down at last, out of the way.
Unwounded;— stout lad, too, before that strafe.
Malingering? Stretcher-bearers winked, "Not half."
Next day I heard the Doc.'s well-whiskied laugh:
"That scum you sent last night soon died. Hooray!"

Wilfred Owen

DISCUSSING THE POEM

1. What sort of position, do you think, did the writer of this poem hold? What leads you to think this?
2. What did the soldier mean when he said in a low voice, "It's Blighty, p'raps, he sees"? (The word "Blighty" has two possible meanings.)
3. Who, in this soldier's opinion, was the man referring to when he whined, "I'll do 'em in"?
4. Why should the man want to murder these people?
5. What opinions of the man were held by the stretcher-bearers, and the doctor? What sort of person did the doctor seem to be?
6. Do you think that the man was putting on an act in order to avoid being sent into battle, and that he was a coward? Can you find any evidence in the poem to support your view? Although the poet does not openly state his own opinion, how, do you think, did he feel about this situation? How does he convey his feelings without actually stating them?

7. Remembering that the man was unwounded, can you suggest why, if he was not bluffing, he might have become deranged, and also why he might have died that very night? (Find out what the word "strafe" means, and discover all you can about a condition known as "shell-shock".)

TECHNIQUES

The Use of Language, and Style

1. *Logical Thinking.* (i) The evidence on which Mitchem, Macleish, Evans and Johnstone decided that their Japanese prisoner had stolen his cigarettes from a British soldier, or even killed one in order to get them, was circumstantial evidence. The facts themselves did not prove the prisoner had stolen the cigarettes; they indicated that this was a possible conclusion—not, however, the only one. If they had seen him taking the cigarettes, they would have had conclusive evidence that he was a thief.

When presented with information to support a particular case, you must decide whether it provides circumstantial or conclusive evidence. If it is the former, you must consider carefully which of the inferences that can be drawn from it is the most likely, and whether this deduction is certain enough to decide on a course of action.

If you were presented with the following sets of circumstantial evidence, what conclusions would you reach? What other explanations are possible? What further evidence would you require in each case to strengthen or prove your deduction? How would you set about getting it?

(*a*) The Japanese prisoner of war has a British cigarette case, which Bamforth admits that he has not given him.

(*b*) In the past, Mary has always scored very low marks in the Mathematics examination. This year she scored much higher marks. The following day she was caught cheating in the History examination.

(*c*) After the leader of a youth club has been replaced by another man, the register shows the attendance to be much lower than previously.

(*d*) Paul and Ronald dislike each other. After a P.E. lesson, Paul reports that his watch is missing. The next day one of Paul's friends finds it in Ronald's desk.

(ii) Comment on the logic of the following arguments.

(*a*) If no-one liked fighting wars, obviously there would be no more wars.

(*b*) Young people never die from lung cancer, so there is no need to warn them about the danger of getting lung cancer from cigarettes.

2. *Colloquialisms and Slang.* An expression which is used in everyday conversation but which is normally considered out-of-place in formal written English is referred to as a colloquialism. The majority of idioms are colloquial. Slang can be thought of as an extreme form of colloquialism, much of it being regarded as inappropriate not only for written English but also for polite conversation.

For many years the inclusion of colloquialisms in a novel was thought to be justified only in the characters' conversations; the narrative had to be written in conventional English. Now, particularly when the story is told by an "ordinary" person, a colloquial style throughout has become more accepted.

Which of the extracts and books you have read, would you say were written in such a style?

Consider these colloquialisms used in "The Long and the Short and the Tall". Can you place any of them as regional idioms (i.e. characteristic of a particular part of Britain)? How many of them would you class as slang?

fags	to have a drag
a Nip	a slob
it gets my hump	to have a crack at something
to knock something off	hold it a sec
a Herb	to lift something
smokes	waiting for the hump
a dim nit	to slip somebody something
to grease up to somebody	to slot somebody
to whip something	a shufti
to go the bundle	to once it over
snouts	nubs
Blighty	half-inching
guts	jack it in

Give a more conventional expression for each of the above colloquialisms. Then, where possible, give another colloquialism with a similar meaning.

3. *General Punctuation.* Study the punctuation of the dialogue in "The Long and the Short and the Tall". Is punctuation as important in a play, so far as style is concerned, as in a novel or a poem?

What effect is gained through using short, jerky sentences? Where could semicolons be substituted for full stops? Could this change make any difference to an actor's interpretation of the lines?

Where has Willis Hall used grammatically incomplete sentences? What changes in punctuation or wording are needed to make these grammatically complete? Do these changes detract in any way from the realism and the impact of the dialogue?

What does the use of dots . . . within the dialogue tell an actor about the way in which he should speak his lines? Where do these occur in the extract, and why do these particular lines need to be spoken like this?

Consider the use of dashes in both dialogue and stage directions. By what punctuation marks could they be replaced? Are there any instances where you think dashes would be more appropriate than the punctuation actually used by Willis Hall?

Correct English, and Vocabulary

4. *Verbosity.* In conversation, people often include words and phrases that are unnecessary.

e.g. BAMFORTH: . . . finish *off* the job.

The word *off* is superfluous—"finish the job" means the same. Try to avoid unnecessary words in your writing.

Rewrite the following verbose sentences, omitting unnecessary words and phrases.

(*a*) I personally do not think you should let him borrow your rifle on loan.

(*b*) On many occasions the man often returns back from the barracks by means of a taxi.

(*c*) I want you all to check up on your supplies of ammunition and, at 2 p.m. this afternoon, report to the neighbouring camp nearby, where we shall meet up with the other partrols to discuss about the next raid.

(*d*) The reason why we shall continue to remain here in this hut is because the enemy has completely surrounded us and would shoot us up if we stepped outside of the door.

(*e*) When the sergeant saw with his own eyes that the men were assembled together in the canteen, he was really and truly very angry, because, in his opinion, he did not think they had any right whatsoever to be there.

5. *Abbreviations.* What do the two abbreviations used in the extract—P.O.W. and N.C.O.—stand for?

Give the full versions of these military abbreviations.

Brig.-Gen.	C. in C.
Maj.	F.M.
Capt.	N.A.A.F.I.
Cpl	N.A.T.O.
Pte	R.E.M.E.

Notice that two of these abbreviations do not require full stops. The exceptions do not need full stops (although it is certainly not incorrect to use them), because each ends with the last letter of the word itself. Similarly it is not necessary to put a full stop after Mr or Mrs.

Make a list of other abbreviations that do not require full stops.

Three of the abbreviations given do not usually have their letters pronounced separately; instead they are pronounced as complete words. How are these three words pronounced?

List other abbreviations that are usually pronounced as complete words.

6. *Direct Speech.* Rewrite part of the extract as direct speech, in either the past or the present tense. Use a wide range of verbs to indicate the manner of speaking. Incorporate the stage directions. Make sure you paragraph and punctuate your version correctly.

TOPICS FOR WRITTEN WORK

1. Write a play in which the characters are involved in some sort of conflict.

Hints

You will write a more convincing play if you use characters with whom you are familiar, and a setting that you know something about. Here are three possible situations.

(a) Articles have been stolen from the school cloakroom. Suspicion falls on one member of your class, but several people are doubtful about his or her guilt.

(b) A father accuses his son (or daughter) of creating a disturbance in the street late at night. This is denied. The mother believes the boy (or girl) and tries to persuade her husband that he has made a mistake.

(c) A group of teachers are discussing how to deal with one of their pupils who has been badly behaved and has done no school work for a long time. Some of the teachers are in favour of severe punishment, others are not.

Decide how you will develop the situation you have chosen and make your characters put forward the relevant evidence and opinions, both sides pointing out the illogicalities and inadequacies in the arguments of their opponents. Include slang and colloquialisms where appropriate. Make sure that you set out your script correctly.

2. Imagine that you are a soldier in the trenches during the war. Write a poem about your experiences.

Hints

It is early morning and you are expecting another attack by the enemy. Describe your thoughts and feelings as you await the dawn. Portray as harshly as you can the physical conditions—the cold, the damp, the rats, the mud—and your own physical discomfort. The photograph below may help you to describe the scene.

3. Give a summary of any conflict that has recently been in the news.
Hints
   The conflict can be of any kind—a war, a strike, a political argument, a clash between two individuals, or one individual and established authority, and so on. Your summary should be unbiased, and should include an account of the cause of the conflict, the arguments put forward by the parties involved, the steps they have taken, the effects of these moves, attempts to solve the conflict, and the present state of the situation. If it is still unresolved, put forward your own suggestions for solving the problem.

Pupils' Work

Assault

Gas;
faces turned,
eyes scanned the sky,
hands feverishly ripped open canisters
and masks were soon covering faces.
A man choked
as the white cloud
swirling around him like fog caught him
unawares.
Then his body flopped over.
Shells floated across
as if suspended by hidden strings
and then tired
they sank earthwards.
A command
like a cold shower
to revive the mumbling shadows.
I fixed my bayonet
scrambled over the open trench
and struggled through
the thick pasty mud.

It was quiet
as we walked,
except for the sucking
groaning squelching sound
which came from the wet earth
as it tried
to creep into our stockings.
The wind cut me
with the skill of an executioner
as it came roaring down the ridge
towards which we were marching
over the wall.
Then a whistle:
"Good luck, mates."
Mind that hole! Through the wire,
over the top.
And kill.
"God. This is fun!"

                                        Erno Muller

79

ORAL WORK

1. Act or tape-record the extract from "The Long and the Short and the Tall." Give each character an appropriate accent. In addition to this, you can act or tape-record some of the plays written by the class. If you decide to act the extract or any of your own plays, work out an appropriate layout for each of the scenes. If you tape-record the work, try to include some sound effects.

2. Using the information in the passage and the notes below, give a short talk, in your own words, on "The Treatment of Prisoners of War". You may re-arrange the order of the material if you wish.

(a) Primitive and barbarous tribes had no idea of giving special treatment to prisoners of war. When prisoners were captured in the kind of battles that were fought in pre-Roman times, and for many centuries later among smaller tribes and primitive peoples, they were either summarily slaughtered or permanently enslaved, and little distinction would be made between the fighting men and any women, children or other civilians who might be captured.

The Roman idea of conquest was more concerned with imposing law and order on the civilian population, and in the Roman Empire it was possible for captured enemies to become freed men in the course of time, as well as for members of subject races to become Roman citizens. The practice in Medieval Western Europe was also sometimes quite humane, because the widespread habit of paying ransom money for the release of captives often made prisoners quite valuable and therefore worth preserving.

The Treaty of Westphalia in 1648 is often taken as marking the beginning of modern thinking about prisoners, because it allowed for the release of prisoners without ransom. During the 17th and 18th centuries civilised nations generally came to accept that humane treatment of prisoners was not only right but also expedient, since it might mean that one's own prisoners would be better treated by the enemy.

The Geneva Conventions of 1864, 1906, 1929 and 1949 sought to regulate the treatment of prisoners by international agreement, and laid down that prisoners, although confined, should be treated generally as well as one's own soldiers, and returned home immediately hostilities were ended.

(b) 1929 Geneva Convention—all military prisoners covered—principles of treatment: 1. full information on prisoners taken. 2. sanitary quarters away from military zone. 3. sufficient, wholesome food. 4. medical attention. 5. pay on agreed scales. 6. free passage for letters and parcels. 7. non-officers given reasonable work of non-military kind—

1949 Convention extended definition—included volunteers, resistance fighters, civilians accompanying army or resisting invasion—forbad: reprisals, physical violence or insult, extorting information (except for name, date of birth, service no., rank)—punishments and discipline on same principles as for captors themselves.

3. Hold a class discussion on "The Treatment of Prisoners of War".
4. Suggest some of the camera shots you might use if you were to make a film of this chapter's extract from "The Long and the Short and the Tall". Compare your ideas with those put forward by other people in the class and discuss which of the shots would be the most effective. (Do not write out a scenario, however.)

ACTIVITIES AND RESEARCH

1. Collect more information about the treatment of P.O.W.'s as laid down in the rules of the Geneva Conventions, by consulting the entry under *Prisoners of War* in the "Encyclopaedia Britannica" and referring to other reference books.
2. Compile your own "Dictionary of Modern Slang". Make a list of all the current slang words and colloquialisms in common use among your contemporaries. Give an accurate translation and, where possible, the origin of each one. For example, the words "hep" and "hep cat", which were in common use among teenagers in the early 1960's, meant "in the know, or having good taste" and "a follower of the current trends in fashion". They derive from the cry "help!" which North American horse-drivers called to their teams; hence "to get hep" meant "to liven up".
3. "The Long and the Short and the Tall" contains a number of swear words. Some people object to these being used on the stage and demand stricter censorship. Find out what you can about the history of censorship in this country, and the position as it stands at the moment. Who is responsible for licensing plays, and what kinds of plays are refused permission? Can performances of unlicensed plays be given? A useful summary of the current procedure will be found in the "Writers' and Artists' Year Book", which is available in the reference section of most public libraries. Compare the censorship of plays with the regulations covering film censorship, and those applying to the publication of books.

FURTHER READING

The Long and the Short and the Tall by Willis Hall (Heinemann; Penguin).

As you will have gathered from the extract, this gripping play is concerned with the predicament of the British patrol, who cannot decide what they should do with their Japanese prisoner, with whom they become friendly but who still remains a source of danger, and who, when one of the patrol shoots him in a fit of panic, finally becomes the indirect cause of their discovery.

A Glimpse of the Sea, with *Last Day in Dreamland,* and *Return to the Sea* (Evans Plays).

The setting for *Last Day in Dreamland* is an amusement arcade on the last day of the season; the employees are about to lose their jobs and have to face the prospect of six month's unemployment. The central character, Fentrill, is very similar in personality and temperament to Bamforth. *A Glimpse of the Sea* is about a seaside infidelity, and is in quite a different style.

Air Mail from Cyprus in *The Television Playright* (Michael Joseph).

The action of this play revolves around a girl's battle to keep the secret of her brother's cowardice from her mother.

Much of Hall's other work, apart from over eighty radio and television scripts that he has written on his own, has been in collaboration with Keith Waterhouse.

Celebration by Willis Hall and Keith Waterhouse (Michael Joseph).

Two large working class families in the North of England are faced with two of the biggest events in their lives—a wedding and a funeral. They are anxious that everything should be done properly, but are bedevilled by a series of minor catastrophies.

CHAPTER 6

Modern Fables

The fable is a short story, frequently illustrating a moral. Those of the best known fabulist, Aesop of Ancient Greece, were usually of an instructive and serious nature, and this is how the fable has generally come to be regarded. But these absurd and witty pieces by James Thurber show that the fable form can be used in quite a different way.

The Little Girl and the Wolf

One afternoon a big wolf waited in a dark forest for a little girl to come along carrying a basket of food to her grandmother. Finally a little girl did come along and she was carrying a basket of food. "Are you carrying that basket to your grandmother?" asked the wolf. The little girl said yes, she was. So the wolf asked her where her grandmother lived and the little girl told him and he disappeared into the wood.

When the little girl opened the door of her grandmother's house she saw that there was somebody in bed with a nightcap and nightgown on. She had approached no nearer than twenty-five feet from the bed when she saw that it was not her grandmother but the wolf, for even in a nightcap a wolf does not look any more like your grandmother than the Metro-Goldwyn lion looks like Calvin Coolidge. So the little girl took an automatic out of her basket and shot the wolf dead.

Moral. It is not so easy to fool little girls nowadays as it used to be.

The Glass in the Field

A short time ago some builders, working on a studio in Connecticut, left a huge square of plate glass standing upright in a field one day. A goldfinch flying swiftly across the field struck the glass and was knocked cold. When he came to he hastened to his club, where an attendant bandaged his head and gave him a stiff drink. "What the hell happened?" asked a sea gull. "I was flying across the meadow when all of a sudden the air crystallized on me," said the goldfinch. The sea gull, and a hawk, and an eagle all laughed heartily. A swallow listened gravely. "For fifteen years, fledgling and bird, I've flown this country," said the eagle, "and I assure you there is no such thing as air crystallizing. Water yes; air no." "You were probably struck by a hailstone," the hawk told the goldfinch. "Or he may have had a stroke," said the sea gull. "What do you think, swallow?" "Why, I—I think maybe the air crystallized on him," said the swallow. The large birds laughed so loudly that the goldfinch became annoyed and bet them each a dozen worms that they couldn't follow the course he had flown across the field without encountering the hardened atmosphere. They all took his bet; the swallow went along to watch. The sea gull, the eagle, and the hawk decided to fly together over the route the goldfinch indicated. "You come, too," they said to the swallow. "I—I—well, no," said the swallow. "I don't think I will." So the three large birds took off together and they hit the glass together and they were all knocked cold.

Moral: *He who hesitates is sometimes saved.*

The Shrike and the Chipmunks

Once upon a time there were two chipmunks, a male and a female. The male chipmunk thought that arranging nuts in artistic patterns was more fun than just piling them up to see how many you could pile up. The female was all for piling up as many as you could. She told her husband that if he gave up making designs with the nuts there would be room in their large cave for a great many more and he would soon become the wealthiest chipmunk in the woods. But he would not let her interfere with his designs, so she flew into a rage and left him. "The shrike will get you," she said, "because you are helpless and cannot look after yourself." To be sure, the female chipmunk had not been gone three nights before the male had to dress for a banquet and could not find his studs or shirt or suspenders. So he couldn't go to the banquet, but that was just as well, because all the chipmunks who did go were attacked and killed by a weasel.

The next day the shrike began hanging around outside the chipmunk's cave, waiting to catch him. The shrike couldn't get in because the doorway was clogged up with soiled laundry and dirty dishes. "He will come out for a walk after breakfast and I will get him then," thought the shrike. But the chipmunk slept all day and did not get up and have breakfast until after dark. Then he came out for a breath of air before beginning work on a new design. The shrike swooped down to snatch up the chipmunk, but could not see very well on account of the dark, so he batted his head against an alder branch and was killed.

84

A few days later the female chipmunk returned and saw the awful mess the house was in. She went to the bed and shook her husband. "What would you do without me?" she demanded. "Just go on living, I guess," he said. "You wouldn't last five days," she told him. She swept the house and did the dishes and sent out the laundry, and then she made the chipmunk get up and wash and dress. "You can't be healthy if you lie in bed all day and never get any exercise," she told him. So she took him for a walk in the bright sunlight and they were both caught and killed by the shrike's brother, a shrike named Stoop.

Moral: *Early to rise and early to bed makes a male healthy and wealthy and dead.*

The Bear Who Let It Alone

In the woods of the Far West there once lived a brown bear who could take it or let it alone. He would go into a bar where they sold mead, a fermented drink made of honey, and he would have just two drinks. Then he would put some money on the bar and say, "See what the bears in the back room will have," and he would go home. But finally he took to drinking by himself most of the day. He would reel home at night, kick over the umbrella stand, knock down the bridge lamps, and ram his elbows through the windows. Then he would collapse on the floor and lie there until he went to sleep. His wife was greatly distressed and his children were very frightened.

At length the bear saw the error of his ways and began to reform. In the end he became a famous teetotaller and a persistent temperance lecturer. He would tell everybody that came to his house about the awful effects of drink, and he would boast about how strong and well he had become since he gave up touching the stuff. To demonstrate this, he would stand on his head and on his hands and he would turn cartwheels in the house, kicking over the umbrella stand, knocking down the bridge lamps, and ramming his elbows through the windows. Then he would lie down on the floor, tired by his healthful exercise, and go to sleep. His wife was greatly distressed and his children were very frightened.

Moral: *You might as well fall flat on your face as lean over too far backward.*

(from *Vintage Thurber* by James Thurber)

APPRECIATION AND DISCUSSION

1. On which folk tale is "The Little Girl and the Wolf" based?
2. What is the "Metro-Goldwyn lion"? Who was Calvin Coolidge?
3. The style of "The Little Girl and the Wolf" is similar to the style used for many children's stories. What are the characteristics of this style, and where has Thurber employed these techniques.
4. The stories depend, for some of their effect, upon bizarre contrasts, e.g. colloquialisms which are not in keeping with the general style. What other contrasts are there, and where do they occur?
5. What sort of animal is a chipmunk? Why are chipmunks particularly suitable characters for this story? Why not have wolves or snakes? What other animals would be suitable?
6. What human attitudes to life could the male and the female chipmunk stand for? Do you think that Thurber intended such a comparison?
7. What was it that the brown bear could "take or let alone"? What does this saying mean?
8. Explain more fully the moral of "The Bear Who Let It Alone".
9. (a) Inventing a completely bizaare and pointless moral (b) making up a moral which gives a useful piece of advice (c) taking a well known moral and altering it—are three of the techniques James Thurber has used to construct his fables. Say which technique has been used for each of his stories printed in this chapter, and each of the fables in the "Pupil's Work" section.
10. How many fables do you know? How many of them had talking animals as characters? What moral did each one illustrate?
11. The fable has often been used as a form of criticism—to attack individuals, policies and situations. What advantages does it have that make it suitable for this purpose (particularly when criticism is not favourably received)?
12. The moral or message of a fable is always stated quite explicitly at the end of the story. This does not mean, however, that other sorts of stories do not contain a message. Many novels, films and plays put forward a particular point of view or, perhaps, give a warning of some kind. One story, for example, might show that money cannot buy happiness; another, that colour prejudice is unjustified; and another, the danger of allowing nuclear arms to spread. Can you refer to a novel, film or play and explain to the rest of the class what the basic theme is, and what message is being conveyed?

TECHNIQUES

The Use of Language, and Style

1. *Jargon.* Remembering that Thurber has used and even exaggerated the simplified style often found in children's stories, say what changes you would make to the vocabulary and sentence structure of "The Little Girl and the Wolf" to give it a more mature tone. Take care, however, not to become verbose and pompous, for such English is even less acceptable than that written in an over-simplified style.

A verbose, pompous style is particularly ugly when it contains jargon. This is the sort of language used by specialists of various kinds. Thus we refer to legal jargon, commercial jargon, medical jargon, and so on. In its proper context, jargon can serve a useful purpose, but when it is used unnecessarily, because the writer cannot be bothered to express himself in clearer, more meaningful English, it is often difficult to understand and unpleasant to listen to.

Consider, for example, how James Thurber's fable would sound if it were written in the jargon of a police report (deliberately exaggerated here, of course).

At 3-15 on the afternoon of December 12th, the young lady in question commonly believed to go under the name of Little Red Riding Hood, was proceeding in a westerly direction through the local forest, which at the time was inadequately supplied with lighting facilities. This excursion was in the normal course of her duties, namely, the delivery of a basket of food to her grandmother. While patrolling the main path, I noticed a heavily built wolf loitering in a suspicious manner within the confines of the forest, apparently with the intention of accosting the young lady when she reached the vicinity in which he had stationed himself . . . .

Comment on the expressions used in this, and on the general style of police reports. Give other examples of police report jargon, e.g. "unknown assailants". Can you suggest why police reports, particularly those which are to be used as evidence in a trial, rely so heavily on these set expressions?

Complete "The Little Girl and the Wolf" in the style of a police report. N.B. Do *not* use such a style on any other occasion. This exercise is intended only to give you practice in recognising such jargon, so that you can avoid it in future.

Give examples of other kinds of jargon,
e.g. the jargon used in sermons—"we are gathered here today".

2. *Climax and Anti-climax.* (i) When a story rises to its highest level of excitement, it is said to have reached a climax. (Look up the origin of this word.)

At what point in "The Wall" (Chapter 4) does the climax occur? Does the author take long to tell us the outcome once the climax has been reached?

In "The Long and the Short and the Tall" (Chapter 5), events look as though they are moving towards a climax while Bamforth is outside the hut. In fact, Bamforth's return relaxes the tension; but shortly afterwards it begins to build up again, and the play takes another step towards the climax. Compare this technique with that which uses a steady progression.

A build-up to a climax can also be achieved in the space of one or two sentences, each statement being stronger and more important than the one before.

    e.g. I came, I saw, I conquered.

He trembled, whimpered, and finally screamed with terror.

Write sentences of your own on the following topics, building each one up to a climax.

 (*a*) someone growing angry
 (*b*) someone attacking the "evils of drink"
 (*c*) one person threatening another
 (*d*) one person praising another
 (*e*) an audience becoming very excited

(ii) When a writer appears to be working up to a climax, and then ends with something unexpectedly ridiculous, he is using anti-climax (or bathos). This usually has a comic effect. As with a climax, an anti-climax can occur both at the end of a complete story, and within a single sentence. Did any of the Thurber fables in this chapter end in or contain anti-climax?

Consider this example, and then complete each of the sentences below by adding an anti-climax.

> e.g. Over the last ten years he has acquired a beautiful wife, a luxurious home, a vast fortune, and a bald head.

(a) Falling upon his knees, her lover cried, "I offer you my body, my mind, my life, my love, and ———."

(b) The president settled himself in a chair, picked up the document, studied it carefully, and pondered on it for several hours before ———.

(c) With my own razor, you have slashed my clothes to ribbons, cut my face and hands, and threatened to kill me; not only that, you have ———.

(d) He took great care, every advantage, full command and ———.

(e) I came, I saw, I conquered, I ———.

3. *Note-making.* (i) The notes below give the outline of another of Thurber's fables. Expand these into a story, writing in the style that Thurber has used for the fables printed in this chapter.

> Scotty dog to country for visit. Decided farm dogs cowards. All afraid of animal with white stripe down back. Scotty—I will lick him. Farm dog—Any questions? No. Went to woods. Short fight. Scotty beaten. Claimed animal threw vitriol at him. Later, farm dog—Another animal all afraid of. Scotty—I will lick him. Farm dog—Any questions? No. To woods. Short fight. When Scotty regained consciousness, farm dog pulling out quills. Scotty claimed animal pulled knife on him. Then Scotty threatened to beat up farm dog. Held nose with one paw to ward off vitriol. Covered eyes with other to keep out knives. Couldn't see, couldn't smell, so badly beaten up. Back to city. Nursing home.

> *Moral: Better to ask some of the questions than know all the answers.*

(ii) Reduce to notes, one or more of the fables printed in this chapter, then, working only from your notes, rewrite the story in your own words. Afterwards, check your version against the original. Remember that you are *not* being asked to summarise, i.e. shorten, the story. Your version should be about the same length as the original.

Correct English, and Vocabulary

4. *Confused Words.* (i) Read aloud these pairs of words to show that you know the difference in pronunciation. Then compose short sentences to show the difference in meaning.

e.g. The chipmunk *hopped* back into his cave.

The chipmunk *hoped* that his wife would leave him.

bellow, below	dully, duly	fussed, fused
bitter, biter	filling, filing	scarred, scared
dinner, diner	furry, fury	stripped, striped

(ii) Compose short sentences to show the difference in meaning between the words in these pairs.

bare, bear	mail, male	root, route	tail, tale
fair, fare	mare, mayor	scene, seen	taught, taut
fate, fête	pair, pear	scent, sent	their, there

5. *General Punctuation.* A semicolon, full stop, dash, hyphen and comma are to be inserted in the sentences below—one punctuation mark in each sentence.

(*a*) This nerve shattering experience convinced the large birds that they were wrong.

(*b*) The attendant gave him a drink bandaged his head and drew up a chair.

(*c*) James Thurber Esq has been invited to the reception.

(*d*) His wife was greatly distressed his children were very frightened.

(*e*) The birds learnt their lesson the hard way through experience.

TOPICS FOR WRITTEN WORK

1. Write a humorous fable of your own.

Hints

To construct your fable, employ one of the techniques mentioned in Question 9 of the "Appreciation and Discussion" section. Use the same simplified, children's-story style that Thurber has used. You could also introduce colloquialisms and facts that are out of keeping with the tone and content of the rest of your story, in order to achieve bizarre contrasts as he has done. Work out your story and your moral in the form of notes first, dealing with such points as climax and anti-climax at this stage.

2. Expand your answer to Question 12 "Appreciation and Discussion" into an essay.

Hints

Start by giving an outline of the plot of the novel, film or play. Describe the appearance, background and attitudes of the main characters. Say what theme was being dealt with, and what point of view the story conveyed. What techniques did it use to convey and emphasise this message (e.g. emotive description and characterization, evocative music)?

3. Rewrite the following example of legal or official jargon in clear, concise English.

Trespass

If a police officer is requested by the lawful occupier to aid in ejecting a person improperly on his premises, although in law that person is simply a trespasser, the officer may, when he can place reliance on the statement of the applicant, properly give his assistance, using no more force than is necessary for that purpose.

An officer should only act in the presence and on the expressed application of the lawful occupier, and after the person has refused to leave on a formal request being made to him in the presence of the officer. He should himself first use persuasion and bear in mind that he must not take the person into custody, but leave him perfectly free as soon as the street or public road is reached; for, although the intruder in such a case is wrongfully on the premises he has not been guilty of any offence against the criminal law and the intervention of a police officer is, strictly speaking, not as a police officer but as a private person aiding the occupier.

Hints

Read through the passage once in order to grasp what it is about. Read it through again, noting any words or phrases that you do not understand; find out what they mean. On the third reading, rewrite it in clear, concise English.

Pupils' Work

Walley Bee

Once upon a time there was a kangaroo named Walley Bee. He was a very agile kangaroo and could jump 30 metres in one pace; he could even jump across a whole valley in a few strides. But Walley was very careless and did not worry if he knocked down his neighbours' wheat fields or fences or even his neighbours themselves.

After a while Walley's neighbours decided that it was about time they had a talk to him about his irresponsibility.

Walley, after being told off and threatened by his neighbours, decided to be careful from then on. He looked before he jumped over a valley or a fence; and after doing this for a few days decided that it was quite the best thing to do in future.

One day Walley went up into the mountains. While he was hopping along, he came across a gaping hole in the ground and, doing as his neighbours had told him, he looked over the edge to see what was there before he jumped. But the sight of the great space of nothing below made him giddy and he fell headlong into the deep hole and was killed.

Moral: Leap before you look.

K. R. Catchpole

Three Bears

Once upon a time there were three bears, and in the evening they all used to watch Noddy on the "telly". One evening one bear said, "I am going to chop wood for the old man down the road." Now this was very unusual, for this particular bear didn't like work and it was well known he would rather sit by the "telly" and watch Noddy than chop wood. The smarter of the other two bears deduced that his companion must have a good reason for going to chop wood for the old man. So he decided to go with him. The third bear did not want to stay and watch Noddy alone, so he went too. When the bears got to the old man's place they started chopping wood. Soon all the wood was chopped and the old man said, "Here is the reward I told your friend I would give you if you came and chopped wood for me." And he gave the three bears 3p. Two of the bears were delighted about this unexpected reward. But the one who didn't like work was not at all pleased. For he had been hoping to get the 3p to himself and buy three 1p. gumsnakes. Because the others had interfered he only got one 1p gumsnake.

Moral: Many hands make less gumsnakes.

P. Herd

Fryatt's Fable

Twice upon a time (well, it goes something like that) there was a man who had a head shaped like an egg, and who lived in a town called Lagoon. This lollop was always lounging on a couch and never went to work, so his only income was the dole.

But one day his wife sent him out to work, and he got a job sitting on a wall counting sheep.

One day he was counting sheep and it was a warm summer's day so he fell asleep. After about an hour a strong wind blew him off the wall, onto the cobbled courtyard below. This was very unfortunate because the cobbled courtyard was very hard and it broke his egg-head, and he died.

So then his wife had no regular income at all, not even the dole money she used to get when her husband was alive.

Moral: It's better to have a live lollop in Lagoon than a dead egg-head somewhere else.

R. Fryatt

ORAL WORK

1. Read to the rest of the class the fable you have written, or, if you do not think yours is good enough, choose a fable by a well known writer such as Aesop. If the fables written by the class are popular, you could make a tape-recorded anthology for playing to other classes.

ACTIVITIES AND RESEARCH

1. Look up *Fables* in an encyclopaedia (consult the Index Volume first), and other reference books such as the "Oxford Companion to English Literature". Gather information about Aesop ("Fables of Aesop" translated by S. A. Mandford, published Penguin 1954), La Fontaine and others.

2. You could draw a series of cartoons to illustrate the fable you have written, or any others that you think would lend themselves to comic illustration.

3. Cut out from newspapers and magazines any examples of jargon, and bring them to school to show to your colleagues.

4. Orators are very aware of the power of climax in a speech. Consider, for example, this famous passage from one of Sir Winston Churchill's war speeches, which uses climax and repetition very successfully.

   ". . . we shall defend our island, whatever the cost may be, we shall fight on the beaches, we shall fight on the landing grounds, we shall fight in the fields and in the streets, we shall fight in the hills; we shall never surrender."

Study some of Sir Winston Churchill's other speeches, and speeches made by present day orators, and analyse them for climax, repetition, and similar techniques.

FURTHER READING

Fables For Our Time, are included in *Vintage Thurber* (Hamish Hamilton) and in *The Thurber Carnival* (Hamish Hamilton; Penguin).

The latter selection of James Thurber's work has been made from nine books. In addition to *Fables For Our Time*, there is *My Life and Hard Times*, and, from *The Owl in the Attic, The Pet Department. The Night the Ghost Got In* and *The Dog that Bit People* are two typical Thurber stories dealing with ridiculous domestic catastrophes. *The Secret Life of Walter Mitty* also provides a good introduction to this author's brand of humour. His drawings, frequently showing men and women at their worst and animals at their best, are as amusing as his text, perhaps more so to some people.

Further Fables For Our Time (Hamish Hamilton).

More fables in the same witty, sophisticated and absurd mould as those printed in this chapter.

A Thurber Garland (Hamish Hamilton).

Those of you who appreciate Thurber's illustrations will certainly enjoy this selection of twenty-five drawings that have now become comic classics.

The White Deer (Hamish Hamilton; Penguin).

This collection of "mad, beautiful, fairy stories", again illustrated by the author, was intended for children but has probably been enjoyed even more by adults.

Some of his other books are:

Thurber's Dogs (Hamish Hamilton).

The Years with Ross (Hamish Hamilton).

The Wonderful O (Hamish Hamilton).

Lanterns and Lances—humorous essays (Hamish Hamilton; Penguin).

CHAPTER 7 ## Daydreams and Nightmares

Although Dylan Thomas's style may be puzzling at times, the pictures he presents are always rich and exciting, as in this account of "A Visit to Grandpa's".

In the middle of the night I woke from a dream full of whips and lariats as long as serpents, and runaway coaches on mountain passes and wide, windy gallops over cactus fields, and I heard the old man in the next room crying, "Gee-up!" and "Whoa!" and trotting his tongue on the roof of his mouth.

It was the first time I had stayed in Grandpa's house. The floorboards had squeaked like mice as I climbed into bed, and the mice between the walls had creaked like wood as though another visitor was walking on them. It was a mild summer night, but curtains had flapped and branches beaten against the window. I had pulled the sheets over my head, and soon was roaring and riding in a book.

"Whoa there, my beauties!" cried Grandpa. His voice sounded very young and loud, and his tongue had powerful hooves, and he made his bedroom into a great meadow. I thought I would see if he was ill, or had set his bed-clothes on fire, for my mother had said that he lit his pipe under the blankets, and had warned me to run to his help if I smelt smoke in the night. I went on tiptoe through the darkness to his bedroom door, brushing against the furniture and upsetting a candlestick with a thump. When I saw there was a light in the room I felt frightened, and as I opened the door I heard Grandpa shout, "Gee-up!" as loudly as a bull with a megaphone.

He was sitting straight up in bed and rocking from side to side as though the bed were on a rough road; the knotted edges of the counterpane were his reins; his invisible horses stood in the shadow beyond the bedside candle. Over a white flannel nightshirt he was wearing a red waistcoat with walnut-sized buttons. The over-filled bowl of his pipe smouldered among his whiskers like a little, burning hayrick on a stick. At the sight of me, his hands dropped from the reins and lay blue and quiet, the bed stopped still on a level road, he muffled his tongue into silence and the horses drew softly up.

"Is there anything the matter, Grandpa?" I asked, though the clothes were not on fire. His face in the candlelight looked like a ragged quilt pinned upright on the black air and patched all over with goat-beards.

He stared at me mildly. Then he blew down his pipe, scattering the sparks and making a high, wet dog-whistle of the stem, and shouted: "Ask no questions."

After a pause, he said slyly: "Do you ever have nightmares, boy?"

I said: "No."

"Oh, yes, you do," he said.

I said that I was woken by a voice that was shouting to horses.

"What did I tell you?" he said. "You eat too much. Who ever heard of horses in a bedroom?"

He fumbled under his pillow, brought out a small tinkling bag, and carefully untied its strings. He put a sovereign in my hand, and said: "Buy a cake." I thanked him and wished him good night.

As I closed my bedroom door, I heard his voice crying loudly and gaily, "Gee-up! gee-up" and the rocking of the travelling bed.

In the morning I woke from a dream of fiery horses on a plain that was littered with furniture, and of large, cloudy men who rode six horses at a time and whipped them with burning bed-clothes. Grandpa was at breakfast, dressed in deep black. After breakfast he said, "There was a terrible loud wind last night," and he sat in his arm-chair by the hearth to make clay balls for the fire. Later in the morning he took me for a walk, through Johnstown village and into the fields on the Llanstephan road . . . .

On the last day but one of my visit I was taken to Llanstephan in a governess cart pulled by a short, weak pony. Grandpa might have been driving a bison, so tightly he held the reins, so ferociously cracked the long whip, so blasphemously shouted warning to boys who played in the road, so stoutly stood with his gaitered legs apart and cursed the demon strength and wilfulness of his tottering pony.

"Look out, boy!" he cried when we came to each corner, and pulled and tugged and jerked and sweated and waved his whip like a rubber sword. And when the pony had crept miserably round each corner, Grandpa turned to me with a sighing smile: "We weathered that one, boy."

When we came to Llanstephan village at the top of the hill, he left the cart by the "Edwinsford Arms" and patted the pony's muzzle and gave it sugar, saying: "You're a weak little pony, Jim, to pull big men like us."

(from *Portrait of the Artist as a Young Dog* by Dylan Thomas)

APPRECIATION AND DISCUSSION

1. What had the boy who tells this story been dreaming about before he was woken up?
2. What had he been doing before he went to sleep? Was there any connection between this and his dream?
3. What connection was there between his dream and what he heard upon waking?
4. Why did the boy go to Grandpa's room?
5. What was Grandpa doing?
6. Was he doing this in his sleep, or was he awake and aware of what he was doing?
7. Why was Grandpa (a) "trotting his tongue on the roof of his mouth" (b) "rocking from side to side" (c) holding "the knotted edges of the counterpane"?
8. Why, do you imagine, was Grandpa wearing a waistcoat in bed?
9. What did he say to his grandson, and why did he give him a sovereign?
10. Why did Grandpa say, after breakfast the following morning, "There was a terrible loud wind last night"?
11. Would you say that Grandpa deliberately evoked his fantasies, or that he drifted into them because he was an old man whose mind was deteriorating? Quote from the passage to support your opinion.
12. How did the boy feel about his grandpa? How did the old man feel about his grandson? Was their relationship a close one? How does the story establish a bond between them?

The Hero

Young Jimmy Stone lived a life of his own,
but he shared a small room with his brother.
He woke up at six from a kick in the head,
the alarm-clock bawling beside his bed;
he envied his kid-brother, Ken, sleeping sound,
but he had to get up for his paper-round.
His hand wouldn't grip; he closed one fist;
kneading his eyes to clear the mist,
he fought off sleep with a yawn and a groan,
then he knocked out the clock with the other.

The house was still, the air was chill,
and his teeth began to chatter.
He sized himself up in the long wardrobe glass
and decided his chest and his biceps would pass,
pulled a black woollen windcheater over his head,
rummaged round for his socks at the foot of the bed,
half-considered a wash, but decided the strain
wasn't worth it, he'd get a good rinse in the rain,
so he guzzled his thermos-flask off at a swill,
and was off down the road at a clatter.

To cover the mile from his house to the shop,
Jimmy stretched his imagination.
On the six-minute run he'd scored many a goal
As left-winger for Spurs, but this morning his role
was cast as a gun-slinging, wild desperado
who cantered alone through the streets of Laredo.
Beneath him his stallion, a powerful roan,
rang echoing rhythms of steel upon stone;
Jimmy felt for his gun-butt and reined to a stop
In the courtyard in front of the station.

It wasn't the bank he was going to crack,
nor the Wells-Fargo strongroom to plunder;
he'd robbed plenty before, and he'd rob 'em again
but he knew they'd unloaded just then from the train
some freight much more precious than gold, a great stack
of papers that carried death-warrants in black
banner headlines: 'The Stone Brothers break out of jail!
One wounded—gone East—full descriptions.' The tale
mustn't break till a doctor had dressed Kenny's back,
then they'd ride for the border like thunder.

Kicking open the door, he strode into the store;
the news-sheets were stacked on the counter.
The storekeeper hardly looked up from the scales,
unpacking tobacco from seven-pound bales
into dark, lacquered jars, and checking the weight;
not another soul near, by a good stroke of fate.
Leaning over the counter, Jim pitched a half-dollar
to roll past the storekeeper's feet; with a holler
the old guy was grubbing about on the floor.
Counterfeit beat the draw, this encounter.
Jimmy grabbed all the papers up under one arm,
while the storekeeper grovelled and grumbled,
then ran out to his horse, waiting, patient, on guard,
in the rain-washed, deserted, dawn-desolate yard,
swung up in the saddle and gave a quick chuck
to the rein, heading home, laughing out at his luck.
When a doctor had strapped Kenny's back good and tight
and he'd rested a while, they would hit out at night;
no time could be lost, for he knew an alarm
would be raised when his trick had been rumbled.

Unpursued and alone, he steadied the roan
to a canter, checked chamber and trigger.
In the thud of his newly shod boots on the stone
and the turf of the verge, he could feel through the bone
the power of the steel-sinewed stallion's stride.
"Steady, Smoky," he murmured, "we'll easy outride
any posse"—he woke startled-stiff as a van
pulled up sharp at his side and his governor, a man
whose one driving ambition was simply to own
twenty thousand, leaned out with a snigger.

"Who you talking to, Jimmy? You'd better take care—
people might think you're getting half-witted.
Here, give us your papers—you took the wrong stack—
and snap out of your dreaming! Next time it's the sack!"
Jimmy stared at the shop-keeper's bumptious behind,
despising his shop-shape, cash-register mind.
A man whose one dream is of winning the pools
thinks those who make stories are liars or fools;
the sharp schemer and dreamer have nothing to share,
and each by the other is pitied.

                                    Gordon Gridley

DISCUSSING THE POEM

1. Was Jimmy Stone woken up literally by "a kick in the head"? If not, explain what this phrase refers to. How is this idea of a fight extended to the rest of the verse?
2. Why did Jimmy indulge in daydreams on his way to the newsagent's shop?
3. In your own words, outline the plot of the daydream that he conjured up on this particular morning. What other sort of daydream did he indulge in?
4. In what ways did Jimmy connect what he was doing in his imagination with what he was doing in reality?
5. Explain more fully what is meant by "counterfeit beat the draw, this encounter". Can you quote a well known saying which means much the same?
6. What sort of person was the shopkeeper who was Jimmy's employer?
7. Why did the shopkeeper and Jimmy despise and pity one another? What expression does Gordon Gridley use to sum up the two types of people they represent?
8. Work out the rhyme scheme of this poem. Were you very conscious of the rhyme when reading the poem?
9. Pick out and comment on examples of alliteration, onomatopeia, simile and metaphor, and any other figures of speech in the poem.

TECHNIQUES

The Use of Language, and Style

1. *Figures of Speech.* There are many techniques that a writer can use to make his work vivid and interesting. So far we have encountered:

    simile   metaphor   alliteration   onomatopoeia
    exaggeration   understatement   climax   anti-climax.

   These techniques are called figures of speech.

   The prose of Dylan Thomas contains many figures of speech. Identify these figures of speech taken from the passage and explain how each one creates its effect.

(a) "The over-filled bowl of his pipe smouldered among his whiskers like a little burning hayrick on a stick."

(b) " . . . I heard Grandpa shout, 'Gee-up!' as loudly as a bull with a megaphone."

(c) " . . . so tightly he held the reins, so ferociously cracked the long whip, so blasphemously shouted warning to the boys who played in the road, so stoutly stood with his gaitered legs apart and cursed the demon strength and wilfulness of his tottering pony."

(d) "wide, windy gallops" and "roaring and riding".

(e) "At the sight of me, his hands dropped from the reins and lay blue and quiet, the bed stopped still on a level road, he muffled his tongue into silence and the horses drew softly up."

(f) He put a sovereign in my hand and said: "That should be enough to buy a cake."   (adapted)

(g) " . . . his tongue had powerful hooves, and he made his bedroom into a great meadow."

(h) " . . . upsetting a candlestick with a thump" and "a high, wet dog-whistle" and "a small, tinkling bag"

2. *Contrast.* (i) Another technique that writers use is to put close together two or more words with opposite or very different meanings. Such contrast (or antithesis) is a figure of speech often found in proverbs.
    e.g. You cannot teach an *old* dog to perform *new* tricks.
Just as white paint appears whiter, and black paint seems even blacker when the two are put next to one another, so the words *old* and *new* stand out through being brought close together.
Complete these sentences by inserting contrasting words.

(a) ——— rush in where wise men will not go.

(b) Actions are worth more than ———.

(c) Before you can understand others, you must understand ———.

(d) This gamble will either ——— me, or ——— me.

(e) A firework lasts for ———, but a candle burns for ———.

(ii) Explain where the contrast lies in these quotations from the poem.

(a) "Young Jimmy Stone lived a life of his own,
    but he shared a small room with his brother."

(b) "the alarm-clock bawling beside his bed;
    he envied his kid-brother, Ken, sleeping sound"

(c) "pulled a black woollen windcheater over his head,
    rummaged round for his socks at the foot of the bed,"

(d) "Counterfeit beat the draw, this encounter."

(e) "the sharp schemer and the dreamer have nothing to share,"

3. *Mixed Metaphors.* When using a number of metaphors, packed closely together, you must be careful not to confuse them.

    e.g. The *key* to his success proved to be a *web* of lies.

    A *web* cannot possibly act as or be compared to a *key*.

This is known as a mixed metaphor.

The absurdity of mixed metaphors becomes even more apparent when they are illustrated literally.

    e.g. When he lost the thread of his argument and found himself all at sea, with his back to the wall, he buried his head in the sand.

Rewrite the following mixed metaphors in straightforward, literal English.

(*a*) By letting the cat out of the bag, he stabbed his friend in the back.

(*b*) He remained sitting on the fence because, although he appeared to have his head in the clouds, his feet were, in fact, planted firmly on the ground.

(*c*) He was a lion in battle, bulldozing his way through the ranks of the enemy, and filling their hearts with fear as he sailed into action.

(*d*) He left no stone unturned in his attempt to get to the bottom of the fishy affair which had begun to rear its ugly head.

(*e*) With one eye firmly fixed on the future, he put his shoulder to the wheel, his nose to the grindstone, kept an ear to the ground, took the bit between his teeth—and promptly kicked the bucket.

4. *Onomatopoeia.* Both the prose and poetry of Dylan Thomas gain from being read aloud, because the very sounds of the words he uses

can often create moods and images. To enjoy such an effect it is not even necessary to understand the meaning of words. Consider, for example, this poem by Lewis Carroll, in which he has used words of his own invention.

Jabberwocky

'Twas brillig, and the slithy toves
Did gyre and gimble in the wabe;
All mimsy were the borogoves,
And the mome raths outgrabe.

"Beware the Jabberwock, my son!
The jaws that bite, the claws that catch!
Beware the Jubjub bird and shun
The frumious Bandersnatch!"

He took his vorpal sword in hand:
Long time the manxome foe he sought—
So rested he by the Tumtum tree,
And stood awhile in thought.

And as in uffish thought he stood,
The Jabberwock, with eyes of flame,
Came whiffling through the tulgye wood,
And burbled as it came!

One, two! One, two! And through and through
The vorpal blade went snicker-snack!
He left it dead, and with its head
He went galumphing back.

"And hast thou slain the Jabberwock!
Come to my arms, my beamish boy!
O frabjous day! Callooh! Collay!"
He chortled in his joy.

'Twas brillig, and the slithy toves
Did gyre and gimble in the wabe;
All mimsy were the borogoves,
And the mome raths outgrabe.

Lewis Carroll

What sort of animals do you imagine the "slithy toves", and the "Jabberwock" to be? What sort of actions are suggested by the verbs "gyre" and "gimble"? Compare your impressions of these and other words invented by Lewis Carroll with the impressions gained by other members of the class. To what extent do the interpretations agree? (One of the words coined by Lewis Carroll—"chortle"—has now become an accepted part of the English language.)

Make up words and use them in sentences.

e.g. A squibble was winting in the mirn.

Decide beforehand what impression you want to create, try to convey meaning through the sound of your words, and afterwards ask the rest of the class to comment on your choice.

Correct English, and Vocabulary

5. *Commas and Ambiguity.* It is not generally necessary to use a comma when two things are separated by "and". Sometimes, however, ambiguity can arise if a comma is not inserted. In the following sentence from the passage, not only the verb "waved" but "pulled", "tugged", "jerked" and "sweated" could all refer to what Grandpa was doing with his whip.

" 'Look out, boy! he cried when we came to each corner, and pulled and tugged and jerked and sweated and waved his whip like a rubber sword."

How would you punctuate the sentence in order to avoid this ambiguity?

Explain the ambiguity in these sentences and say how you would punctuate them in order to avoid it.

(*a*) I woke from a dream full of cowboys and lariats as long as serpents.

(*b*) We had fish and chips and peaches and cream for dinner.

(*c*) When she had finished ironing and milking the cow, my grandmother prepared my tea.

(*d*) Artists and writers and politicians have nothing in common.

6. *Commas and Correction of Adjectives for Adverbs.* Study this quotation from the passage.

"There was a terrible loud wind last night." (Incorrect)

It can be corrected in two ways.

There was a terrible, loud wind last night.

There was a terribly loud wind last night.

Say why these corrections are necessary, and explain the difference in meaning between them.

Now make similar corrections to each of the sentences below.

(*a*) The new G.P.O. tower is a tremendous high building.

(*b*) I was struck by the unusual coloured design.

(*c*) She has a beautiful clear voice.

(*d*) The flashing light has a horrible hypnotic effect.

104

TOPICS FOR WRITTEN WORK

1. Write a vivid prose description of an old person.
Hints
   You may write about an old person you know or have seen, or use the photograph on this page as the basis for your description. Pay close attention to small details so that your description is not a vague one that could apply to any old person, but conjures up a picture of a particular individual. (Notice how specific is Dylan Thomas's description of his grandfather.) Include not only details of appearance, but movements, speech, mannerisms, etc. Make your description really vivid by using figurative language as extensively as possible. Be careful, however, not to mix your metaphors.

2. (*a*) Give an account, in poetry or prose, of a dream or nightmare that you have experienced. (*b*) Alternatively, you may describe a daydream in which you have indulged at some time.

Hints

(*a*) Choose a dream or a nightmare that affected you deeply at the time and that you remember clearly. When describing it, try to evoke in the reader the same feelings that the dream brought about in you as you experienced it. For how long did you feel like this after you had woken up? What might have caused you to have the dream?

(*b*) When did you indulge in this daydream? Did you indulge in it frequently? Did you keep to one version, or did you vary the plot? Did you connect events in the daydream with reality, as Jimmy Stone did in "The Hero", or were they completely removed from what was going on around you? Can you say why you evoked this daydream?

3. Write a poem for which you invent most of the words, as Lewis Carroll did for "Jabberwocky".

Hints

You may write this as a rhymed poem if you wish, since you will find it fairly easy to complete the rhymes if you are using words of your own invention. Try, however, to convey a definite meaning through the sound of your words. If you cannot think of a suitable plot for your poem, use "Jabberwocky" as a basis, replacing Lewis Carroll's words with your own.

Pupils' Work

Dreams

To eat . . . cheese,
Is to dream . . . . nightmares.
To sleep . . . . soundly
Is to dream . . . . pleasantly.
To know,
To dream,
Nightmares of reality.
To be in . . . .
The unknown,
To be trapped,
To go on,
To gradually . . . .
Disappear.
And yet . . . .

106

Appear in another place.
To see
Big iron railings,
To see friends,
Turn into enemies.
To see things of the unknown,
Change their form
To the bodies of your friends.
To put you
In a cell
With giant spiders,
Flies,
And insects;
To see them
Close in on you,
Come nearer,
Nearer,
To grab you.
And yet
To wake up
In a nice warm bed.
To be away
From harm,
But to be
Shouting,
Screaming,
And trembling.
To see a fly
Upon your pillow,
To be scared
Of the fly
But safe
Back in this
Safe world.

Jacqueline Dewar

The Oldest Member of My Family

I cannot be quite sure, but I think that my oldest relative is my great-uncle, Albert.

He was brought up in the country around Norfolk and Suffolk. He is about eighty years old, but looks not a day over sixty. He has a fine ruddy complexion and silver hair, and is rather short, being less than 1·75 metres. One thing I have always remembered is his large black boots. I noticed these the first time I saw him when I was about five. Another thing I can remember is his spitting. I do not wish to give the idea that he is always spitting, for this is definitely not so. His spitting attacks seem to come only when he is sitting in my grandfather's garden. For no apparent reason he sometimes looks around him, sees that no-one is watching, and then spits. This is followed by a satisfied "Ah!" His wife, my great-aunt Ethel, generally gives a disapproving "Albert!" with the stress on the last syllable. She is about two years younger than he, but looks a good many older. She has wrinkles on her face and around her neck. She is going slightly bald, but conceals this fact with a peculiar bonnet. She wears her National Health glasses on the end of her nose and peers over them, never through them, at her knitting or her book, which is usually an Agatha Christie.

My great-uncle has, as he puts it, "put up with her nigh on fifty years and ain't fed up with her yet." I think among many of my family, this has become one of those tiresome things known as a "family joke".

My great-uncle Albert likes his beer now and again, as most men do, but he is not a heavy drinker, for which my great-aunt praises the heavens every time she thinks about it.

When young, I always thought my great-uncle a miserly old man, but last Christmas this was disproved, as he gave me 25p and I only saw him for half an hour.

P. R. Edwards

ORAL WORK

1. Tape-record "Jabberwocky" and some of the poems written by the class, for which words were invented. Introduce peculiar interruptions and sound effects (e.g. hysterical giggles, weird plopping noises) when recording the poems.

2. If you can borrow a fairly portable tape-recorder, you could tape-record interviews with old people. Remember that much of the success of such an interview will depend upon the skill of the interviewer, so prepare a full list of questions beforehand but be ready to compose others on the spot if you feel that the person being interviewed needs prompting.

3. Practise reading aloud the following passage, and then use the questions given below it as the basis for a discussion about old age.

Improved standards of living, together with better medical services available to a greater number of people, and a general increase in medical knowledge have changed our pattern of life. Each generation is bigger and stronger than the previous one, certain diseases have disappeared, many others are much less common, and where they occur are more easily treated. A greater variety of food is available, and more people are able to afford to buy it. Probably as a result of all this the average age of the population is increasing. In other words, people are tending to live longer. At the same time National Insurance and Retirement Pensions ensure that most people retire from active work at the age of sixty or sixty-five, rather than continuing in employment as long as possible.

It is obviously very desirable that this should be so, and yet the change in the pattern of living has brought about an unexpected problem—the problem of old age. It seems that today more than ever before, large numbers of older people are left in circumstances which make one feel that something must be done about the problem.

Retired pensioners, often after many years of useful work and happy married life, are left alone, without husband or wife, to fend for themselves in old age. They have little money for the necessities of life, none at all for its luxuries. But over and over again we are told that the greatest of their burdens is that of loneliness, of lack of company. What can we do for these old people? Surely some solution can be found besides the obvious one of herding them together into old people's homes. Surely it was never intended that as our society advances in social welfare, those who are too old to play an active part should be left to die alone and neglected.

And when we consider what can be done to help these unfortunate older people it is as well for us to remember that as we too grow older, many of us will in time become part of the problem ourselves.

(a) Do you think everyone should retire at sixty or sixty-five?
(b) Do you think the problem of elderly people is as bad as the writer suggests? Have you any personal experience of this?
(c) What can be done to help these people?
(d) How do you think you will manage in old age? Have you any fears?

munt RutIRmENTretirementR

109

ACTIVITIES AND RESEARCH

1. Discuss the implications of the figures in the graph and the chart on this page. Collect other figures as to the distribution of old people in the population, how the numbers have risen, and how figures for Britain compare with those for other parts of the world. The *Annual Abstract of Statistics,* published by the Central Statistical Office, is a good source of up-to-date information about Britain, and is available in good reference libraries.

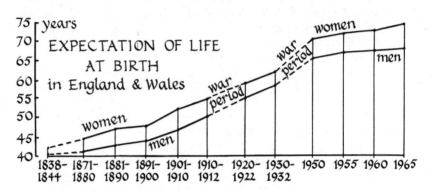

EXPECTATION OF LIFE AT BIRTH IN ENGLAND & WALES
from p. 10 of BRITAIN: AN OFFICIAL HANDBOOK, H.M.S.O.

Year	1955	1965	1975	2000
U.K. Population in 1,000's Under 20 years 20 - 64 years 65 years and over	 15,030 30,426 5,765	 16,973 31,066 6,556	 19,414 31,761 7,732	 27,005 39,119 8,450
TOTALS	51,221	54,595	58,907	74,574

2. Find out what opportunities there are in your district to go out and help old people at weekends and in the evenings. Many schools and youth clubs have their own schemes. If yours has not, see if one can be started. The organisation called *Task Force* works in a number of London Boroughs, directing the volunteers from schools and youth organisations. The Chief Welfare Officer at your local council offices can probably help you to help those whose need is greatest.

110

3. "Your sons and daughters shall prophesy, and your young men shall see visions, and your old men shall dream dreams." (Acts 2, verse 17, and Joel 2, verse 28.) Study some of the references to dreams and visions that occur in the Bible and, after enough information has been collected, discuss their significance.
4. Listen to any records by Stanley Unwin, who distorts the pronunciation of words so that they are almost unrecognisable but who still manages to convey a peculiar sense of reality.
5. Illustrate the mixed metaphors given in Exercise 3, as in the example on page 102.

FURTHER READING

A Visit to Grandpa's from *Portrait of the Artist as a Young Dog* by Dylan Thomas (Dent).

Dylan Thomas first won fame as a poet, and his poetic talents are evident in all his writing. Much of it may seem puzzling at first, but it is always full of rich and exciting images which can often by enjoyed without being fully understood. *Portrait of the Artist,* described as a "fictional autobiography", is probably the least demanding of his prose works. If you enjoy it, try his other books, but be prepared to find them more difficult.

A Prospect of the Sea (Dent).

Stories of childhood, madmen, fantasy and the subconscious, plus a satirical essay entitled *How to be a Poet,* make up this collection.

Quite Early One Morning (Dent).

This is a collection of Thomas's broadcast talks. The title piece, a description of the morning hours in a small, Welsh seaside town, formed the basis for his remarkable radio play *Under Milk Wood.*

Under Milk Wood (Dent).

In this play, which was not completed until ten years after his radio talk, we hear first the dreams of the sleeping inhabitants, then we follow the people as they get up and go about their business, until night falls at the end of the Spring day.

As with most of Dylan Thomas's work, *Under Milk Wood* must be *heard* to be fully appreciated. The complete play, with the original radio cast, is available on two long-playing records, issued by the Argo Record Company, who have also issued *Homage to Dylan Thomas,* which includes *A Visit to Grandpa's,* read by Emlyn Williams. Two records of Dylan Thomas reading his own prose and poetry have also been issued by Caedmon.

A retired actress, Miss Porteus, a reserved and lonely person who kept a milliner's shop, has been found dead by Mr. Sprake, the owner of the watchmaker and jeweller's shop next door. Miss Porteus, wearing a pink nightgown, was lying on her bathroom floor, shot in the chest. On the afternoon of her death, Mrs. Sprake had seen a middle-aged man in the backyard of the milliner's.

LATEST

Search for Shot Actress
Assailant Goes On

FULL STORY

ACTRESS FOUND DEAD

ACTRESS MURDERED

CHAPTER 8   **The Press**

BY afternoon the crowd was packed thick right across the street. They were pressed tight against my window. I put the shutters up. Just as I was finishing them, four men came up and said they were newspapermen and could I give them the facts about Miss Porteus.

Before I could speak they pushed into the shop. They shut the door. Then I saw that there were not four of them but twelve. I got behind the counter and they took out notebooks and rested them on my glass showcases and scribbled. I tried to tell them what I had told the local man, the truth, and nothing more or less than the truth, but they didn't want that. They hammered me with questions.

What was Miss Porteus like? Was her real name Porteus? What else besides Porteus? What colour was her hair? How long had she been there? Did it strike me as funny that an actress should run a milliner's shop? When had I last seen the lady? About the bathroom . . . about her hair.

I was flustered and I said something about her hair being a little reddish, and one of the newspapermen said:

"Now we're getting somewhere. Carrots." and they all laughed.

Then another said: "Everybody says this woman was an actress. But where did she act? London? What theatre? When?"

"I don't know," I said.

"You've lived next door all this time and don't know? Did you never hear anybody say if she'd been in any particular play?"

"No. I . . . Well, she was a bit strange."

"Strange?" They seized on that. "How? What? Mysterious?"

"Well," I said, "she was the sort of woman who'd come out in big heavy fox furs on a hot summer day. She was different."

"Crazy?"

"Oh, no!"

"Eccentric?"

"No, I wouldn't say that."

113

"About her acting," they said. "You must have heard something."

"No." Then I remembered something. At a rehearsal of the Choral Society, once, her name had come up and somebody had said something about her having been in *Othello*. I remember it because there was some argument about whether Othello was a pure black or just a half-caste.

"*Othello?*" The newspapermen wrote fast. "What was she? Desdemona?"

"Well," I said, "I don't think you ought to put that in. I don't know if it's strictly true or not. I can't vouch for it. I don't think —"

"And this man that was seen," they said. "When was it? When did you see him? What was he like?"

I said I didn't know, that I hadn't seen him, but that my wife had. So they had my wife in. They questioned her. They were nice to her. But they put down, as in my case, things she did not say. Yellow tie? Dark? How dark? Foreign looking? Actor? Every now and then one of them dashed out to the post office. They questioned us all that afternoon.

The next morning the placards of the morning newspapers were all over Claypole. "Shot Actress—Full Story." It was my story, but somehow, as it appeared in the papers, it was not true. I read all the papers. They had my picture, the picture of Miss Porteus's shop, looking somehow strange and forlorn with its drawn blind, and a picture of Miss Porteus herself, as she must have looked about 1920. All over these papers were black stabbing headlines: "Search for Shot Actress Assailant Goes On"; "Police anxious to Interview Foreigner with Yellow Tie"; "Real Life Desdemona: Jealousy Victim?"; "Eccentric Actress Recluse Dead in Bathroom"; "Mystery Life of Actress who wore Furs in Heat Wave"; "Beautiful Red-Haired Actress who Spoke to Nobody"; "Disappearance of Dark-looking Foreigner".

It was Saturday. That afternoon Claypole was besieged by hundreds of people who had never been there before. They moved past Miss Porteus's shop and mine in a great stream, in cars and on foot and pushing bicycles, staring up at the dead actress's windows. . . . Hundreds of people who had seen Miss Porteus's shop every day of their lives suddenly wanted to stare at it. . . .

There sprang up, gradually, a different story about Miss Porteus. It began to go all over Claypole that she was a woman of a certain reputation, that the milliner's shop was a blind. "Did you ever see anybody in there, or going in? No, nor did anybody else. Did anybody ever buy a hat there? No. But the back door was always undone." That rumour gave cause for others. "Sprake," people began to say,

114

"told me himself that she lay on the floor naked. They put the night-gown on afterwards." Then she became not only a woman of light virtue and naked, but also pregnant. "That's why," people began to say, "she either shot herself or was shot. Take it which way you like. But I had it straight from Sprake."

As the story of Miss Porteus grew, the story of my own part in it grew.

I used to belong, in Claypole, to a Temperance Club, the Melrose; we had four full-sized billiard tables and in the evenings I went there to play billiards and cards, to have a smoke and a talk and so on. Next to the billiard room was a small cloakroom, and one evening, as I was hanging up my coat, I heard someone at the billiard table say:

"Old Sprake knows a thing or two. Ever struck you it was funny old Sprake knew the colour of that nightgown so well?"

I put on my coat again and went out of the club. I was trembling and horrified and sick. What I had heard seemed to be the crystallization of all the rumours that perhaps were and perhaps were not going round Claypole. It may have been simply the crystallization of my own fears. I don't know, I only know that I felt that I was suspected of things I had not done and had not said; that not only had she been murdered but that I knew more than I would say about the murder. I was harassed by fears and counter-fears. I did not know what to do.

Then something happened. It was important and it suddenly filled the front pages of the newspapers again with the mystery of Miss Porteus's death. The police found the man with the yellow tie. It was a sensation.

That was the end. It was established, beyond doubt, that Miss Porteus had taken her life. And suddenly all the mystery and sensation and horror and fascination of Miss Porteus's death became nothing. The papers were not interested in her any longer and her name never appeared in the papers again.

I no longer live at Claypole. All those odd, unrealised rumours that went round were enough to drive me mad; but they were also enough to kill my wife. Like me, she could not sleep, and the shock of it all cracked her life right across, like a piece of bone. Rumour and shock and worry killed her, and she died just after the facts of Miss Porteus's death were established. A month later I gave up the business and I left the town. I could not go on . . . .

Poor Miss Porteus. She took her life because she was hard up, in a fit of despair. There is no more to it than that. But nobody in Claypole ever believed that and I suppose very few people ever will. In Claypole they like to think that she was murdered; they know, because the papers said so, that she was a strange and eccentric woman; they know that she acted in a play with a black man; they know, though nobody ever really said so, that she was a loose woman and that she was pregnant and that somebody shot her for that reason; they know that I found her naked in the bathroom and that I was a bit queer and that I knew more than I would ever say.

They know, in short, all that happened to Miss Porteus. They can never know how much has happened to me.

(from *Shot Actress—Full Story* H. E. Bates)

APPRECIATION AND DISCUSSION

1. Sprake said that he tried to tell the reporters "nothing more or less than the truth", but "they didn't want that". Why weren't they satisfied with straightforward facts?

2. What sort of details were they interested in? Why did they pursue these so avidly?

3. "It was my story, but somehow, as it appeared in the papers, it was not true." Had the reporters deliberately put in lies? If not, what had they done?

4. Judging from newspaper reports that you have read, about cases similar to the one described in this story, do you think reporters sometimes distort or obscure the truth in order to achieve sensational effects?

5. Why did hundreds of people visit Claypole to view the scene of the crime, and others, who had lived in Claypole all their lives, suddenly want to stare at the shop? Would you have gone if you had been living nearby? Can you cite other occasions when people behave in a similar manner? Do you disapprove of such behaviour?

6. "There sprang up, gradually, a different story about Miss Porteus." Can you suggest why people made up this story?

7. Why do such rumours grow and spread so easily? Why was Sprake included in these rumours?

8. Why did the newspapers suddenly lose interest in the death of Miss Porteus?

9. Who was responsible for the death of Mrs. Sprake—the reporters, the people of Claypole, Mrs. Sprake, Miss Porteus?

10. Why didn't people want to believe that Miss Porteus "took her life because she was hard-up, in a fit of despair"?

116

11. "they know, because the papers said so" . . . How much reliance do you place on what you read in the newspapers? Have you ever been involved in or witnessed an incident about which you later saw a "distorted" report in a newspaper? If so, what form did the distortion take? What aspects of the incident were emphasised or exaggerated? How much of the report consisted of personal opinion, or rumour?

12. Have you ever encountered situations that gave rise to ugly stories, or known people about whom rumours were spread? Did these rumours hurt anybody? If so, did the people who spread the rumours realise that they could have such an effect? Would they have continued, had they known?

HEADLINE HISTORY

GRAVE CHARGES IN MAYFAIR BATHROOM CASE,
ROMAN REMAINS FOR MIDDLE WEST,
GOLFING BISHOP CALLS FOR PRAYERS,
HOW MURDERED BRIDE WAS DRESSED.

BOXER INSURES HIS JOIE-DE-VIVRE,
DUCHESS DENIES THAT VAMPS ARE VAIN,
DO WOMEN MAKE GOOD WIVES?
GIANT AIRSHIP OVER SPAIN.

SOPRANO SINGS FOR FORTY HOURS,
COCKTAIL BAR ON MOORING MAST,
"NOISE, MORE NOISE!" POET'S LAST WORDS,
COMPULSORY WIRELESS BILL IS PASSED.

ALLEGED LAST TRUMP BLOWN YESTERDAY,
TRAFFIC DROWNS CALL TO QUICK AND DEAD,
CUP TIE CROWD SEES HEAVENS OPE,
"NOT END OF WORLD", SAYS WELL-KNOWN RED.

WILLIAM PLOMER

The British Journalist

> You cannot hope
>   to bribe or twist
> thank God! the
>   British journalist,
> But, seeing what
>   the man will do
> unbribed, there's
>   no occasion to.
>
> *Humbert Wolfe*

DISCUSSING THE POEMS

1. What is "joie-de-vivre"? What sort of person is a "Red"?
2. Which details in this poem show that it was written in the 1930's?
3. Do you think the lines of this poem are typical of real newspaper headlines? Do you feel that the poet has had to distort them at all, to make them fit into the rhyme scheme of the poem or to maintain a regular beat?
4. Which of these headlines do you think refer to important events, and which are concerned with gossip? Consider the information given in each one and explain how it achieves its effect. For example, would "Bishop Calls For Prayers" be as sensational and eye-catching as "Golfing Bishop Calls For Prayers"?
5. Make up a rhyming verse consisting of four headlines. (See A. D. Rogers' poem in the "Pupils' Work" section). This could be done verbally as a class activity; one person supplies the first headline, the next person the second, and so on. It could even become a competition: when a member of one side fails to complete the rhyme satisfactorily, he drops out of the game and it is passed to the next person.
6. Explain briefly in your own words the comment that Humbert Wolfe is making in "The British Journalist".
7. Do you agree with this judgement?
8. Why, do you think, did Humbert Wolfe break his poem into eight short lines, instead of writing one four-line verse?
   > e.g. You cannot hope to bribe or twist
   >   thank God! the British journalist,
   >   etc.

TECHNIQUES

The Use of Language, and Style

1. *Press Styles and Emotive Language.* (i) The following passage was composed by Professor Richard Hoggart as an example of a certain newspaper style.

IT BEATS ME

Here we go again, chums!

Who is it *this time*?

Only the 60-year-old bachelor Archprelate of Pontyholoth.

He was talking the other day to the League of Christian Women (average age 62) about "The Way We Spend our Spare time".

Well . . . well . . .

Do *you* like a spot of TV after a hard day's work?

. . . You shouldn't—not according to the bachelor Archprelate.

. . . "Too many people," he said, "take their recreations passively nowadays. This can do them no good."

Do *you* like a mild flutter on the pools every week?

. . . Sorry, pal, you shouldn't—not according to the 60-year-old Archprelate.

. . . "It may be," he said, "that we should think much more about the freedom we allow to such organizations in our national life."

BLIMEY, THAT SURE IS FIGHTING TALK.

Who would have thought that a Christian leader in 1961 could forget the first essentials of democracy?

We may be a bit simple, but we always understood that Christian leaders should inspire us with the virtue of TOLERANCE.

Perhaps we got it wrong, because we also thought that Christian leaders were on the side of FREEDOM and EQUALITY.

But maybe these ideas are only all right for the Archprelate and his pals.

Anyway, I hope that someone in the poor old worried League of Christian Women got up and reminded him of those ideas.

. . . And that someone whispered a short word or two about the dangers of REACTION—and of HUMBUG—and of HYPOCRISY—and of SMUGNESS, for our Christian leaders.

. . . and that someone else suggested that the Archprelate could do with meeting *ordinary folk* a bit more and with getting a better understanding of their *good sense*.

If they didn't—

IT BEATS ME

(from *The Uses of Literacy*)

Say which newspaper (or newspapers) you think the passage is typical of. How well has Hoggart captured this particular style? Has he exaggerated it all?

Pick out the colloquialisms. Would you agree that these help to create a feeling of "Them" (the object of the attack) and "Us" (the newspaper and its readers)?

Where have emotive words been used? Can any of these be condemned as irrelevant to the argument?

Where does the writer use sarcasm and ridicule? Is it justified?

What details of information have been included with the obvious intention of prejudicing the reader?

What effect is achieved through the frequent use of block capitals and italics?

Analyse the arguments put forward. To what extent are they emotive, and to what extent logical?

(ii) Consider the facts and arguments in the passage below and then write an article, in the same style as Richard Hoggart's example, either putting forward the same point of view, or denying the truth of these opinions. N.B. Unless instructed to do so, you should not normally use this emotive, colloquial style for putting forward arguments.

An examination of our newspapers shows that the great majority of them are extraordinarily uniform with regard to what news is reported. This is not, on reflection, surprising, since most of the newspapers with the biggest circulations are owned by a comparatively small group of men. Fourteen of London's eighteen newspapers (nine daily, two evening and seven Sunday papers) are owned by six groups of proprietors; six of them are controlled by only two proprietors. Papers belonging to one group naturally give the same news in much the same sort of way. The owners of these newspapers have an almost unlimited power to form the opinions of the reading public. The danger lies in the fact that the majority of people are not aware of the ownership. Consequently, when they see different newspapers providing the same news and expressing very similar opinions they are not aware that the news and the evaluation of the news are determined by a single group of persons, perhaps mainly by one man—a Press Lord.

(adapted from *Thinking to Some Purpose* by Susan Stebbing)

2. *Headlines.* What is the function of a headline?

Which of the headlines quoted in "Shot Actress—Full Story" do you think is the most sensational and eye-catching?

Make up sensational headlines for the following, giving no more information than that supplied.

(*a*) A young pop singer is injured by a group of hysterical fans.

(*b*) A British sportsman breaks a world record.

(*c*) An elderly lady prevents two teenagers from robbing a Post Office.

(*d*) There is a rise in the country's unemployment figures.

Now write a short paragraph about each of these four topics, maintaining the sensational effect created by your headlines. You must, however, keep to the truth, which is:

the pop singer received one slight scratch;

the world record was for tiddlywinks;

the teenagers were small, thirteen year old girls who had taken a 3p stamp, and the lady, though elderly, was a judo expert and weighed 100 kg;

only 20 more people were unemployed.

The above facts must be included in your reports. Can you avoid a sense of anti-climax?

3. *Euphemisms.* A euphemism is a mild, polite expression used in place of a more forthright or unpleasant one.

The following euphemisms were used by reporters to describe part of a cricketer's anatomy.

Sunday Telegraph: "not unsubstantial stern"
Sunday Citizen: "considerable posterior"
Sunday Mirror: "rear portion"

How would you have described this in straightforward terms?

Euphemisms are sometimes used deliberately for comic effect; generally however, they should be avoided.

Rewrite the following sentences, replacing the italicised euphemisms with more direct expressions.

(*a*) He has *passed away from us.*

(*b*) Journalists are sometimes *a little shy of the truth.*

(*c*) The rough sea caused many of the boat's passengers to *make offerings to Neptune.* (Neptune was god of the sea.)

(*d*) The judge decided that the accused should *take an enforced holiday at Her Majesty's expense* for two years.

(*e*) He was *invited to offer his resignation.*

newsSENSATIONALISMnews

4. *The Colon.* Basically the colon is an introductory punctuation mark. It is most often used to introduce a list.

> e.g. The reporter visited the following countries: America, Japan, Australia, and South Africa.

It is sometimes used instead of a comma to introduce direct speech or a quotation.

> e.g. I heard someone at the billiard table say: "Old Sprake knows a thing or two".

The headline in the local paper was: "Council Cuts Rates".

It can also be used to introduce an explanation. In this use, it marks a stronger pause than a semicolon.

> e.g. It took Smith only three months to rise from his first position as tea-boy to that of editor: his father owned the newspaper.

Rewrite the following sentences, inserting one colon in each.

(*a*) They were all there reporters, photographers, radio and television commentators, camera-men and publicity agents.

(*b*) The news editor of a popular paper should remember that there are four subjects in which the public is always interested Crime, Love, Money and Food.

(*c*) I heard him say "You can't believe anything you read in the papers."

(*d*) This is the ideal purpose of the popular press, as defined by the Press Council "to expose injustices, to right wrongs, to befriend the friendless and to help the helpless."

(*e*) Miss Porteus is dead she committed suicide.

5. *General Punctuation.* Punctuate the following.

(*a*) people do not read the daily mirror they merely look at it.

(*b*) i consider it a sign of snobbery to sneer at the daily mirror for this newspaper performs a valuable service by presenting complex issues in simple everyday language it does this so successfully that 33% of its readers attempt the editorial each day.

(*c*) look for examples of the following in national newspapers distortion exaggeration lying biased selection of news emotive argument and cliches.

(*d*) a newspapers character is often indicated by the headlines that it uses the times for example will lead with cheering crowds hail major gagarin the daily sketch will use ga-ga over gaga.

(*e*) the editor an astute man decided to print the photograph which showed the actress wearing a low cut dress.

6. *Vocabulary*. Miss Porteus was described by one of the reporters as a "real-life Desdemona". In what play does Desdemona appear? What characteristics and circumstances are associated with her?

What do we mean when we refer to someone as: a Romeo; a Jesabel; a Judas; a Shylock; a Solomon; a Midas?

Find out from which characters these four adjectives are derived: herculean; machiavelian; tantalising; quixotic.

Define, in one sentence for each, the following types of people:

an eccentric; a miser; an extravert;

an introvert; a recluse; a spendthrift.

If you keep a "Vocabulary Notebook", copy in any of the above words with which you are not familiar.

TOPICS FOR WRITTEN WORK

1. Write one paragraph about each of the following newspapers: "Daily Mirror", "Daily Express", "The Times", "The Guardian", and your local paper.

Hints

Indicate the size and type of readership each newspaper has. (See the table on page 125). Comment on the amount of space it devotes to news, sport, cartoons, advertisements etc., its political attitude, its literary style and its approach to its readers. Plan your essay carefully: the simplest approach is probably to deal with each newspaper separately, and to make any comparisons or judgements in your concluding paragraph.

2. Write a letter to your local newspaper.

Hints

This will be set out as a business letter. Choose a topic about which you know something and about which you feel strongly. You might find a topic by reading the letters printed in the last few issues of the paper. Or you could write about a subject of local interest which has not yet been discussed by readers.

Follow this plan for your letter.

Introduction: In the first sentence or two, state what you are writing about.

Development: Set out your facts and arguments in a logical order. If you use emotive words and phrases when presenting your case, choose them with care.

Conclusion: End by giving your views about what should be done.

3. Give a short account of the production and distribution of a national newspaper.

Hints

Make a list of the various people who take part in the production and distribution of the newspaper, including the printing, and describe briefly what each one does. Imagine that your account is intended for children of about 11 years of age. Select, therefore, only the main facts and make your explanation very clear and logical.

Pupils' Work

THE NEWS

MAN CHARGED WITH MURDER
NOW TWISTING'S THE TREND
THE WORLD CUP FOR ENGLAND
SCHEDULE A TAX TO END

ROCKET SHIP OFF COURSE
BEER IS THE BEST
BANK RAID IN PUTNEY
BARDOT'S KNITTED VEST

H BOMB EXPLOSION
ELVIS OUT OF TOP TEN
FILM STAR REVEALS ALL
THE RUSH KILLS TEN MEN

A. D. Rogers

1. Study the following table of figures carefully, and discuss the questions raised below:

ADULT READERSHIP OF NATIONAL DAILY AND SUNDAY
NEWSPAPERS (1965-66)

Newspaper	*Percentage of Adult Readership by Social Class*				
	Total	A, B	C(1)	C(2)	D, E
Daily Mirror	38%	13%	26%	48%	42%
Daily Express	29%	31%	34%	29%	25%
Daily Mail	16%	23%	20%	14%	12%
The Sun	11%	3%	8%	14%	14%
Daily Telegraph	8%	29%	14%	4%	2%
Daily Sketch	8%	4%	5%	9%	8%
The Guardian	2%	8%	3%	1%	1%
The Times	2%	8%	3%	1%	1%
Financial Times	1%	5%	2%	*	*
News of the World	40%	16%	27%	47%	49%
The People	39%	20%	32%	45%	43%
Sunday Mirror	35%	15%	28%	44%	36%
Sunday Express	26%	46%	38%	20%	16%
Sunday Times	9%	29%	13%	5%	3%
The Observer	6%	18%	10%	3%	1%
Sunday Telegraph	5%	16%	8%	3%	1%
Sunday Citizen	2%	1%	2%	2%	1%

Notes: The figures are quoted by kind permission of the I.P.A. National Readership Survey (1966). All figures are percentages; the asterisk * represents less than 1%. The social grades A and B represent "upper middle" and "middle" class people in higher and intermediate managerial, administrative or professional occupations, then earning £1,000 or more p.a. C1 represents "lower middle" class people in supervisory or clerical or junior managerial, administrative or professional occupations under £1,000 p.a. C2 are skilled working class manual workers, then earning £14-£22 weekly. The D and E grades are working class and other people doing semi-skilled or unskilled work, casual and lowest grade workers, state pensioners, widows, etc. earning less than £14 weekly.

(a) Which are the three most popular national daily newspapers (i) with the total adult population, (ii) with each social class group? Consider each class in turn.

125

(*b*) Which are the three most popular Sunday newspapers with the total population and with each social class in turn?

(*c*) Add up the total percentages of readers for (i) all dailies and (ii) all the Sunday newspapers. If either (or both) of these figures comes to more than 100%, explain this.

(*d*) The "Daily Telegraph" and the "Daily Sketch" both have a readership of 8% of the total adult population, yet if you add the percentages for the four social classes together, one total is 49% and the other only 26%. Explain this, if you can.

(*e*) Is there any evidence for saying (i) that Sunday papers generally are more popular than daily papers, or (ii) that the newspaper reading habit is more widespread in one social class than in another?

(*f*) "The Times" has 8 times as great a percentage of A, B class readers as of D, E class readers. Make the same kind of calculation for other newspapers. Which has the greatest and which the least difference in class of readership?

(*g*) Divide the newspapers into three categories: (i) those with mainly upper and middle class readers, (ii) those with mainly working class readers and (iii) those with a mixed class readership.

(*h*) If you were responsible for advertising goods that would appeal (i) to a wealthy, exclusive market, (ii) to a cheap, mass market, and (iii) to people of all classes and levels of income, which newspapers would you recommend most strongly in each case, to carry your advertisements?

2. When you have examined and discussed the above figures, and have completed "Activities and Research" No. 1, give a short talk entitled "Britain's Newspapers". It is your task to call attention to interesting conclusions and trends, and not just to quote figures.

3. Discuss statements (*b*) and (*d*) in Exercise 4, and (*a*) and (*b*) in Exercise 5.

4. Practise reading aloud the extract from "the Uses of Literacy" (Exercise 1(i)). Try to bring out the tone of the passage in your reading, paying particular attention to the parts printed in capitals and italics. Then read aloud the passage adapted from "Thinking to Some Purpose" (Exercise 1(ii)), and compare the way in which this should be read with the approach needed for the previous extract.

5. Prepare a short talk entitled "My Ideal Newspaper".

126

ACTIVITIES AND RESEARCH

1. From reference books such as "Whitaker's Almanack",,or "Britain, an Official Handbook" (*H.M.S.O.*) collect up-to-date information about the main, national daily and Sunday newspapers. The last-mentioned book sets out its information like this:

Title	General Political Tendency	Ultimate Control-ing Company	Circulation Average (*Jan-June* 1965)
Daily Mirror	Left of Centre	International Publishing Corporation	4,956,997

Try to find out what newspapers have ceased publication, have been amalgamated, have changed hands, or have been launched in the last twenty years.

2. Find out the meaning of the following terms.

the editorial	the N.U.J.
the leader writer	Our Own Correspondent
a sub-editor	From a Correspondent
a "scoop"	a Lobby Correspondent
a press agency	the financial columns
classified advertisements	banner headlines.

3. Collect a set of national daily papers for one week to: (*a*) compare the front page headlines (*b*) contrast the treatment of identical news items (*c*) study the content and attitude of the editorials.

127

4. The form might like to produce one copy or one edition of its own "sensational" newspaper. Each person could choose one aspect of school life and write a popular-press-style report about it. You could include such features as (*a*) a "gossip column" based on current form-room gossip and rumours (*b*) a "moving, exciting, touching" biography of a well known personality in the school (*c*) an "exposure" of some apparent injustice (*d*) "The Confessions of . . ." (*e*) cartoons (*f*) readers' letters. Remember that the whole point of this activity is to make perfectly ordinary school events seem *extraordinary* by presenting them in a gimmicky, eye-catching manner. You will need to pay particular attention, therefore, to the headlines that you use.

FURTHER READING

Shot Actress—Full Story from *Twenty Tales* by H. E. Bates (Cape).
Thirty One Selected Tales (Cape).
The latter volume, selected from books published between 1934-40, provides a good introduction to this writer's short stories.
Stories of Flying Officer X (Cape).
During the Second World War, H. E. Bates served in the R.A.F. and, under the pseudonym of "Flying Officer X", wrote some of the best stories about the war in the air. Several of his most successful novels, such as: *Fair Stood the Wind for France, The Purple Plain* and *The Jacaranda Tree* also deal with the Second World War in Europe and in Burma.
The Fallow Land (Cape) and *My Uncle Silas* (Cape).
The characters and scenes in these books, as in many of his others, are drawn from English country life. The first is about life on a farm at the end of the nineteenth and beginning of the twentieth centuries. It is a serious study of some of the more elemental human qualities—loyalty, passion, recklessness, fortitude. In contrast, the stories in *My Uncle Silas* are gems of comedy; they are about a cranky, crotchety, little man who is a poacher and a liar, with an unquenchable thirst for cowslip wine and an ever-open eye for the ladies.
The Darling Buds of May, A Breath of French Air, and *When the Green Woods Laugh* (Michael Joseph; Penguin).
For sheer entertainment, this triology of books about the Larkin family is unbeatable. Pop—"Larkin by name. Larkin by nature"— Ma, munching crisps and laughing like a jelly, their numerous and magnificently named offspring, and the newly recruited Mr. Charlton provide hilarious comedy.

CHAPTER 9

The Absurd

The sort of play written by N. F. Simpson is known as "Drama of the Absurd", and the world it presents on the stage appears completely nonsensical and eccentric. In this extract, two comedians are putting on a short, "goonish" sketch, for no explicable reason, in a room adjoining the living room of a suburban house.

(*FIRST COMEDIAN is sitting at his improvised desk writing. He leans forward, presses a button, and says "Ping". The door from the living room opens to admit a man of no particular age between forty and sixty, whose nondescript appearance and defeated air contrast with the brisk ebullient manner the First Comedian has assumed. This is the SECOND COMEDIAN. He approaches the desk and sits diffidently down. When after a few minutes the FIRST COMEDIAN disengages his attention from what he is writing, the SECOND COMEDIAN leans forward.*)

SECOND COMEDIAN: It's my feet, Doctor.

FIRST COMEDIAN: What's the matter with your feet?

SECOND COMEDIAN: I was rather hoping you might be able to tell me that, Doctor.

FIRST COMEDIAN: Let me see them.

(*SECOND COMEDIAN takes off shoes and socks.*)

SECOND COMEDIAN: They're all right now. It's when they suddenly swivel round they catch me.

(*SECOND COMEDIAN holds out both legs quite straight in front of him. FIRST COMEDIAN stands over them.*)

FIRST COMEDIAN: What are these?

SECOND COMEDIAN: They're my kneecaps, Doctor.

FIRST COMEDIAN: They ought to be much higher up your legs than this.

SECOND COMEDIAN: I can't seem to keep them up, Doctor.

FIRST COMEDIAN: Take everything off except your trousers and lie down over there.

(*FIRST COMEDIAN goes to wash-basin where he begins washing his hands, while SECOND COMEDIAN goes into the corner, where the desk conceals him, to undress.*)

FIRST COMEDIAN: Eardrums still getting overheated?

SECOND COMEDIAN: Only when I listen to anything, Doctor.

(*SECOND COMEDIAN comes out and lies down on the couch. FIRST COMEDIAN examines his chest.*)

FIRST COMEDIAN: Breathe in deeply. Again. Yes—you're having trouble with your breathing. Breath out. Do you notice any difference?

SECOND COMEDIAN: None at all, Doctor.

FIRST COMEDIAN: And do you know why? The reason you notice no difference is that there isn't any. All the time while you're breathing out, there's air forcing its way in. It's trying to push past. Breathe in again. (*He reflects for a moment.*) Do you ever feel as though the air you're getting is the wrong kind of air?

SECOND COMEDIAN: I just don't get the air, Doctor.

FIRST COMEDIAN: Somebody must have it if you don't.

SECOND COMEDIAN: It's my lungs, Doctor.

FIRST COMEDIAN: Nonsense. There's nothing wrong with your lungs. They're both perfectly fit.

SECOND COMEDIAN: I don't think they hit it off, Doctor. They're at daggers drawn practically the whole time. Over the air.

FIRST COMEDIAN: And your breathing's twisted to blazes as a result. Let me see your tongue. Open your mouth. (*He looks inside.*) You've had this jaw to pieces, haven't you?

SECOND COMEDIAN: It was some years ago, Doctor.

FIRST COMEDIAN: It doesn't matter how long ago it was. It's not a question of time. You laymen start dismantling these parts, but you've no idea how to put them together again. Here's a tooth which has been put back upside down. You're biting on the root.

(*FIRST COMEDIAN begins to use the stethoscope.*)

SECOND COMEDIAN: I've been told I can expect all my teeth to turn turtle eventually.

FIRST COMEDIAN: What are you doing about it?

SECOND COMEDIAN: Consulting you, Doctor.

FIRST COMEDIAN: I thought you'd come to me about your feet.

(*FIRST COMEDIAN grimaces as he continues to sound SECOND COMEDIAN'S chest.*)

FIRST COMEDIAN: What on earth are you carrying round in this blood stream of yours?

SECOND COMEDIAN: Only my blood, Doctor.

FIRST COMEDIAN: You've got a hell of a noisy circulation.

130

SECOND COMEDIAN: I have, Doctor. It keeps me awake.

FIRST COMEDIAN: I should think so. It sounds like a mobile iron foundry. You need a silencer for it. I'll give you a letter to take to the King's Cross Blood, Brain, and Bowel Hospital. You can have it under the National Health.

SECOND COMEDIAN: I'd like them to look at my arteries while I'm there as well, Doctor. They seem to have venous blood in them.

FIRST COMEDIAN: It's when you get arterial blood in the veins that you need to begin worrying. Turn over and let me look at your back.

(*SECOND COMEDIAN turns painfully over and FIRST COMEDIAN stands looking for some moments in silence.*)

SECOND COMEDIAN: I've had it some time, Doctor.

FIRST COMEDIAN: I can see that. And we can write off these kidneys.

SECOND COMEDIAN: I hardly ever use them, Doctor.

FIRST COMEDIAN: How long have your ribs been like this?

SECOND COMEDIAN: As long as I can remember, Doctor.

FIRST COMEDIAN: And how long is that? Months? Years?

SECOND COMEDIAN: I can't altogether recall, Doctor.

(*FIRST COMEDIAN goes back to his desk where he takes up a pen and begins writing briskly.*)

FIRST COMEDIAN: You can get your clothes on.

(*While SECOND COMEDIAN gets dressed, FIRST COMEDIAN goes on writing. When SECOND COMEDIAN reappears, he puts down his pen.*)

FIRST COMEDIAN: Sit down, Mr Avalanche.

(*SECOND COMEDIAN sits down hesitantly and waits for FIRST COMEDIAN to begin.*)

FIRST COMEDIAN: I don't suppose there's much I can tell you that you don't know already. It's an obsolete body, of course, as you realize. And I'm afraid you'll have to do the best you can with it. You must learn to co-operate with your organs.

SECOND COMEDIAN: The small of my back is too big, Doctor.

FIRST COMEDIAN: There's nothing to be gained by pretending it isn't. In fact I'll be quite frank with you, Mr Avalanche—it's a great deal larger than it should be. Not only in your case, but with a surprisingly large number of people. But there's absolutely no need for you to have any misgivings about it. People go on—some of them with far less wrong with them than you have by a long way—they go on living active lives sometimes for years. There's no reason at all,

131

Mr Avalanche, why given time you shouldn't have a good twenty or thirty years in front of you.

SECOND COMEDIAN: With a transparent pelvis, Doctor?

FIRST COMEDIAN: The main thing is to keep that blood circulating. Take precautions, but don't overdo it. Sleep whenever you can with your eyes closed. Keep off strong poisons of all kinds—and breathe. Breathe all the time. If it doesn't seem to be showing results, make sure it isn't because you're under water. Keep at it: the more you breathe the better you'll feel.

SECOND COMEDIAN: I've been having a lot of trouble with my slanting bowel since I became allergic to smells, Doctor.

FIRST COMEDIAN: You will for a time, but it's nothing to worry about. Take this letter to the Blood, Brain, and Bowel Hospital and they'll give you a thorough overhaul.

SECOND COMEDIAN: I shall feel a lot easier, Doctor.

FIRST COMEDIAN: And get those feet seen to. They'll be no good to you while they swivel. You should be seeing somebody about them. The feet should never swivel. Hand that letter in to the almoner and you can come back here when the specialist has seen you.

SECOND COMEDIAN: Thank you, Doctor. And I'll come in again as you say when I've been examined.

FIRST COMEDIAN: Next Thursday. I can't see you before then. And I'll give you something for those elbows to see if we can't get them bending the right way.

SECOND COMEDIAN: Very good, Doctor.

(*SECOND COMEDIAN goes listlessly out, switching off the light as he does so.*)

(from *A Resounding Tinkle* by N. F. Simpson)

APPRECIATION AND DISCUSSION

1. How should the parts of the doctor and the patient be played? Suggest the appropriate dress, properties and mannerisms for the two characters.
2. Why is the doctor-patient relationship good material for comedy? Can you think of other situations that provide comedy writers with plenty of scope?

3. The absurd tone of this play is reflected even in the title—"A Resounding Tinkle". Why is this phrase absurd?
4. Relate any jokes that you think would come into the category of "comedy of the absurd".

   e.g. "What is yellow and dangerous?"
   "An E-type banana."
   "No."
   "A mad canary."
   "No, no. Shark-infested custard."

5. How far do the jokes in this sketch depend upon misconceiving the body as a machine? What other comic ideas of the body are used?
6. In what ways are the remarks of the doctor and patient in this sketch typical of doctors and patients generally? Is there an element of satire here?
7. Explain what is involved in the following forms of comedy: (*a*) slapstick (*b*) character (*c*) situation (*d*) satire (*e*) verbal repartee (*f*) sick humour. Give examples of each, by referring to books and films, etc.
8. Is the comedy of the absurd a distinct form of humour? Give the names of comedians, television series, films, novels, etc. that employ comic absurdities.
9. What do people find funny about absurdities? Is comedy of the absurd, the world of comic fantasy, more, or less effective when played absolutely straight, against a completely normal background?
10. Which forms of humour appeal most to you? Give examples.
11. Express the following colloquialisms, used in the passage, in more formal English.

    "I don't think they hit it off"
    "your breathing's twisted to blazes"
    "we can write off these kidneys"
    "keep at it"
    "get those feet seen to"

12. Explain the meaning of the following words and phrases taken from the passage, and then use them in sentences of your own.

nondescript appearance	grimaces
defeated air	obsolete
ebullient manner	to have misgivings
diffidently	allergic
disengages his attention	listlessly

Scorflufus
By a well-known National Health Victim No. 3908631

There are many diseases,
That strike people's kneeses,
Scorflufus! is one by name
It comes from the East
Packed in bladders of yeast
So the Chinese must take half the blame.

There's a case in the files
Of Sir Barrington-Pyles
While hunting a fox one day
Shot up in the air
And *remained hanging there*!
While the hairs on his socks turned grey!

Aye! Scorflufus had struck!
At man, beast and duck.
And the knees of the world went Bong!
Some knees went Ping!
Other knees turned to string
From Balham to old Hong-Kong.

Should you hold your life dear,
Then the remedy's clear,
If you're offered some yeast—don't eat it!
Turn the offer down flat—
Don your travelling hat—
Put an egg in your boot—and beat it.

Spike Milligan

134

DISCUSSING THE POEM

1. Try reading the poem aloud in various comical, "goony" voices. Which is the most suitable?
2. From verse 3 pick out one example of anti-climax, and one incongruous contrast, and from verse 4, a pun.
3. Pick out one metaphor and one example of alliteration in the poem.
4. Which word has Spike Milligan twisted slightly in order to achieve a comic effect?
5. Which of the absurd pictures conjured up by this poem do you find the most comical?

TECHNIQUES

The Use of Language, and Style

1. *Humorous Writing.* (i) There are many ways in which a comic effect can be achieved in a few words. We have already seen that anti-climax can create such an effect, as can exaggeration and understatement.
How are these figures of speech used in the following sentences?
   (a) The nurses watched anxiously as the doctor performing the operation used first a scalpel, then a screwdriver, next a hammer, and finally resorted to a hacksaw—before managing to open his bag.
   (b) You will appreciate that performing an operation on the heart is slightly more difficult than slicing the Sunday joint.
   (c) Mrs. Stickybeak's nose was so long that she used to wrap it round her neck and pose as a petrol pump.
Make up comic sentences of your own, using these techniques; or tell any jokes that use them.
(ii) Using the notes in brackets at the end of this exercise as a guide, explain how each of the following extracts achieves its effect.
   (a) 1st COMEDIAN: Open your mouth. (*He looks inside*). You've had this jaw to pieces haven't you?
   (b) 1st COMEDIAN: The main thing is to keep that blood circulating . . . Sleep whenever you can with your eyes closed. Keep off strong poisons of all kinds—and breathe. Breathe all the time.
   (c) 1st COMEDIAN: I'll give you a letter to take to the King's Cross Blood, Brain, and Bowel Hospital. You can have it under the National Health.

135

(*d*) 2nd COMEDIAN: I've been having a lot of trouble with my slanting bowel since I became allergic to smells, Doctor.

(*e*) 2nd COMEDIAN: I've been told I can expect all my teeth to turn turtle eventually.

1st COMEDIAN: What are you doing about it?

2nd COMEDIAN: Consulting you, Doctor.

(an absurd impossibility; ridiculously obvious statements; comic imitation of a conventional statement; illogical sequence of ideas; repartee)

Use these techniques to compose humorous statements of your own.

2. *Puns.* (i) Another form of verbal humour is the pun. This figure of speech is a play on words, either on two meanings of the same word or phrase, or on words which sound alike.

Explain the play on words in these puns.

(*a*) 2nd COMEDIAN: The small of my back is too big, Doctor.

(*b*) When he died, they told the sexton; and the sexton tolled the bell.

(*c*) Whether life is worth living often depends upon the liver.

(*d*) "What do you think of Britain's current rôle in the world?" asked the politician.

"Delicious," replied the comedian.

(*e*) My mother-in-law is at death's door; I hope the doctor will pull her through.

(ii) Complete these sentences by inserting suitable punning words. The first letter of each word has been given.

(*a*) The cobbler put his heart and *s*—— into his work.

(*b*) The surgeon lost his *patience*; and his *p*—— lost their lives.

(*c*) The champion walker set a new record by walking for three weeks without shoes on. Everyone was impressed by his great *f*——.

(*d*) The girls in this town are frequently *chased* by the young men, but they usually get away, so they remain *c*——.

(*e*) Follow the exciting new strip cartoon printed on your packet of **BLUGGO BREAKFAST FOOD.** Enjoy the *s*—— on the back while you munch the *c*—— inside.

3. *Logical Thinking.* Consider the following arguments and explain clearly what is wrong with the reasoning and the conclusions.

(*a*) Today, more infants are made ill by the injections given to protect them against various diseases than are made ill by the diseases themselves. Therefore, we should no longer inject them against these diseases.

136

(b) All doctors in this hospital wear white coats. Since that man is wearing a white coat, he must be a doctor.

(c) Your kidneys are larger than average. But that's nothing to worry about. Everybody's kidneys are larger than average nowadays.

(d) I don't believe that smoking cigarettes causes lung cancer. My uncle smoked twenty cigarettes a day for thirty years and he didn't die of lung cancer. He was knocked down and killed by a bus at the age of fifty.

(Refer to "Oral Work" No. 1 for further examples).

Correct English, and Vocabulary

4. *Malapropisms.* Another form of verbal humour—often unintentional —is a malapropism. This is the confusion of two words that have a resemblance to each other in sound, but have very different meanings. Errors of this kind are called malapropisms because the conversation of Mrs. Malaprop, a character in Sheridan's play "The Rivals", contains many of these blunders.

e.g. "Oh, it gives me the *hydrostatics* to such a degree."

Mrs. Malaprop has confused *hydrostatics* with *hysterics*.

Substitute correct words for the malapropisms in the sentences below. The number of incorrect words is shown in brackets.

(a) The only way to improve your speech is to have electrocution lessons. (1)

(b) The young doctor—a very edible bachelor—was extremely populous with the nurses. (2)

(c) The patient was suffering from chronological defammation of the liver. (2)

(d) This irritation scheme will ennoble us to cultivate vast areas of dessert. (3)

(e) The heat is generated infernally by eccentricity and then distributed by conviction. (3)

5. *Ambiguity.* Explain the different meaning each of the sentences below can have. Then re-write each sentence, making one meaning quite clear each time.

(a) He made his patients remove their clothes and then threw them into the incinerator.

(b) She took the stethoscope from his neck and twisted it nervously in her hands.

(c) The surgeon told the man that he would be in a deep sleep throughout the operation.

(*d*) While the nurse was talking to the woman, she put a thermometer in her mouth.

(*e*) All the sleeping tablets that arrived yesterday have been swallowed by the patients, who thought they were vitamin pills; they didn't last long, I'm afraid.

6. *Reported Speech.* Discuss what changes would be necessary to convert any part of the script of "A Resounding Tinkle" to reported speech. To avoid ambiguity of pronouns you may assume that the patient is a woman, and the doctor a man.

   e.g. After asking her to breathe in again, the doctor reflected for a moment. He then asked her whether she ever felt as though the air she was getting was the wrong kind of air. The patient told him that she just didn't get the air.

TOPICS FOR WRITTEN WORK

1. (*a*) Write a "comedy-of-the-absurd" sketch. (*b*) Or you may write a prose story in a similar vein.

Hints

You could use one of the situations suggested by the class when discussing Question 2. "Appreciation and Discussion". Here are a few more suggestions:

(*a*) a husband and wife about to retire for the night;
   GERT: Have you put the tiger out, Henry?
   HENRY: Not yet, my dear.—Rover, Rover. Come here, boy.

(*b*) a policeman questioning a suspect;
   P.C. 48: What were you doing riding a woolly rhinoceros through the Council Rest Home for Unmarried Noddy Makers?
   SUSPECT: I was riding a woolly rhinoceros through the . . .

(*c*) two old people comparing the past and present;
   1st PENSIONER: It wasn't like this when I was a girl.
   2nd PENSIONER: That's probably because you were a boy.

(*d*) a man applying for a job;

(*e*) a workman (e.g. a plumber, an electrician) comes into a house to repair a fault.

Your sketch or story should last for about five minutes when read aloud.

138

2. Review a comedy that you have recently seen and enjoyed.
Hints

You may choose a play, a film, or an episode from a television comedy series. Imagine that you are writing the review for publication in a particular newspaper or magazine. Study a number of reviews from the newspaper or magazine of your choice. Notice what sort of style is used, what details the reviewer includes and what sort of comments he makes. What is the general construction of the reviews? Do they all follow much the same pattern?

3. Write an "absurd" poem of the kind composed by Spike Milligan.
Hints

Your poem can be of any length. You may invent words, or twist existing words to suit your purpose. Choose a title which reflects the absurd tone of the poem.

Pupils' Work

A Too Eager Salesman

A ring at the door-bell.

Self: Yes? Well, what do you want?

Salesman: Here sir, I have the most advanced wife-despatcher in the world today.

S.: Oh! All right, let me hear more. Yes, this looks interesting.

Sm.: It is recommended, sir, by all leading widowers; it gave them complete satisfaction; works without any attention; and the husband—or I should say widower—can come home and find an otherwise messy job carried out by a product specially designed for the purpose having done an excellent job.

S,: You mean to say that they—the manufacturers—have actually made a machine which has been wanted by poor unfortunates all over the world for the last couple of thousand years?

Sm.: Eh? Well, you could put it like that and may I say that, besides the manufacturer's guarantee, I can proudly say that I actually watched this marvellous machine work with all its magic on my dear wife; God rest her soul.

You should have seen how with expert precision it despatched her; a perfect treat to watch I can assure you, and no mess; no blood, no bruises, no cuts, not even one swear word was uttered by either of us.

S.: It certainly sounds very good. Could I have a look do you think?

Sm.: Why of course, sir. Here we are, this model is our latest: "The Wife Disposal-Unit Mk. II."

S.: But what happened to the Mk. I?

Sm.: Oh, that was a nasty business. Yes, we found after intensive tests that the machine tended to blow up. This, of course, made the clearing up quite a difficult matter, and as the motto of all the Company's goods is: efficiency, reliability, economy, well, we just had to take it off the market.

The Mk. II, now there's one of the best pieces of machinery the company has ever put out. Just look! (*Hands the machine to me*). No sharp corners, we always put safety first you know, the sleek finish, and the exceptionally good mechanism and easiness ensure that not even the most neurotic buyer will have the least trouble in setting it. Oh, and it also comes in a range of colours: white, pink, black, and sky-blue— we like to add an air of natural glamour and attractiveness to all our products. Well, sir, what do you think of it?

S.: Yes, well come back tomorrow, could you, because I will have to discuss it with my wife first? Goodbye!

Jon Brass

The Amorous Adventures of Betty Crumbleweed

Betty Crumbleweed was a vastly beautiful, vivacious young woman of eighty. She lived alone with her two cats, four dogs, eighteen pigeons, twenty chickens and one butler in a quaint and secluded medieval fortress.

One hot day in December there was a loud tap on her door. Betty was taking a bath (in her bath-chair) so she grabbed the nearest article to her in order to answer the door; she tightly pulled it around her slim 125-centimetre waist. She opened the door; her lower lip trembled and dropped 20 centimetres. (Coolly, the caller picked it up from her bosom and handed it back). There stood a handsome giant of a man (all one metre of him) who introduced himself as Baron Joseph von Cheesemuncher, self-styled soap salesman. Betty invited the Baron in to tea, her mind (what there was of it) swirling with evil thoughts of murder and lust.

Once over the threshold Betty sized the Baron up (six and seven-eighths head; size ten shoe; height: one metre; chest: 125 centimetres; 50-centimetre waist and so on). She found out that the Baron was literally stinking rich and that he had only two hours and six and a half minutes to live. With her seductive, hypnotic charm she gained control of his will and became sole heir to his soap fortune ($52\frac{1}{2}$p). With the help of her butler, Frank N. Styne, a couple of thousand panel pins and a hammer she suspended Baron Joseph von Cheesemuncher from a strong balsa wood beam in the cellar, to join the hundred other rentmen, milkmen, pools collectors, insurance men and unsuspecting callers there.

Yes, once again Betty Crumbleweed had nailed her man.

Jeff Daunton

A Rare Bird

A bent toenail zum zum zigger
is a small bird about the size of a sixpence.
One of the rarest birds in the world,
breeding only in teacups,
it is often seen flying backwards;
this is to keep the dirt out of its eyes.

S. Moore

ORAL WORK

1. The sort of twisted reasoning and absurd conclusions to be found in
"A Resounding Tinkle" are, of course, used for comic effect.
   e.g. 1st COMEDIAN: . . . There's no reason at all, Mr. Avalanche,
   why given time you shouldn't have a good twenty or thirty years
   in front of you.

   Dishonest and illogical statements are, however, not confined to
comedy, as you will have realised (e.g. see Exercise 3). In serious
discussion they are much more dangerous, since they may appear
logical and convincing.
   e.g. I am quite impartial about this matter, but I am also quite convinced, whatever they may say, that the Government are wrong
   about it.

   This is an abuse of the word "impartial" (which should mean
"unbiased to either side") in order to make the condemnation of the
Government seem fairer than it is.
   Discuss the following statements, pointing out in what ways they
are illogical and dishonest.
   (*a*) A: Of course, I am against cruelty to animals.
       B: But you go fox-hunting!
       A: Yes, but that's different; you can't call that cruel. The fox
          enjoys it.
       B: Surely he doesn't enjoy being caught and killed?
       A: Perhaps not, but he enjoys the chase, and anyway he usually
          gets away.
   (*b*) A: I believe that we should cut our expenditure on arms so that
          we can give more help to under-developed countries.
       B: That is an unpatriotic suggestion. Aren't you prepared to
          defend your country?

(c) Extremists are always dangerous. If I had my way, I would put them all in prison, or shoot them, and would only tolerate reasonable people of moderate views.

(d) The Germans started two world wars within thirty years: I wouldn't trust a German girl to look after *my* children.

(e) The demonstrators are getting out of hand: some are threatening to attack the police and break into the Embassy. They are behaving like wild dogs, and when a dog goes mad, the only thing you can do is shoot him!

2. Act or tape-record this chapter's extract from "A Resounding Tinkle", and the plays written by members of the class.

3. Each member of the class can tell a joke, preferably one that comes into the category of "comedy of the absurd". Then try arranging these jokes in such an order that they form a continuous script; you will, of course, have to provide a certain amount of "linking" material. Choose six people who told their jokes very effectively and get each of them to rehearse the script, or a part of it. One of them could then be selected to perform the script before an audience from other classes.

ACTIVITIES AND RESEARCH

1. Find out all you can about the "Drama of the Absurd" and the dramatists who specialise in this field. Look at some of the work of Eugene Ionesco, Harold Pinter, N. F. Simpson, and Samuel Beckett. Martin Esslin's book "The Theatre of the Absurd" (*Eyre and Spottiswoode*) might be useful; and you could collect biographical details from such sources as "Who's Who". Refer also to the "Goon Show", which was popular on the radio and later on television, and to magazines such as "Mad" and "Private Eye".

2. There are a number of films which have a strong element of absurd fantasy, such as "The Running, Jumping and Standing Still Film", starring Spike Milligan, and "The One Way Pendulum" by N. F. Simpson. See these and any others if you have an opportunity.

3. Listen to records of the "Goon Show" and any other comedy records that you can borrow. There is, for example, one by Tony Hancock called "The Blood Donor" which demonstrates another treatment of the doctor-patient relationship.

142

FURTHER READING

A Resounding Tinkle appears in the collection *The Hole—Plays and Sketches* by N. F. Simpson (Faber).

The plays of N. F. Simpson are the dramatic counterparts to the nonsense literature and poetry of Lewis Carroll and Edward Lear. In addition to writing the film script of *The One Way Pendulum*, he has also created a large number of plays for television about the domestic tribulations of Bro and Middie Paradock, who appear in *A Resounding Tinkle*.

The Room and *The Dumb Waiter* by Harold Pinter (Methuen).

If you enjoyed your first taste of the drama of the Absurd, these two short plays by another outstanding British playwright will provide a very suitable follow-up. Pinter's style is not so "goonish" as Simpson's; although he too uses the clichés of everyday conversation as his basic ingredient, he usually combines them into what has been described as an "unnerving comedy of menace". Another volume, *A Slight Ache*, contains three one-act plays originally written for radio and television, and five review sketches.

Waiting for Godot by Samuel Beckett (Faber).

Beckett is one of the most profound of the dramatists of the Absurd, and this play, first produced in 1952, earned him a world-wide reputation. In it, two tramps stand, talk, try to make a decision—and wait.

Absurd Drama (Penguin).

This volume contains four plays. They are Eugene Ionesco's first full-length play, *Amédé*, and three shorter pieces, Arthur Adamov's *Professor Taranne*, Fernando Arrabal's *The Two Executioners*, and *The Zoo Story* by Edward Albee.

A Resounding Tinkle, The Dumb Waiter and *The Long and the Short and the Tall* are also available in one Penguin volume.

Jim Raeder is taking part in a television "thrill show" contest. In order to win the prize of two hundred thousand dollars he has to avoid being killed by a gang of professional gunmen who are allowed to hunt him for one week. He now has less than five hours to go before the time limit expires.

Take care!
BEWARE of your killer

Which way?

Jim Raeder

They've got you boxed

Look out!

Your life is at stake!

CHAPTER 10

Television

H e closed his eyes again and remembered, with mild astonishment, a time when he had been in no trouble . . . .

He had been a big pleasant young man working as a truck driver's helper. He had no talents. He was too modest to have dreams.

The tight-faced little truck driver had the dreams for him. "Why not try for a television show, Jim? I would if I had your looks. They like nice average guys with nothing much on the ball. As contestants. Everybody likes guys like that. Why not look into it?"

So he had looked into it. The owner of the local television store had explained it further.

"You see, Jim, the public is sick of highly trained athletes with their trick reflexes and their professional courage. Who can feel for guys like that? Who can identify? People want to watch exciting things, sure, but not when some joker is making it his business for fifty thousand a year. That's why organized sports are in a slump. That's why the thrill shows are booming."

"I see," said Raeder . . . .

"It's a marvellous opportunity. Take you. You're no better than anyone, Jim. Anything you can do, anyone can do. You're *average*. I think the thrill shows would go for you." . . .

* * * * * *

There was a heavy truck approaching. He kept on walking, pulling his hat low on his forehead. But as the truck drew near, he heard a voice from the television set in his pocket. It cried, "*Watch out!*"

He flung himself into the ditch. The truck careered past, narrowly missing him, and screeched to a stop. The driver was shouting, "There he goes! Shoot, Harry, shoot!"

Bullets clipped leaves from the trees as Raeder sprinted into the woods.

"*It's happened again!*" Mike Terry was saying, his voice high-pitched with excitement. "*I'm afraid Jim Raeder let himself be lulled into a false sense of security. You can't do that, Jim! Not with your life at stake! Not with killers pursuing you! Be careful, Jim, you still have four and a half hours to go!*"

The driver was saying, "Claude, Harry, go around with the truck. We got him boxed."

"*They've got you boxed, Jim Raeder!*" Mike Terry cried. "*But they haven't got you yet! And you can thank Good Samaritan Susy Peters of twelve Elm Street, South Orange, New Jersey, for that warning shout just when the truck was bearing down on you.. We'll have little Susy on stage in just a moment . . . Look, folks, our studio helicopter has arrived on the scene. Now you can see Jim Raeder running, and the killers pursuing, surrounding him . . .*"

* * * * * *

One week ago he had been on the *Prize of Peril* stage, blinking in the spotlight, and Mike Terry had shaken his hand.

"Now, Mr. Raeder," Terry had said solemnly, "do you understand the rules of the game you are about to play?"

Raeder nodded.

"If you accept, Jim Raeder, you will be a *hunted man* for a week. *Killers* will follow you, Jim. *Trained killers,* men wanted by the law for other crimes, granted immunity for this single killing under the Voluntary Suicide Act. They will be trying to kill *you* Jim. Do you understand?"

"I understand," Raeder said. He also understood the two hundred thousand dollars he would receive if he could live out the week . . . .

"Very well!" cried Mike Terry. "Jim Raeder, meet your wood-be-killers!"

The Thompson gang moved on stage, booed by the audience.

"Look at them, folks," said Mike Terry, with undisguised contempt. "Just look at them! Antisocial, thoroughly vicious, completely amoral. These men have no code but the criminal's warped code, no honour but the honour of the cowardly hired killer. They are doomed men, doomed by our society which will not sanction their activities for long, fated to an early and unglamorous death."

The audience shouted enthusiastically.

"What have you to say, Claude Thompson?" Terry asked.

Claude, the spokesman of the Thompsons, stepped up to the microphone. He was a thin, clean-shaven man, conservatively dressed.

"I figure," Claude Thompson said hoarsely, "I figure we're no worse than anybody. I mean, like soldiers in a war, they kill. And look at the graft in government, and the unions. Everybody's got their graft."

That was Thompson's tenuous code. But how quickly, with what precision, Mike Terry destroyed the killers' rationalizations! Terry's questions pierced straight to the filthy soul of the man . . .

"We'll get him," Thompson said.

146

"And one thing more," Terry said, very softly. "Jim Raeder does not stand alone. The folks of America are for him. Good Samaritans from all corners of our great nation stand ready to assist him. Unarmed, defenceless, Jim Raeder can count on the aid and good-heartedness of *the people*, whose representative he is. So don't be too sure, Claude Thompson! The average men are for Jim Raeder—and there are a lot of average men!"

* * * * * *

Raeder thought about it, lying motionless in the underbrush. Yes *the people* had helped him. But they had helped the killers, too.

A tremor ran through him. He had chosen, he reminded himself. He alone was responsible. The psychological test had proved that.

And yet, how responsible were the psychologists who had given him the test? How responsible was Mike Terry for offering a poor man so much money? Society had woven the noose and put it around his neck and he was hanging himself with it, and calling it free will.

Whose fault?

"Aha!" someone cried.

Raeder looked up and saw a portly man standing near him. The man wore a loud tweed jacket. He had binoculars around his neck, and a cane in his hand.

"Mister," Raeder whispered, "please don't tell!"

"Hi!" shouted the portly man, pointing at Raeder with his cane. "Here he is!" . . .

The killers were shooting again, Raeder ran, stumbling over uneven ground, past three children playing in a tree house.

"Here he is!" the children screamed. "Here he is!"

Raeder groaned and ran on. He reached the steps of the building, and saw that it was a church.

As he opened the door, a bullet struck him behind the right kneecap. He fell, and crawled inside the church.

The television set in his pocket was saying, *"What a finish, folks, what a finish! Raeder's been hit! He's been hit, folks, he's crawling now, he's in pain, but he hasn't given up! Not Jim Raeder!"*

Raeder lay in the aisle near the altar. He could hear a child's eager voice saying, "He went in there, Mr. Thompson. Hurry, you can still catch him!"

Wasn't a church considered a sanctuary, Raeder wondered.

Then the door was flung open, and Raeder realized that the custom was no longer observed. He gathered himself together and crawled past the altar, out the back door of the church.

147

He was in an old graveyard. He crawled past crosses and stars, past slabs of marble and granite, past stone tombs and rude wooden markers. A bullet exploded on a tombstone near his head, showering him with fragments. He crawled to the edge of an open grave.

They had deceived him, he thought. All of those nice average normal people. Hadn't they said he was their representative? Hadn't they sworn to protect their own? But no, they loathed him. Why hadn't he seen it? Their hero was the cold, blank-eyed gunman, Thompson, Capone, Billy the Kid, Young Lochinvar, El Cid, Cuchulain, the man without human hopes or fears. They worshipped him, that dead, implacable robot gunman, and lusted to feel his foot in their face.

Raeder tried to move, and slid helplessly into the open grave.

(from *The Prize of Peril* by Robert Sheckley)

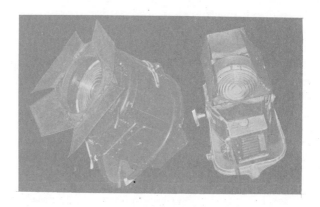

APPRECIATION AND DISCUSSION

1. What is meant when a viewer is said to "identify" with a character in a television programme?
2. Do you think the desire to identify with characters in television shows and in films and books is a strong one?
3. Name and discuss television shows which involve ordinary people who have to undergo some sort of test in order to win a reward. Do viewers identify with the participants in these shows? If not, what motives prompt people to watch them?

148

4. Speedway riders and lion tamers could be quoted as examples of "highly trained athletes with their trick reflexes and professional courage", who make it their business to perform exciting feats for high rewards. According to one theory in this story, ordinary people would not identify with such performers. Do you agree with this? What is the attraction of these feats? Was there a similar attraction about *The Prize of Peril* show?

5. Do people like to imagine themselves as the central characters in exciting stories about the war, gangsters, the Wild West, and romantic involvements? What, do you think, is the basic attraction of such forms of entertainment?

6. If you were responsible for a television quiz show which had ordinary people as contestants, and your audience-viewing figures began to fall, would you consider replacing the quiz with a more exciting form of test in order to revive the interest of the public? If so, what sort of tests would you invent?

7. Bearing in mind the answers to the above questions, say whether you think such a show as *The Prize of Peril* could ever become a reality.

8. Compare Mike Terry's commentary on the chase with commentaries that you have heard about exciting events. Is it at all similar to these, and if so, in what respects? Compare also his introduction at the start of the programme with those of some actual television shows.

9. "Terry's questions pierced straight to the filthy soul of the man." Did the author intend this as a straight forward description of Thompson, or is he, in fact, exaggerating in order to mock Mike Terry?

10. What, do you imagine, were the motives of "Good Samaritan Susy Peters" and the other Good Samaritans who helped Jim Raeder?

11. In what sense was Jim Raeder the "representative" of the people?

12. The people's hero, Raeder bitterly concluded, was not, after all, the average, normal person like themselves, but "the cold, blank-eyed gunman", the superman who, whether he acted for good or bad, was "without human hopes or fears". Do you agree with this conclusion? Are any of the arguments raised by Question 5 relevant to this discussion?

149

Aunts Watching Television

The aunts who knew not Africa
But spoke of having been to Weymouth in the spring—
Not last spring but the year the lilac was so good—
Who never saw prize-fighters in a ring,
But could recall a fox-hunt in the neighbourhood.

Two aunts who never went abroad,
Nor travelled far in love, nor were much wronged, nor sinned
A lot—but for such peccadillos as to damn,
With tiny oaths, late frost or some chill wind,
Slugs at the dahlias or wasps at home-made jam.

Two aunts who, after silences,
Spoke knowingly of angels passing overhead:
But who prayed little and slept well, were worried less
By death than weeds; but hoped to die in bed,
Untouched by magic or by economic stress.

This age's beneficiaries
For whom our century endows this box of dreams,
Conferring prize-fighters, dancers of unimaginable grace,
Glimpses of Africa, of football teams,
Of statesmen, of the finish of a classic race.

Vestals of the impalpable,
Dazed by its prodigality, by acrobats
On bicycles, by lovers speaking Shapespeare's lines,
Mazed by murders, by speeches from democrats,
Wooed by cooking hints and the Paris dress designs.

Flirt on, soft spinsters, flirt with time.
Order the crowded hours, vicariously tranced.
Know Africa and judge which prize-fighter was hurt,
How well the latest ballerina danced,
How cake, or love, was made. O flirt, my two aunts, flirt!

John Pudney

150

DISCUSSING THE POEM

1. The first three verses describe the two spinsters—what they had and had not done, the sort of lives they led and the sort of experiences they had missed. How many of these points are mentioned again when the poet describes in the next three verses the contents of the television programmes?
2. Describe, in your own words, the two aunts, using information in the poem as a guide, and then adding other details that seem appropriate.
3. In what way would the aunts "order the crowded hours"?
4. In what sense were the two aunts "flirting"? What sort of relationship is implied by the word "flirt"? If you flirt with somebody (or something) do you have a close, meaningful relationship?
5. Explain in simpler terms what is meant by:

    "peccadillos"   "economic stress"
    "beneficiaries"   "Vestals of the impalpable"
    "Dazed by its prodigality"   "vicariously tranced".

TECHNIQUES

The Use of Language, and Style

1. *Clichés.* Television consumes material at a tremendous rate. Inevitably, the standard of some of the material is low. Dialogue, for example, may be riddled with clichés. Consider the hackneyed expressions below and give the titles of programmes in which they might have occurred.

    (a) Now remember what I told you, boys—no rough stuff!
    (b) I don't like the lyric much but I think the backing's great.
    (c) There's only one man for this job.
    (d) This doesn't concern you, Matt. Just keep out of my way.
    (e) Things can never be the same between us again.
    (f) Do you think I like doing this?
    (g) A man's gotta do what he thinks is right.
    (h) It's touch and go. I've done everything I can. All we can do now is wait and pray.
    (i) You're running away from yourself, Joe.
    (j) You must see how I feel about you.
    (k) Look! What's this all about?
    (l) It's a boy!

List other clichés that occur regularly, and give the programmes in which they appear. Are there any clichés in Mike Terry's commentary from the "Prize of Peril" extract?

151

2. *Contrast and Anti-climax.* Throughout the poem "Aunts Watching Television" different ideas are contrasted very effectively.

> e.g. "The aunts who knew not *Africa*
> But spoke of having been to *Weymouth* in the spring—"

Find other examples of contrast in the poem. Very often, as in the above example, exciting or dramatic ideas are put first and then contrasted with insignificant or homely details, so that there is a sense of anti-climax and incongruity.

Rewrite these sentences, replacing the words and phrases in italics with incongruous contrasts of your own invention.

(*a*) I was intending to go to *Brazil*, but the journey back from *Bournemouth* was too much for me.

(*b*) He was worried more by *woodworm* than by *World War II*.

(*c*) They spoke of *the angels overhead* and swore at *the draught under the door.*

(*d*) They shunned *reality* and flirted with *dreams.*

(*e*) She was captivated by *cream cakes*, and ignored by *love.*

3. *Definitions: Metaphorical and Literal.* (i) John Pudney used a striking metaphor to define a television set: he called it a "box of dreams". Complete these sentences with suitable metaphors of your own.

(*a*) A television set is a ———.

(*b*) A motor car is a ———.

(*c*) An aeroplane is a ———.

(*d*) Money is ———.

(*e*) A school is ———.

(ii) Now write a literal definition of each of the above items.

> e.g. A television set is a device for receiving electrical impulses and converting them into pictures and sounds.

REALISMrealism
REALISM

4. *Emotive Language.* (i) The words that a person chooses to describe something will often depend upon the response he wishes to evoke. For example, one critic may describe a television programme as "frank and outspoken", another as "rude and vulgar".

Each of the phrases in the left-hand column can be matched in basic meaning with a phrase in the right-hand column, but they are very different in implication. Pair them off and comment on the difference.

Complimentary	*Uncomplimentary*
tough quality	a small, old-fashioned house
generous size	long term expense
a compact, traditional cottage	coarse strength
gay colours	a slippery top
easy payments	inconvenient bulk
a trend-leading breakthrough	a bewildering variety
a polished, glossy surface	a daft, decrepit countryman
a wide range	gaudy appearance
a simple, old rustic	a sickening stench
a rich odour	an untried experiment

(ii) Now write two, short, emotive descriptions of each of the following —one that is favourable, and another that is critical or insulting.

a strong alcoholic drink	an old building
a fast car	a manual worker
a man's beard	warm sunshine
a long journey	fried food
snow in a town	snakes

Correct English, and Vocabulary

5. *Confused Words.* (i) The verbs "to lie" and "to lay" are often confused.

Present	*Past*
I lie (he lies)	I lay *and* I have lain
I lay (he lays)	I laid *and* I have laid

Remember that the verb "to lay" is followed by the name of the thing being put down. The verb "to lie" refers to the performer of the action.

Say which of these two verbs is used in the extract in the first sentences of paragraphs 2 and 16 on page 127.

For each of the sentences below, choose the correct form of the verb from those in brackets.

(*a*) If you (lie lay) on the ground, you will get dirty.
(*b*) I watched him (lie lay) his gun on the table.
(*c*) The man (lay laid) motionless in the undergrowth.
(*d*) Yesterday we (lay laid) several kilometres of cable.
(*e*) They (have lain have laid) the carpet in the dining room.
(*f*) These books (have lain have laid) here for several months.

(ii) Make sure that you can also distinguish between the various forms of these pairs of verbs.

(*a*) to rise   to raise   (*b*) to bear   to bore   (*c*) to set   to sit
(*d*) to fall   to fell   (*e*) to see   to saw

6. *Prefixes and Suffixes.* (i) Mike Terry described the Thompson gang as *amoral*. This word is formed from *moral* and the prefix *a-*, meaning *without*. We can also form another word, with a slightly different meaning, by adding the prefix *im-*, meaning *not*, i.e. *immoral*.

Two other words can be formed from each of those below by using prefixes from the list. Give these words and their meanings.

(*a*) conscious   (*b*) dependent   (*c*) human   (*d*) mature   (*e*) migrate

Prefix	*Meaning*
e-	out of
im-	into
im-	not
in-	not
inter-	between
pre-	before
sub-	under
super-	above
un-	not

(ii) Form another version of each of the above words by adding the correct suffix from those below. (In one case the existing suffix has to be replaced, in two others a slight alteration to the end of the word is necessary.)

Suffixes   -ancy   -ity   -ion   -ness

These four suffixes all have the same meaning. What is it?

TOPICS FOR WRITTEN WORK

1. Imagine that you are producing a short film for television. Write a brief outline of your aims, and give part of your scenario for the film.

Hints

You may choose any subject that you wish, bearing in mind that the film is to last no more than five minutes. Here are a few suggestions:

(*a*) a pop group, singing their latest song

(*b*) the reading of a poem

(*c*) an appeal on behalf of a charity

(*d*) a review of local events

(*e*) a profile of a well known person, or an interesting building in your area.

In the first few sentences of your outline, state what your film is about and give your reasons for choosing this subject. Then explain the main effect you wish to create and how you intend to achieve this through your camera shots, any musical accompaniment, etc. Describe the appearance of characters in the film. Set out your scenario as shown in the example below. Remember that just as you can contrast words for effect (Exercise 2), so you can contrast camera shots and sounds.

My Friend Maloney (poem in Chapter 13)

Vision	*Sound*
1. Close up shot of Maloney's face Camera moves back to show Maloney leaning against a street corner.	Trumpet playing "St Louis Blues"
2. Long distance shot of Maloney moving off down the street. Camera follows behind him.	Music slowly fades
3. Middle distance shot of Maloney stopping by an expensive car. He wrenches the handle.	My friend Maloney, eighteen Swears like a sentry.
4. C.U. of Maloney's hand.	Got into trouble two years back.
5. M.D. of two boys looking round the corner.	
6. L.D. of the boys running down the street to a policeman talking to the owner of the car. They point back to the corner.	With the local gentry. Parsons.and squire's sons
7. L.D. of Maloney driving away the car as the policeman, owner and boys run towards it.	Informed a copper.
8. Shot from above, looking down into the courtroom.	Music "Rule Britannia"
9. C.U. of the magistrate's face.	Ditto
10. C.U. of the policeman's face.	Ditto
11. C.U. of the car owner's face.	Ditto
12. C.U. of Maloney's face.	Music becomes distorted and fades

2. Write a letter of complaint to the manufacturers of your new television set, which has not functioned properly since you bought it.

Hints

Make up the name and address of the manufacturers when you write this business letter. Make your complaint firmly and politely; do not become abusive. Explain that the set is only three months old and is still under guarantee, and that the local supplier has taken it away six times in order to repair faults. State what the faults were, and ask the firm to replace the set with a new one.

3. "Watching Television". Write about anything that is suggested to you by this title.

Hints

This piece of work can be either a poem, a play, or a piece of prose (factual or imaginative).

Watching Television

"At last," I sighed to myself, as the orgy of door-shutting stopped and everyone was settled in their places. "Now for some relaxation, and the pleasantest way of spending an evening." Everyone was quiet, and as the television warmed up, "I Love Lucy" appeared on the screen.

For ten minutes everything was fine. The programme was well on its way, and already Dad had laughed, for what seemed ages, at something which to me was not worth all the noise, and prevented us from hearing the next few lines.

Then disaster! "O me miserum!" I thought, and everyone else leant back and groaned. The television, which had offered the sound-track and film of what had seemed to be the funniest "I Love Lucy" ever had suddenly gone completely and absolutely blank.

The chair creaked as Dad heaved himself up and slowly lumbered towards that unfaithful, unthinking, selfish television set. He poked cautiously round with one finger for five minutes, and then, gaining courage, he went on with both hands. A moment later, his face was contorted into a picture of excruciating agony, and everyone knew that he had touched a red-hot valve. He jumped back, trod on the dog, and poured forth a volley of mild exclamations.

We exchanged startled glances. Mum stood up, trying to look cheerful, and said. "Well, that seems to be that," and went to turn on the light. The switch was down, the room should have been flooded with light, but darkness still prevailed.

I groaned again, and murmured . . . well, that really doesn't matter. Mum resignedly drew the curtains, and let in as much light as can get past the tall garage which is practically built on to the house. The torches gave only a feeble glow owing to the fact that a certain person had used them to search the shed for something last seen three years ago.

The whole family sat there for a few minutes, wondering how to occupy the time before going to bed. Then, what joy, what delight! The light flashed on and the television began to warm up. Evidently there had been a power cut. Soon we settled down again to watch the good, faithful old television.

Nobody had seen a stealthy figure slip the fusebox back into its place. No-one had heard the click as the front door was opened and closed again. Nobody missed the fifteen pounds towards our holidays until the next morning. Yes, it was bliss to sit back, forget your troubles, and watch television.

Jacqueline Archer

1. Each take one of the following technical terms (or jargon), which are used frequently in the world of television, and explain what it means.

commentator	test card	pan
compere	outside broadcast	zoom
interviewer	on location	track
news-caster	boom	traverse
scriptwriter	camera script	adapted by
script supervisor	captions	devised by
floor manager	dissolve	dramatised by
animation	fade-out	edited by
live or recorded material	wide-angle	introduced by
sound effects	close-up	narrated by
video tape	long shot	based on an idea by

2. Discuss these criticisms of television Westerns and crime stories.
   (*a*) Scenes, characters and situations are hackneyed.
   (*b*) The heroes are mainly admired for their toughness and self-confidence, and not for really admirable qualities such as sympathy, generosity or intelligence.
   (*c*) The stories frequently look upon Red Indians, negroes and foreigners generally as inferior to the American or British heroes.
   (*d*) They glamourise sordid and degrading pursuits such as gambling, drinking and searching for wealth.
   (*e*) They give the impression that law and order must be based upon violence and the use of force, which is a totally wrong idea.
   (*f*) The over-simplified picture of independent heroes and treacherous villains which they present is so unreal that it is pointless to go on portraying it.
3. Robert Sheckley's story, "The Prize of Peril", does not end at the point reached in this chapter's extract. Suggest possible endings to the story and discuss them. If possible, get the anthology "Second Orbit" and find out how Sheckley concluded his story.

ACTIVITIES AND RESEARCH

1. (*a*) Make a survey of the kinds of programme offered on a typical day, or during a typical week, by all the channels available in your area. In order to draw some comparisons and contrasts, it will be necessary to decide on certain categories into which nearly all programmes can be fitted. Limit the number of these categories, extending them to include all programmes if possible; here is a suggested list of headings:

More Serious	*Lighter Entertainment*
News and background	Sports news, comment, etc.
Discussions, talks, etc.	Light plays, comedy series
Documentaries	Travel and nature films
Serious plays and films	Western, crime and spy films
Serious music, opera, ballet	Light and pop music, dancing, etc.
Educational programmes	"Magazine" programmes, etc.
Religious programmes	(for women, children, the deaf).

First, add up the broadcast time devoted to each category on each channel. Then note how much of this time is "live" broadcasting, how much is television recording, how much is film; and, in the case of smaller commercial television companies, how much time is given to their own programmes, and how much is "networked"?

(*b*) Where different channels broadcast similar programmes, attempt some comparison of their styles. Here the judgement is bound to be largely a matter of personal opinion, but it should be interesting to note differences in the way in which news, documentaries, quiz shows, etc. are presented.

2. Watch a television programme which, in your opinion, usually demonstrates some effective camera work. Make a list of the shots used in part of the programme. To do this, you will have to make very rapid notes, using abbreviations.

   e.g. 1. C. U. dancer's ft. 5 secs.
   2. Shot fm abv. audience. 6 secs.
   3. M. D. singer. Pan to drummer. Dissolve. 15 s.

You will find it easier, of course, if you can get two other people to help you, taking it in turn to take notes on each shot. Afterwards you can discuss with the rest of the class the way in which the camera work added to the effect of the programme (whether it was a play, a pop music programme, a documentary, etc,) by referring to specific shots and sequences.

159

3. If possible, arrange for the class or a small group to visit a television studio, to see a broadcast as part of a studio audience, or to be shown round. Tickets for shows are usually free, but not always easy to obtain! Make a report on what you saw, and learned from the visit.

FURTHER READING

The Prize of Peril by Robert Sheckley appeared in *Second Orbit* edited by G. Doherty (Murray).

Robert Sheckley is one of the most talented of science fiction writers. In an original and intriguing way, his short stories examine human values, institutions, and patterns of behaviour to be found in contemporary society. And, although it is a fair criticism that the use of words by many science fiction writers is on the same level as popular journalism, Robert Sheckley's style often rises considerably above this level.

The anthology in which this chapter's story is to be found, and its forerunner, *Aspects of Science Fiction*, also edited by G. Doherty provide a good introduction to worthwhile science fiction.

Listed below are other anthologies that contain stories of considerable merit in the quality of values implied, in manipulation of plot, and in invention of incident.

Penguin Science Fiction, More Penguin Science Fiction, Yet More Penguin Science Fiction, edited by Brian Aldiss (Penguin).

Best S.F. series edited by Edmund Crispin (Faber).

Connoisseur's S.F. edited by Tom Boardman (Penguin).

The Starlit Corridor edited by Roger Mansfield (Pergamon Press).

CHAPTER 11

A Defeat

The story from which this extract is taken is an account of the relationships, fights and escapades of childhood in a working class area of a northern town

The whole school knew about the fight next morning. I was a bit frightened in case any of the teachers got to know about it, but proud in a way because I was so famous. All day me and Raymond Garnett kept out of each other's way. I thought I could beat him with one hand tied behind my back, but as the day wore on I started getting like a sinking feeling and wanting to go to the lavatory all the time. I didn't want to go back to school after dinner and I wished I could break my leg. But I knew I would have to go, and on the way back to school, Ted shouted after me: "Have you made your will out?"...

The bell went for going-home time and Old Ma Bates said everyone could go . . . .

We walked out of the playground and round by Parkside towards the fighting field. We walked without saying anything. The only one who spoke was Ted who said: "Got any chewy?" to Little Rayner, and that was the only thing that was said.

I was frightened when we got down on to the field, not by Raymond Garnett but by this big crowd of kids who had waited to see the fight. At the same time I was happy because they were waiting to see me and Raymond Garnett and nobody else . . . .

I had never had a fight before. I felt important and pleased at the crowds who were round us, none of them touching us but leaving it to us to have our fight.

"Back a bit," I said, and I was right pleased when they moved back. I took off my coat and handed it to a kid I did not know. He took it and held it carefully over his arm, and this pleased me too.

Raymond Garnett took off his coat and his glasses. I had never seen him without his glasses before, except that time when we were playing in Clarkson's woods with Marion. He had a white mark over his nose where he had taken them off and it gave me the feeling that I could bash him easy. He gave them to a kid to look after and as the crowd started pushing the kid went: "*Mi-ind* his glasses!"

We both stepped forward to meet each other and put our fists up. We stood staring at each other and dancing round a bit like they do on the pictures, then I shot out my right hand to Garnett's chin but it missed and caught his shoulder. The next thing I knew was that his fist had caught me a stinging clout over the forehead. I was surprised and worried at the size of the blow and I began to notice, in a far-off sort of way, that he was a lot bigger than me and that his arms were thicker and longer.

I don't know how I got time to look at the people in the ring around us, but I did, and I noticed that I didn't even know most of them. Little Rayner was at the front shouting: "Go it, Garno!" and this hurt me, don't ask me why. Ted was at the back, jumping up and down to get a good look . . . .

I remember reading in the "Hotspur" or somewhere about all these boxers, they always hit with their left. I tried to hit Garno with my left hand but I couldn't aim it properly and I missed. Little Rayner started going: "Cur, call this a fight!" One or two kids at the back had started their own little fights.

I started trying to look in Garno's eyes all the time. This was something else I remembered. If you look the other man in the eyes all the time, well you can tell what he's going to do.

You couldn't tell what blinking Garno was going to do. He seemed surprised that I was staring at him all the time, and for a minute I thought he was going to start saying: "Have you seen all?" His mouth was pursed up and he looked as though he was getting his mad up. Suddenly, for no reason at all as far as I could see, he went: "Right! You've asked for it now!" and he started laying into me. I started dancing round backwards like proper boxers do. There was a bump or a stone or something and I tripped over it and fell, sprawling. Little Rayner shouted: "What you doing on the floor, man?" Garno stood over me, breathing through his mouth.

"Do you give in?" he said.

The question seemed cocky and unfair. I said: "We haven't started yet!" I got up on my feet and he hit me with his fist in the face. I didn't fall this time but I turned round to stop him hitting me. I was all hunched up and almost cringing and I could feel his knuckles on the back of my head. Some kids were drifting away from the back of the crowd and that was even worse. Ted at the back started shouting: "One - two - three - four, who - are - *we* - for - GARno!" Nobody took up the cry and he sounded silly.

162

Garno had stopped moving round the ring now. He just stood there and every time I came near him he hit me. He hit me in the lip again and it started bleeding.

We stood staring at each other, our fists clenched, breathing heavily I said to the kid who had my coat: "Get us my hanky," because the blood was going down my chin.

The kid said: "Clean your boots for fourpence." He dropped my coat on the floor and started going: "Yurrrks" as though it were all over lice or something.

"Do you give in?" said Raymond Garnett.

I didn't answer him, I couldn't. Suddenly Garno lifted his hand and slapped me across the cheek. It wasn't with his fist, it was with his open hand. I had to bite into my bleeding lip to stop myself from crying. The tears came up into my eyes.

"*So-ock* him, man!" said Little Rayner.

"Do you give in?" said Raymond Garnett. He slapped me across the face again. I couldn't stop the tears rolling down my cheeks.

"Yer," I muttered.

(from *There is a Happy Land* by Keith Waterhouse)

1. Why, do you think, did Raymond Garnett and the narrator keep out of each other's way before the fight?
2. What was the narrator's attitude to the fight and to its audience before the fight took place? How did he react physically to the pre-fight tension?
3. Why was he so confident that he could beat Garnett?
4. Why would he have been hurt when Little Rayner shouted, "Go it, Garno!"?
5. Was Raymond Garnett any more experienced than the narrator at fighting? How can you tell?
6. "I could feel his knuckles on the back of my head. Some kids were drifting away from the back of the crowd and that was even worse." In what sense was it worse?
7. What was the attitude of the crowd watching the fight (a) before it started (b) after the boys had been fighting for a while? What caused the change?
8. How did the boy holding the narrator's coat act before, and after the fight? Why did he act like this? Would you have acted in this way?
9. Why did tears come to the narrator's eyes after Garno had slapped him? Would he have been so likely to have cried if Garno had punched him?
10. Do fights of this kind ever solve a problem or dispute? On what occasions, if any, are they justified? What other ways are there of resolving disputes?
11. Have you ever been in a fight? Why did the fight occur? How did you feel about it? Were any of your feelings similar to those described in the extract? Did you win or lose the fight?
12. Would you fight if somebody of your own age and size (a) teased you (b) insulted you (c) falsely accused you of stealing (d) bullied a young friend of yours? Would you act in the same way if the person was (a) older and stronger than you (b) smaller and weaker?

HUMILIATION DEFEAT futility despair

Breakfast

He put the coffee
In the cup
He put the milk
In the cup of coffee
He put the sugar
In the *café au lait*
With the coffee spoon
He stirred
He drank the *café au lait*
And he set down the cup
Without a word to me
He lit
A cigarette
He made smoke rings
With the smoke
He put the ashes
In the ash-tray
Without a word to me
Without a look at me
He got up
He put
His hat upon his head
He put his raincoat on
Because it was raining
And he left
In the rain
Without a word
Without a look at me
And I took
My head in my hand
And I cried.

Jacques Prévert,
translated by *Lawrence Ferlinghetti.*

DISCUSSING THE POEM

1. What sort of person could be telling this poem?
2. Which words and ideas are repeated? What effect is created by this repetition?
3. Only at the very end is the narrator's unhappiness described: "And I cried." But throughout the poem there is a sense of defeat, of rejection, of despair. Can you explain how this atmosphere is created?
4. This poem was originally written in French and was rhymed. Do you think the unrhymed English translation still qualifies to be called a poem? Would it still have the same impact if it were written out as punctuated prose? What effect is given by the absence of punctuation?
5. The language of the poem is very simple. Would the poet have described this experience more vividly if he had used more complex words?

TECHNIQUES

The Use of Language, and Style

1. *Colloquial Writing.* "There is a Happy Land" employs the simple vocabulary of a young boy; colloquialisms are used frequently, e.g. "getting his mad up"; and sentences are phrased as if the narrator were actually *speaking* to the reader, e.g. "I started getting like a sinking feeling". What sort of impression does this style create? Is it appropriate for this novel?

It is certainly not appropriate for the following business letter. Rewrite it, replacing the colloquialisms, avoiding ambiguity, and making any other corrections.

Number 22 Friday

Dear head,

I'm writing to let you know that I'd be right pleased if you would let Raymond off from being away from his lessons next Monday afternoon so as he can nip down to his uncle's funeral with us. He kicked the bucket yesterday and that's the reason why he needs the afternoon off, so we can bury him good and proper.

Cheerio for now,
Raymond's mum.

Now read through the passage, each member of the class taking a sentence in turn, and suggest the changes that would have to be made if the extract were to be written in a conventional, formal style. What effect does this have? Does it improve the passage, or weaken it?

2. *Business Jargon.* Colloquial writing, in dialogue and narrative, can be very appropriate for certain types of novels. Some forms of jargon, when used in their proper context, are also quite justified. One form of jargon which should always be avoided, however, is "Business English". Here is part of an article from a magazine issued by I.C.I., one of the largest firms in Britain, explaining why it should never be used.

Anyone who writes a letter from an I.C.I. sales office beginning "Dear Sir, We are in receipt of your esteemed favour of the 5th inst., and beg to inform you . . . " will almost certainly be in receipt of his Sales Manager's displeasure. Since 1953 courses in letter writing have been held for sales staff all over the country, and "esteemed favours", "inst.", "ult.", "prox." and any form of "begging" have become definitely taboo, along with many other words and phrases from that pompous and serpentine language known as Business English.

Business English, the students are taught, is anything but businesslike. It is shorter, sweeter and far more businesslike to refer to a letter as a letter than as an "esteemed favour". And if a husband never says to his wife on a shopping expedition that "the position opposite detergents is difficult", why should a correspondence clerk write to a customer that "the supply position opposite salt is difficult" when there is merely a shortage of salt?

The students are shown how to replace such cumbersome and nebulous phrases as "in respect of", "with a view to" and "with regard to" by simple prepositions. They are urged to use the active rather than the passive voice, to guard against unnecessary adjectives, and to shun euphemisms.

Rewrite the following examples of Business English.

e.g. We are in receipt of your esteemed favour of the 6th inst.
We have received your letter of the 6th April.—(What does inst. mean?)

(a) Your esteemed order of the 2nd inst. is to hand and we thank you for same.

(b) It will be our earnest endeavour to give you the utmost satisfaction.

(c) We shall take the earliest opportunity of acquainting you with our decision in the matter.

(d) We are of the opinion that we can now see our way clear to proceeding with operations as per our agreement of the 12th ult.

(e) Re your esteemed order of the 7th ult., we have to advise you that in view of the fact that the position opposite paper is difficult we cannot ensure delivery until the 20th prox.

3. *General Punctuation.* In order to judge more clearly what effect Jacques Prévert has achieved by omitting all punctuation from his poem "Breakfast", write out the poem, inserting punctuation marks. There are several different ways in which the poem can be punctuated. How do these alter the meaning? Which meaning, in your opinion, did the poet intend?

Correct English, and Vocabulary

4. *Prepositions.* A part of speech known as a preposition was mentioned in the article quoted in Exercise 1. A preposition is a word which shows the connection between other words.

In the example below, one of the cumbersome phrases the writer quotes has been replaced, as he suggests, by a preposition.

> e.g. I have made some comments *with regard* to your scheme.
>
> I have made some comments *on* your scheme.

Certain words have to be followed by certain prepositions. Thus it is incorrect to write:

> *Compare* this extract *against* the previous one.

The correct version is:

> *Compare* this extract *with* the previous one.

Insert the correct prepositions in these sentences.

(*a*) The cumbersome phrase was replaced — a single word.

(*b*) He was very different — his brother.

(*c*) This picture is similar — that one.

(*d*) Everything depends — the weather.

(*e*) He triumphed — his opponent.

Some words can be followed by one of a number of prepositions, depending on the meaning.

> e.g. look *after*   look *into*   look *for*   look *through*
>
> look *around*   look *under*

Use each of the above in a sentence. (Remember that the italicised prepositions must be closely followed by a noun or pronoun; e.g. I shall look *after* the baby.)

5. *Pronouns.* Correct these three sentences adapted from the passage. In each one, a pronoun is incorrectly used.

(*a*) Me and Raymond Garnett kept out of each other's way.

(*b*) I began to notice that he was a lot bigger than me.

(*c*) I said: "Give us my hanky." (The speaker wanted the handkerchief for himself only.)

Explain the difference in meaning between the sentences in these two pairs.

(*d*) We smelt them cooking; it was not a very pleasant smell.
We smelt their cooking; it was not a very pleasant smell.

(*e*) If we looked closely, we could see him washing in the yard.
If we looked closely, we could see his washing in the yard.

TOPICS FOR WRITTEN WORK

1. Write a poem or a piece of prose about a recent occasion when you felt utterly defeated and rejected.

Hints

Fix clearly in your mind the occasion, and the events that took place. Analyse your feelings at the time, noting any changes that occurred. Decide whether you will write in poetry or prose, and what sort of style you will use. Notice that neither Keith Waterhouse nor Jacques Prévert described too emphatically the feelings of despair and defeat; these were often brought out indirectly through the description of events and other people.

2. Imagine that you are a secretary and that your employer, Mr. Nesbitt, has left you a message asking you to write a letter on his behalf. Write the letter, working from the notes given below.

MEMO	SCHOFIELD AND SIMS, LTD., 35, St. John's Rd., Huddersfield, HD1 5DT Yorks.
Miss Henderson	Pl. write King's Head Hotel thanking for excell. catering and entertainment for staff party last Thurs. Ask quotation for bed & bkfst. for 2 (separate rooms) re our American visitors Tues. 12 April. Also dinner for 6 same eve. in private room; start 8 pm. 4 courses, roast duck if poss. Request wine list. Address 81 Lydall Dr., Huddersfield. John N.

Hints

Avoid both colloquial English (Exercise 1) and Business jargon (Exercise 2). Arrange the contents of the letter in a logical order and paragraph accordingly. Find out how you sign a letter on behalf of somebody else. (Look under "P" in the list of abbreviations at the back of your dictionary.)

169

3. Rewrite the following passage, which contains pompous clichés, euphemisms and jargon, in a spontaneous, colloquial style.

With reference to the charge that has been brought against me, I feel I must proclaim my innocence in the strongest possible terms. Far from being the guilty party, I was, whilst perambulating aimlessly in the vicinity of the railway station on the night in question, the innocent victim of an unwarranted assault by the guardian of the peace who has just given testimony against me.

I had been to a musical soirée at the house of a friend, at which, I must confess, the liquid refreshment had flowed with gay abandon. I, myself, had partaken freely of the gifts of Bacchus, but remained, nevertheless, in full control of all my faculties. Having escorted to her domestic residence a charming specimen of the female of the species, with whom I had struck up an acquaintanceship at our little gathering, I continued on my way, pondering upon the attractions of this particular member of the fair sex. Whilst I was thus engaged in the realms of thought, I accidentally came into abrupt bodily contact with one of our custodians of law and order, namely P.C. 51. To cut a long story short, this angel of justice accused me, to use the words of the law, of being "drunk and disorderly", and when I attempted to remonstrate with him, proceeded to use me as a visual aid in a demonstration of the noble art of self-defence. His pugilistic exercises brought me perilously close to the verge of unconsciousness, and it was for this reason that I found myself unable to steer a straight course along the white line upon which he and a superior officer later invited me to tread. And on that point, I shall rest my defence.

Hints

Make your version as lively and as realistic as you can. Use idioms, dialect words and even slang. Make your sentence structure reflect the way in which an ordinary person would talk. Expand on any points for which you can think of more details. You might begin like this:

'Ere, 'ang on. Let's get this straight. All this stuff about me being drunk's a load of old rubbish.

HUMILIATION futility DEFEAT despair

Pupils' Work

Shame

I walk slowly back home
From the fight,
The fight I never had.
Frightened, frightened what
Everybody would say
At school, in the morning.

What a feeble excuse.
"My wrist hurts".
After all I had said,
Had said I would do to him,
"My wrist hurts".

Now, now I have the strength,
The strength to hit him.
But when I face him,
Once more
"My wrist hurts".

Peter Clark

Loneliness

Loneliness is terrible.
No-one is about;
All by myself,
I'm frightened now.
Loneliness is full of fright.
The room is empty,
No-one is about;
Not a soul to be seen,
Not a sound to be heard.
How terrible!
Loneliness is about.

Photini Tryforos

1. Tell the story of the fight in "There is a Happy Land" as it might have appeared from Raymond Garnett's point of view. Make up this version as you go along, using colloquialisms, idioms, dialect words and slang. Refer to incidents mentioned in the extract, but show them in a different light. Include references to Raymond Garnett's state of mind at various stages during the incident. You could start like this:

> Everybody at school seemed to know about the fight. I reckon they were looking forward to it a ruddy sight more than I was. That cheeky little shrimp must have been pretty scared too, 'cause he kept out of my way all day before we were due to have the scrap.

2. The poem "Breakfast" by Jacques Prévert is set out almost as though it was intended to be a series of subjects for a film script, or a collection of still photographs. Discuss what sort of shots you would use if you were recording this incident as a short film, or as a series of still photographs.

HUMILIATION DEFEAT futility despair

ACTIVITIES AND RESEARCH

1. One of the most difficult feats to perform well on a stage is a fight. It is little use trying to have a real fight, since this will look very clumsy and the people watching will become bored. Stage fights are, in fact always very carefully planned and rehearsed. The actors taking part will "pull" their punches so that the blows do not actually land, or if they do, then only gently; they will know when and where they have to fall, and exactly how the fight is to end. Boys could work out mock fights to perform before the rest of the class. As with other miming, actions must be slowed down and exaggerated; the exact timing and degree of exaggeration will come with practice; you will know you have achieved the correct balance when your audience ceases to be aware of it. Positioning is also important, so that those watching do not see you pulling your punches, and so on.

2. Draw or paint a picture entitled "Defeat". It could be an illustration to accompany your poem or story ("Topics for Written Work" No. 1), or it could be a completely separate piece of work.

3. Few countries like to remember their war-time defeats, and these are often glossed over in accounts of any particular war. Find out all you can about the occasions when Britain was defeated at war from the 14th century onwards. Notice how these defeats are portrayed by the reference books that you use. Are they written about in an impartial way? Are many reasons given for the defeat? Is the blame laid at the door of particular individuals? Is the courage of the defeated soldiers and sailors stressed?

FURTHER READING

There is a happy land by Keith Waterhouse (Michael Joseph; Longmans).

This book captures the very essence of childhood, in a way that very few others have managed to do. The narrator is a small boy from the backstreets of a grey Northern suburb (probably Leeds, where Keith Waterhouse grew up). Jingles, games, fantasies, nightmares, conversations in a secret language, fights, bouts of misbehaviour, the sinister Uncle Mad—they are all here, and presented in such a vivid and realistic way that the reader cannot help but recall the events and characters of his own childhood.

Billy Liar (Longmans; Penguin).

Billy Fisher, the central character in this novel, lives in two different worlds. His real environment he finds cramping and soul-destroying, so he builds for himself a dream-world, a romantic land called Ambrosia, into which he escapes whenever his relationships with his family, his employers or his three girl friends become too much for him. Needless to say, when his past lies finally catch up with him, he lands in trouble. Billy Liar has been adapted as a play and has also been made into a film.

Jubb (Michael Joseph; Penguin).

The central character in this novel is an essentially tragic figure—an unwashed, unwanted, middle-aged, fussy pervert—whose leisure hours are spent spying upon women, collecting pornography, and being a nuisance at committee meetings. The tragedy is balanced, however, by just the right proportion of humour. The book is a penetrating and sympathetic study of a lonely and maladjusted personality.

CHAPTER 12

Politics and Satire

Napoleon and Snowball, two young boars on Manor Farm, had led the animals in a rebellion and overthrown the cruel and incompetent farmer, Jones. But Napoleon trained some fierce dogs as a bodyguard, drove Snowball off the farm and made himself dictator. Squealer, another pig, has the job of persuading the animals (including Boxer and Clover, who are hard-working farm-horses) that Snowball is to blame for all their troubles.

But Boxer was still a little uneasy.

"I do not believe that Snowball was a traitor at the beginning," he said finally. "What he has done since is different. But I believe that at the Battle of the Cowshed he was a good comrade."

"Our Leader, Comrade Napoleon," announced Squealer, speaking very slowly and firmly, "has stated categorically—categorically, comrade—that Snowball was Jones's agent from the very beginning—yes, and from long before the Rebellion was ever thought of."

"Ah, that is different!" said Boxer. "If Comrade Napoleon says it, it must be right."

"That is the true spirit, comrade!" cried Squealer, but it was noticed he cast a very ugly look at Boxer with his little twinkling eyes. He turned to go, then paused and added impressively: "I warn every animal on this farm to keep his eyes very wide open. For we have reason to think that some of Snowball's secret agents are lurking among us at this moment!"

Four days later, in the late afternoon, Napoleon ordered all the animals to assemble in the yard. When they were all gathered together, Napoleon emerged from the farmhouse wearing both his medals (for he had recently awarded himself "Animal Hero, First Class", and "Animal Hero, Second Class") with his nine huge dogs frisking round him and uttering growls that sent shivers down all the animals' spines. They all cowered silently in their places, seeming to know in advance that some terrible thing was about to happen.

Napoleon stood sternly surveying his audience; then he uttered a high-pitched whimper. Immediately the dogs bounded forward, seized four of the pigs by the ear and dragged them, squealing with pain and terror, to Napoleon's feet. The pigs' ears were bleeding, the dogs had tasted blood, and for a few moments they appeared to go quite mad. To the amazement of everybody, three of them flung themselves upon Boxer. Boxer saw them coming and put out his great hoof, caught a dog in mid-air, and pinned him to the ground. The dog shrieked for mercy and the other two fled with their tails between their legs. Boxer looked at Napoleon to know whether he should crush the dog to death or let it go. Napoleon appeared to change countenance, and sharply ordered Boxer to let the dog go, whereat Boxer lifted his hoof, and the dog slunk away, bruised and howling.

Presently the tumult died down. The four pigs waited, trembling, with guilt written on every line of their countenances. Napoleon now called upon them to confess their crimes. They were the same four pigs as had protested when Napoleon abolished the Sunday Meetings. Without any further prompting they confessed that they had been secretly in touch with Snowball ever since his expulsion, that they had collaborated with him in destroying the windmill, and that they had entered into an agreement with him to hand over Animal Farm to Mr. Frederick. They added that Snowball had privately admitted to them that he had been Jones's secret agent for years past. When they had finished their confessions, the dogs promptly tore their throats out, and in a terrible voice Napoleon demanded whether any other animal had anything to confess . . . .

When it was all over, the remaining animals, except for the pigs and dogs, crept away in a body. They were shaken and miserable. They did not know which was more shocking—the treachery of the animals who had leagued themselves with Snowball, or the cruel retribution they had just witnessed. In the old days, there had often been scenes of bloodshed equally terrible, but it seemed to all of them that it was far worse now that it was happening among themselves. Since Jones had left the farm, until to-day, no animal had killed another animal. Not even a rat had been killed . . . .

The animals huddled about Clover, not speaking. The knoll where they were lying gave them a wide prospect across the countryside. Most of Animal Farm was within their view—the long pasture stretching down to the main road, the hayfield, the spinney, the drinking pool, the ploughed fields where the young wheat was thick and green, and the red roofs of the farm buildings with the smoke curling from the chimneys. It was a clear spring evening. The grass and the bursting hedges were gilded by the level rays of the sun. Never had the farm—and with a kind of surprise they remembered that it was their own farm, every inch of it their own property—appeared to the animals so desirable a place. As Clover looked down the hillside her eyes filled with tears. If she could have spoken her thoughts it would have been to say that this was not what they had aimed at when they had set themselves years ago to work for the overthrow of the human race. These scenes of terror and slaughter were not what they had looked forward to on that night when old Major first stirred them to rebellion. If she herself had had any picture of the future, it had been of a society of animals set free from hunger and the whip, all equal, each working according to his capacity, the strong protecting the weak, as she had protected the lost brood of ducklings with her foreleg on the night of Major's speech. Instead—she did not know why—they had come to a time when no one dared speak his mind, when fierce growling dogs roamed everywhere, and when you had to watch your comrades torn to pieces after confessing to shocking crimes. There was no thought of rebellion or disobedience in her mind. She knew that, even as things were, they were far better off than they had been in the days of Jones, and that before all else it was needful to prevent the return of human beings. Whatever happened she would remain faithful, work hard, carry out the orders that were given to her, and accept the leadership of Napoleon. But still, it was not for this that she and all the other animals had hoped and toiled. It was not for this that they had built the windmill and faced the bullets of Jones's gun. Such were her thoughts, though she lacked the words to express them.

(From *Animal Farm* by George Orwell)

DICTATORSHIP

APPRECIATION AND DISCUSSION

1. In this book, Orwell is satirising human history (especially in countries where there have been political revolutions) by imagining similar situations in the animal world. It is important to realise, therefore, that the animals represent different types of people.

   What dictators does Napoleon remind you of? Can you find parallels for Jones, Snowball, Boxer, the dogs and Squealer in, for instance, the history of the Russian revolution and the U.S.S.R., or in Hitler's Germany? Can you suggest any parallels in the world today?

2. Boxer, the hardworking cart-horse, is chiefly noted for his unquestioning loyalty to the leaders of the revolution. Why then should he have doubts about Snowball's guilt? How does Squealer counter these doubts?

3. Why did Napoleon award himself medals? Do you think he deserved them?

4. What hint is there that a division is emerging between the pigs and the dogs as one group, and all the other animals? Is it significant that the first four "traitors" to be executed were, themselves, pigs?

5. In view of the hysterical fears about Snowball and the way Squealer played upon these, do you find the four pigs' confession convincing? Might they have been saying what Napoleon wanted them to say? Why might Napoleon have picked on these four pigs, and how would their execution have benefited him?

6. What, do you assume, were the "Sunday Meetings" and why would Napoleon have abolished them?

7. Things had gone badly for the animals; they were short of food and finding it difficult to compete with the neighbouring human farmers. Why did Napoleon blame Snowball for all this, rather than accepting responsibility himself?

8. Do you think the dogs' attack upon Boxer was unpremeditated, or had it been ordered beforehand by Napoleon?

9. What seemed to the other animals so terrible about the executions of the "traitors"?

10. Why was Clover determined to go on obeying Napoleon, even after this slaughter? Can you understand and explain why Clover and the other animals felt so attached to Animal Farm?

11. Major was an old boar who had first expounded the idea that one day the animals would revolt and take over from men. What kind of society do you think he had looked forward to? Which countries in the world today would you describe as societies of men "set free from hunger and the whip, all equal, each working according to his capacity"? Which countries do not fit this picture?

12. Would you agree that sudden revolutions inevitably lead to dictatorship and political oppression, instead of liberating those who support them? What could be the reason for this?

177

TECHNIQUES

The Use of Language, and Style

1. *Active and Passive Voice.* (i) The writer of the article quoted in Exercise 2 of the previous chapter said that students were urged to use the active rather than the passive voice. The sentences below show what is meant by active and passive voice.

Active: The dogs killed the sheep.

Passive: The sheep were killed by the dogs.

Active: I have decided upon a plan of action.

Passive: A plan of action has been decided upon.

Active: We have received your order and will deal with it immediately.

Passive: Your order has been received and will be dealt with immediately.

Voice is an important ingredient of style. A writer will use the passive voice more when he wishes to write in a rather detached, impersonal style. The passive voice is widely used in factual books; if it is used too often, however, it gives an impression of clumsiness and vagueness. The active voice is more direct and definite.

Rewrite the following passage, changing it from the passive to the active voice.

A high-pitched whimper was uttered by Napoleon. Immediately four pigs were seized by the dogs and dragged to Napoleon's feet. Then Boxer was set upon. But the dogs' attack was anticipated by the great horse. His hoof was put out and one dog was caught in mid-air and pinned to the ground. Mercy was shrieked for by the wretched animal. Napoleon was looked at by Boxer. Should the dog be crushed to death, or released?

Do you think that the active voice makes the above passage more direct and forceful?

(ii) Rewrite these sentences in the passive voice.

e.g. People find earthworms in the ground.

Earthworms are found in the ground.

(*a*) A bullet has wounded the leader of the revolution.

(*b*) Someone officially launched the new liner last Friday.

(*c*) They are to abolish the Sunday Meetings.

(*d*) The others elected him as their representative.

(*e*) A dictator rules this country.

Why is the passive voice more suitable for the above sentences?

2. *Emotive Language.* The different political opinions of newspapers are reflected, of course, in the language they use to report political events. Rewrite the following account, which supports the Government, as it would have appeared in a newspaper opposed to such views, by replacing each of the italicised words and phrases with one similar in meaning but very different in implication. You may use the phrases given after the passage when you cannot think of suitable replacements. Afterwards, try writing a balanced account of the proceedings.

The Prime Minister had a *hearty* reception yesterday when he gave a *masterly outline* of the negotiations which the Government had so *speedily* initiated. It was clear that he had, as always, remained *strictly impartial* and had *refused to put pressure on either side. A number of hecklers, on one or two occasions,* attempted to *shout him down,* but he *was not to be shaken out of his stride* and *declined their invitations to enter into a slanging match.* In contrast to the Prime Minister's *calm* manner and *confident smile,* the Leader of the Opposition was obviously *unsettled by* the situation. His voice *shook with uncertainty,* but this in no way interfered with his *notorious glibness.*

> rowdy   sketchy account   hastily   sitting on the fence
> been unable to make any positive suggestions   numerous critics
> repeatedly   raise objections   continued plodding through his
> statement   was apparently unable to answer their arguments
> complacent   smug grin   concerned about
> trembled with emotion   famous fluency.

3. *Symbols.* In his satirical fable "Animal Farm", George Orwell chose certain animals to represent certain types of human beings because the characteristics commonly associated with these animals were the same as he wished to associate with the humans. The loyal, industrious but unimaginative worker was represented by a carthorse, the wise old cynic by a donkey, and so on.

Certain qualities are so strongly associated with certain animals that the animals themselves have come to symbolise these qualities. One of the best known examples is probably the lion, which symbolises courage.

Which animals would you choose to symbolise the following qualities?
(*a*) cowardice   (*b*) strength   (*c*) obstinacy   (*d*) wisdom
(*e*) cheekiness   (*f*) dignity   (*g*) ruthlessness   (*h*) cunning
(*i*) laziness   (*j*) stupidity

Correct English, and Vocabulary

4. *Brackets.* (i) Brackets, which are always used in pairs, serve much the same purpose as dashes or commas—to separate an interruption or an afterthought. They do not break the sentence as emphatically as dashes, but they separate more strongly than commas.

Show how brackets can be used in these sentences in the passage, instead of commas or dashes.

(*a*) "That is the true spirit, comrade," . . .   (paragraph 5)
(*b*) When it was all over, . . .   (paragraph 9)
(*c*) Never had the farm— . . .   (paragraph 10)
(*d*) Instead—she did not know why— . . .   (paragraph 10)
(*e*) She knew that, . . .   (paragraph 10)
(*f*) Such were her thoughts, . . .   (paragraph 10)

(ii) Answer these questions about the use of brackets and dashes in the passage.

(*a*) Why would neither brackets nor commas satisfactorily replace the dashes in paragraph 3?
(*b*) Would you use commas or would you use dashes to replace the brackets in the second sentence of paragraph 6?
(*c*) Which punctuation mark could be used instead of the dash in the third sentence of paragraph 9, and the third sentence of paragraph 10? (Refer to Chapter 8, Exercise 4.)

5. *Gender.* (i) The difference between the words in the following pairs is one of sex.

cock	hen	boar	sow
stallion	mare	he	she

Nouns and pronouns which name males are said to be in the masculine gender; those which name females are in the feminine gender.

Some words can refer to either males or females and are in the common gender.

  e.g. animal beast bird society they

Other words have no sex and are in the neuter gender.

  e.g. pool field building windmill it

State the gender of the following nouns:

pig	crowd
chimney	marquis
doe	princess
wizard	hoof
maiden	negro

(ii) Fill in the blanks in these two columns.

Masculine	Feminine
—	cow
fox	—
—	duck
gander	—
—	ewe
dog	—
—	niece
bachelor	—
—	bride
son-in-law	—
—	nun
hero	—
—	duchess
he	—
—	hers

6. *Vocabulary*. Find where the following words occur in the passage; define them, and rewrite Orwell's sentences, replacing the words with others that mean the same.

categorically	tumult	countenances	collaborated
retribution	knoll	spinney	gilded

Now use the above words in sentences of your own, or copy them into your "Vocabulary Notebook".

TOPICS FOR WRITTEN WORK

1. Write a satirical fable.

Hints

Select a situation that you feel should be commented on critically. If possible, choose an incident in which you, yourself, have been involved and which you have never been allowed to criticise in writing before. For example, if your teacher agrees, you could perhaps take some aspect of your life at school and use it as the subject of your fable. (Is there a school rule that you think is unfair? Do you disagree with some way in which the school is organised?) Then substitute appropriate animals for the individuals concerned. (Can you work out who is represented by the animals in Alan's fable in the "Pupils' Work" section?)

Alternatively, you could take an historical event (e.g. the Second

World War) or a national issue (e.g. the action of a political party) and present it in the form of a fable.

You need not put a moral at the end of your fable as Alan has done.

2. The cartoon is one of the most pungent forms of political satire.

Study the cartoon on the opposite page and comment on it.

Hints

The cartoon makes one major point, and that can be seen at a glance. What is the critical comment that it makes? Does it make this comment harshly, or in a gentle way? What do the four figures sitting at the table represent? How are they portrayed? Consider how they are behaving. Look at the expressions on their faces. Why is there so much food on the table? What do the mushroom cloud and rockets represent? What do the reaching hands around the platform and table stand for? Does the cartoon make its point effectively? Say whether a caption would make the cartoon even more telling; if you think so, make one up. Do you agree with what the cartoon says?

3. Give an account of the way in which the British Parliamentary system works.

Hints

This is to be a purely factual account. Do not deal with the historical development of the system, just the existing organisation. Select the most important facts from reference books and express them clearly and simply. The questions below may give you a guide.

What is a constituency? How many of them are there, and to what extent do they vary? Who can put up a candidate, and what is a deposit? Can you explain what is meant by (a) an agent (b) canvassing (c) hustings? What are the Party manifestos and Party political broadcasts? What are (a) returning officers (b) polling stations and booths (c) ballot papers and boxes (d) the count? What are the differences between the House of Lords and the House of Commons? Who are (a) the Speaker (b) Black Rod (c) the Party Whips? What do the following terms mean: a session, an adjournment, question time, and committees of the House? What are (a) White Papers (b) a Royal Commission (c) Parliamentary privilege? Find out how a Bill passes through its various stages, until it receives the "royal assent" and becomes law.

Remember that the passive voice is particularly suitable for this sort of essay.

Pupils' Work

The Job of the Owl

Once upon a time a happy community of animals lived in a small wood. Each day the young animals gathered together in a glade in the middle of the wood to receive instructions from older and presumably wiser creatures. Monsieur Jackdaw showed them how to imitate the noises made by other animals; Miss Spider taught weaving; and Mr. and Mrs. Rabbit gave lessons in addition and multiplication. Presiding over these proceedings was a wise, old owl. As far as the young animals could see, he did nothing to justify this position, but they assumed it must be something important that they did not know about. And since he never interfered with their lessons, they did not mind him. They went on enjoying themselves—although they did not always pay attention to their lessons, and sometimes they left the glade in rather a mess. But nobody, including the gamekeeper, noticed it.

Then one day the young animals were told that a large party of gamekeepers was coming to inspect the wood. Immediately the old owl sprang into action.

"Pay attention to your lessons," he hooted. "More important still, *look* as though you were paying attention. And get this mess tidied up. Clean out your nests, burrows and holes. Pick up these leaves."

And so he went on for several weeks before the gamekeepers arrived, and all the time they were there (though not so loudly). He escorted them round the glade, twit-twooing charmingly. At last the gamekeepers left.

"We are very impressed," they all said. "We have never seen a tidier glade, or better-behaved young animals. Well done."

The young animals were rather puzzled by what had happened.

"If that is all the old owl does, we don't need him in charge," they said. "What he does is not important. There is no point in it."

An intellectual young dormouse, who had pondered the problem, tried to provide an answer.

"The moral of this story is: We can fool some of the people all of the time, and all of the people some of the time, but when we need to fool all of the people all of the time we have to have a public relations expert in charge.— We shall realise the importance of this when we are older," he added.

And I suppose they did.

Alan Jones

ORAL WORK

1. Practise reading aloud the following passage, and then use the questions below it as the basis for a discussion.

There is some talk at present of lowering the voting age to eighteen. It is difficult to understand how such a move can be justified. The old argument of National Service days:—"If you're old enough to die for your country, then you're old enough to have a vote"—was never a very intelligent one, and has no value at all today when so many people, eighteen year olds and others, are noticeably unwilling to die for their country, and when, in any case, in the event of war, two-year-olds will be just as likely to be killed in their cradles as young men and women in uniform.

No. Having the vote has nothing to do with dying for one's country. It is a recognition of one's maturity and responsibility; a reward for being willing to take an interest in the country's economic position, in the influence of the government in foreign affairs, in the maintaining of justice in the law courts, in balancing the rights of the individual against the needs of the community, and above all in maintaining the tradition of freedom and democracy. That is what having a vote means, or at least what it should mean.

How many eighteen-year-olds are interested in these things? Not very many, and a good thing too. They have other things to occupy themselves with—sport, studies, jobs, the opposite sex, clothes, having a good time. There is little enough time in which to enjoy these things. Why waste it through being forced to take an interest in politics?

Another point to remember is that quite a few boys and girls of that age are still at school. Are they to have the vote? Presumably in many cases those still at school are more intelligent than those who have left, so that if the others have it, they must too. What happens then? Mary Brown, in the Upper Sixth at seventeen, head girl and senior prefect, may not vote, but Joe Smith, still in the Fifth at eighteen and a half because he has not yet got three "O" levels, can take his part in governing the country.

It would be a much better idea if nobody could vote until the age of thirty. At least then the voters would be more likely to be interested in what they were doing.

(a) "If you're old enough to die for your country, then you're old enough to have a vote." The writer does not think this an intelligent argument. What do you think of it?

(b) Do you think many people who vote feel about it as the writer does?

(c) Are eighteen-year-olds interested in politics? What makes you think so?

(d) What do you think the voting age should be? What are your reasons?

2. Hold a debate or a discussion on a controversial political issue. Follow the procedure given for formal debates in Book 2, Chapter 3, page 45, and ask your teacher to explain any further details such as "points of order", etc.

3. Each member of the class could give a short talk on a famous revolution, e.g. the Russian Revolution, the French Revolution, the Irish Uprising, or on a well known dictator in modern history, e.g., Napoleon, Lenin, Stalin, Hitler, Mussolini, Mao-Tse-Tung, General Franco.

ACTIVITIES AND RESEARCH

1. From newspapers of different political views, cut out cartoons of the same character or of a certain event. Compare them closely, noticing how the characteristics of one individual will be exaggerated in different ways by different cartoonists, and how they interpret and portray a particular situation to support the political policy of their newspapers. You could mount a display of these cartoons.

2. Try drawing your own cartoons of well known political figures, or of people you see frequently. The best of these could be added to the display of work by professional cartoonists.

3. Holding a realistic mock election can be very interesting, particularly if this is organised at about the same time as any national or local elections are taking place. Instead of a deposit of money, each candidate can perhaps be asked to produce a certain minimum number of supporters' signatures. One of his supporters will then act as his agent. A returning officer and certain polling clerks will also be required. Candidates supporting existing political Parties can, of course, obtain literature and information from local constituency offices, and base their campaigns upon this. A full campaign may not be practicable at school, but at least arrange for an "eve-of-the-poll" confrontation of the candidates, in which each speaker can put his case to the rest of the voters, and answer their questions.

Try to make the polling arrangements as realistic as possible, the kind of instructions to electors that appear in every polling booth are shown on the page opposite. A ballot box can easily be made out of cardboard and a register of electors can be based on school class lists. Each voter has to answer to his name and give his address (or form) to one polling clerk, who then ticks the name on the register and reads out the voter's polling number to the other polling clerk (seated beside him), who writes this number on the counterfoil, tears off one ballot paper, and stamps it on the back. The voter makes his choice by putting a cross against the name of one candidate in the privacy of a polling booth, and then folds his ballot paper once and places it in the ballot box, in such a way as to allow the polling clerks to see the official stamp on the back (but not, of course, the cross indicating his vote).

PARLIAMENTARY ELECTION

DIRECTIONS

FOR THE

GUIDANCE OF THE VOTERS

IN VOTING

1. The voter should see that the ballot paper, before it is handed to him, is stamped with the official mark.

2. The voter will go into one of the compartments, and with the pencil provided in the compartment, place a **cross on the right-hand side of the ballot paper, opposite the name of the candidate for whom he votes, thus X**

3. The voter will then fold up the ballot paper so as to show the official mark on the back, and leaving the compartment will, without showing the front of the paper to any person, show the official mark on the back to the presiding officer, and then, in the presence of the presiding officer, put the paper into the ballot box, and forthwith leave the polling station.

4. If the voter inadvertently spoils a ballot paper, he can return it to the officer, who will, if satisfied of such inadvertence, give him another paper.

5. If the voter votes for more than ONE candidate, or places any mark on the ballot paper by which he may be afterwards identified, his ballot paper will be void, and will not be counted.

6. If the voter fraudulently takes a ballot paper out of the polling station, or fraudulently puts into the ballot box any paper other than the one given him by the officer, he will be liable on conviction to imprisonment for a term not exceeding six months.

187

Ballot boxes are sealed when empty, and the seals are broken only at the official counting station, in the presence of the candidates or their representatives at the count. All the counting has to be done under the strict supervision of the returning officer, whose job it is to announce the result after the count, or to decide whether any re-count can reasonably be asked for.

FURTHER READING

Animal Farm by George Orwell (Secker and Warburg; Penguin; Longmans).

As mentioned in the introduction to the extract, by substituting animals for humans, Orwell is satirising in the form of a fable the course that so many political revolutions have taken. The animals, after driving away the men from their farm, set up their own "democracy", based on seven Commandments, one of which is "All animals are equal". But their leaders, the pigs, soon become "more equal" than the other animals; they copy the manners of men, and rule with the help of the ferocious dogs. And so we have the revolution resulting not in a democracy but in a different, though equally oppressive form of dictatorship.

Nineteen Eighty Four (Secker and Warburg; Penguin; Heinemann).

This is an adult and terrifying book. The world is governed by three totalitarian states, perpetually at war. Nobody is allowed to think or to act for himself; all information is twisted to suit the political viewpoint of the moment; all records are systematically altered so that they conform with this. Everybody is spied upon by the police (there are telescreens in every room). Men and women who rebel—as Winston Smith, the "hero" of this story does—are "converted" by physical and mental torture. The story seems to hold out no hope for Man, but it should be remembered that it was meant as a warning, not a prediction.

Homage to Catalonia (Secker and Warburg; Penguin).

Orwell fought as a British volunteer against Franco in the Spanish Civil War, and this is a combatant's account of that bitter struggle.

Down and out in Paris and London (Secker and Warburg; Penguin).

Here is an unusual and, in parts, very grim record of the early years of a man of considerable talent, down on his luck, ready to take a turn at anything to earn his living and gain experience of life.

CHAPTER 13   **Crime**

The narrator of this story is a Borstal boy, convicted of breaking into a bakery and stealing the cashbox, who takes the opportunity presented to him through his prowess as a cross-country runner to demonstrate his hatred for authority.

I'm in Essex. It's supposed to be a good Borstal, at least that's what the governor said to me when I got here from Nottingham. "We want to trust you while you are in this establishment," he said, smoothing out his newspaper with lily-white workless hands, while I read the big words upside down: "Daily Telegraph". "If you play ball with us, we'll play ball with you." (Honest to God, you'd have thought it was going to be one long tennis match.) "We want hard honest work and we want good athletics," he said as well. "And if you give us both these things you can be sure we'll do right by you and send you back into the world an honest man." Well, I could have died laughing, especially when straight after this I hear the barking sergeant-major's voice calling me and two others to attention and marching us off like we was Grenadier Guards. And when the governor kept saying how "we" wanted you to do this, and "we" wanted you to do that, I kept looking round for the other blokes, wondering how many of them there was. Of course, I knew there were thousands of them, but as far as I knew only one was in the room. And there *are* thousands of them, all over the poxeaten country, in shops, offices, railway stations, cars, houses, pubs—In-law blokes like you and them, all on the watch for Out-law blokes like me and us—and waiting to phone for the coppers as soon as we make a false move. And it'll always be there, I'll tell you that now, because I haven't finished making all my false moves yet, and I dare say I won't until I kick the bucket. If the In-laws are hoping to stop me making false moves they're wasting their time . . . .

As I run and see my smoky breath going out into the air as if I had ten cigars stuck in different parts of my body I think more on the little speech the governor made when I first came. Honesty. Be honest. I laughed so much one morning I went ten minutes down in my timing because I had to stop and get rid of the stitch in my side. The governor

189

was so worried when I got back late that he sent me to the doctor's for an X-ray and heart check. Be honest. It's like saying: Be dead, like me, and then you'll have no more pain of leaving your nice slummy house for Borstal or prison. Be honest and settle down in a cosy six pounds a week job. Well, even with all this long-distance running I haven't yet been able to decide what he means by this, although I'm just about beginning to—and I don't like what it means. Because after all my thinking I found that it adds up to something that can't be true about me, being born and brought up as I was. Because another thing people like the governor will never understand is that I *am* honest, that I've never been anything else but honest, and that I'll always be honest. Sounds funny. But it's true because I know what honest means according to me and he only knows what it means according to him. I think my honesty is the only sort in the world, and he thinks his is the only sort in the world as well. That's why this dirty great walled-up and fenced-up manor house in the middle of nowhere has been used to coop-up blokes like me. And if I had the whip-hand I wouldn't even bother to build a place like this to put all the cops, governors, posh whores, penpushers, army officers, Members of Parliament in; no, I'd stick them up against a wall and let them have it, like they'd have done with blokes like us years ago, that is, if they'd even known what it means to be honest, which they don't and never will so help me God Almighty. . . . .

Our doddering bastard of a governor, our half dead gangrened gaffer is hollow like an empty petrol drum, and he wants me and my running life to give him glory, to put in him blood and throbbing veins he never had, wants his potbellied pals to be his witnesses as I gasp and stagger up to his winning post so's he can say: "My Borstal gets that cup, you see. I win my bet, because it pays to be honest and try to gain the prizes I offer to my lads, and they know it, have known it all along. They'll always be honest now, because I made them so." And his pals will think: "He trains his lads to live all right, after all; he deserves a medal but we'll get him made a Sir"—and at this very moment as the birds come back to whistling I can tell myself I'll never care a sod what any of his chinless spineless In-laws think or say. They've seen me and they're cheering now and loudspeakers set around the field like elephants' ears are spreading out the big news that I'm well in the lead, and can't do anything else but stay there. But I'm still thinking of the Out-law death my dad died, telling the doctors to scat from the house when they wanted him to finish up in hospital (like a bleeding guinea-pig, he raved at them). He got up in bed to throw them out and even followed them down the

190

stairs in his shirt though he was no more than skin and stick. They tried to tell him he'd want some drugs but he didn't fall for it, and only took the painkiller that mam and I got from a herb-seller in the next street. It's not till now that I know what guts he had, and when I went into the room that morning he was lying on his stomach with the clothes thrown back, looking like a skinned rabbit, his grey head resting just on the edge of the bed and on the floor must have been all the blood he'd had in his body, right from his toenails up, for nearly all of the lino and carpet was covered in it, thin and pink . . . .

I'm slowing down now for Gunthorpe to catch me up, and I'm doing it in a place where the drive turns up in to the sportsfield—where they can see what I'm doing, especially the governor and his gang from the grandstand, and I'm going so slow I'm almost marking time . . . . But even so, I say, I won't budge. I won't go for that last hundred yards if I have to sit down cross-legged on the grass and have the governor and his chinless wonders pick me up and carry me there, which is against their rules so you can bet they'd never do it because they're not clever enough to break the rules—like I would be in their place—even though they are their own. No, I'll show him what honesty means if it's the last thing I do, though I'm sure he'll never understand because if he and all them like him did it'd mean they'd be on my side which is impossible. By God I'll stick this out like my dad stuck out his pain and kicked them doctors down the stairs: if he had the guts for that then I've got guts for this and here I stay waiting for Gunthorpe or Aylesham to bash that turf and go right slap-up against that bit of clothesline stretched across the winning post. As for me, the only time I'll hit that clothesline will be when I'm dead and a comfortable coffin's been got ready on the other side. Until then I'm a long-distance runner, crossing country all on my own no matter how bad it feels.

(from *The Loneliness of the Long Distance Runner* by Alan Sillitoe)

191

APPRECIATION AND DISCUSSION

1. What is (or was) a Borstal? What, in your opinion, would a "good Borstal" be like?

2. Smith's portrait of the Governor is highly emotional. Study the emotive adjectives he chooses, e.g. "*lily-white workless* hands", and say what kind of impression they create.

3. Why did Smith say that he "could have died laughing" at the Governor's remarks, especially when they were followed by the "barking sergeant-major's voice"?

4. Throughout Smith's thoughts there runs a clear class division between "them" and "us". What other terms does he use for the two classes? Can you provide yet other names for them?

5. What types of people does Smith class as In-laws? What does Smith say he would do to at least some of the In-laws?

6. What exactly does Smith think is wrong with being honest in the Governor's way? He goes on to accuse the Governor of being "hollow" (lifeless and hypocritical). How does he justify this idea? Do you agree with his judgement?

7. Smith claims to have his own kind of honesty. Clearly he doesn't mean always telling the truth or obeying the law, so what *does* he mean?

8. Is it impossible, as Smith asserts, for the Governor and his friends to ever understand Smith and to be on his side?

9. How and why did Smith's father die? Was it bravery or folly to refuse proper medical attention? What effect did his father's death have on Smith?

10. What did "hitting that bit of clothes line" (winning the race) really mean to Smith? Why did he say he would never do this for the rest of his life, whatever the cost?

11. Has this extract helped you to understand the criminal mentality? Do you sympathise with or understand any of Smith's views? Which of his attitudes do you disagree with? How, in your opinion, should delinquents be treated?

12. In what sort of style has this passage been written? How suitable is it for this story? Does it succeed in conveying the way the boy would talk, and his ideas? Can you suggest any other styles and approaches that would be appropriate for this theme?

My Friend Maloney

My friend Maloney, eighteen,
  Swears like a sentry,
Got into trouble two years back
  With the local gentry.

Parson and squire's sons
  Informed a copper.
The magistrate took one look at Maloney
  Fixed him proper.

Talked of the crime of youth,
  The innocent victim.
Maloney never said a blind word
  To contradict him.

Maloney of Gun Street,
  Back of the Nuclear Mission,
Son of the town whore,
  Blamed television.

Justice, as usual, triumphed.
  Everyone felt fine.
Things went deader.
  Maloney went up the line.

Maloney learned one lesson:
  Never play the fool
With the products of especially a minor
  Public school.

Maloney lost a thing or two
  at that institution.
First shirt, second innocence,
  The old irresolution.

Found himself a girl-friend,
  Sharp suit, sharp collars.
Maloney on a moped,
  Pants full of dollars.

College boys on the corner
  In striped, strait blazers
Look at old Maloney,
  Eyes like razors.

You don't need talent, says Maloney.
    You don't need looks.
All I got you got, fellers.
    You can keep your thick books.
Parson got religion,
    Squire, in the end, the same.
The magistrate went over the wall.
    Life, said Maloney, 's a game.
Consider then the case of Maloney,
    College boys, parsons, squire, beak.
Who was the victor and who was the victim?
    Speak.

Charles Causley

DISCUSSING THE POEM

1. What sort of background did Maloney come from? Do you think this was responsible for him taking to a life of crime? Maloney himself "blamed television". Do you think this could have been at all responsible?

2. Why did the magistrate take just one look at Maloney before deciding to "fix him"? Would he have acted so brusquely if it had been the squire's son or the parson's son appearing before him?

3. Did Maloney's spell in the remand home discourage him from being a criminal? What effect did it have? Explain more fully what the poet meant when he said that Maloney lost his "shirt", his "innocence", and his "old irresolution".

4. What did Maloney do when he was released?

5. What happened to the parson, the squire and the magistrate?

6. What general question is posed at the end of the poem? ("Who was the victor and who was the victim?")

7. This poem suggests that many criminals came from a poor working class background which encourages them to take up a life of crime, while most of the people who enforce the law come from a middle class background and are prejudiced towards such working class people whose background is so very different from their own. Where does Charles Causley bring out this difference and conflict? Can you quote evidence from your own experience to support or to contradict this view?

8. To what extent do the views expressed in "My Friend Maloney" agree with those in "The Loneliness of the Long Distance Runner"?

TECHNIQUES

The Use of Language, and Style

1. *Press Styles and Emotive Language.* Study these extracts from two imaginary newspapers and then discuss or write answers to the questions below.

From the front page of the "Views of the World":—

SHOULD THESE MEN HANG?

Last week a policeman shot in Soho—this week a running battle in Battersea. Dangerous armed men are still loose. VIEWS OF THE WORLD asks its twelve million readers the vital question: Should we bring back hanging for killers of policemen and prison warders?

Can we deny any longer that Britain's underworld is trigger-mad? The time has come to ask ourselves: Were we wrong to abolish the death penalty?

Seven out of ten of your letters are in favour of hanging. The debate is now wide open. What do *you* say? The great British public's voice must be heard again.

Parliament abolished the death penalty for all offences in November, 1965. For eight years before that we had the rope for all "capital" murders—and those included killing of police or prison officers and all second murders.

That year, the Gallup Poll showed that the "abolitionists" in Parliament were defying the will of the nation—that a 3 to 1 majority still supported hanging.

Now we face a new wave of ugly violence. Many responsible men we believe must think again. They argue that a man facing a life sentence for robbery with violence is not going to hesitate to shoot his way out when cornered.

The academics still cling to their statistics showing that hanging does not deter, but a number of M.P.'s have already signed the motion calling for a change in the law. *It is time the people's views were heard.*

From the Editorial of the "National Independent":—

NO QUICK CURE

The Home Secretary is well aware that it would be quite wrong to make any major policy decisions about capital punishment in the shadow of recent tragic incidents in Soho and Battersea. Successive holders of that office have quite correctly maintained that this is a matter to be discussed dispassionately in the light of the available crime figures for this country and for other advanced nations that have abolished the death penalty. The pressure of public opinion, swayed by the heartening wave of sympathy for the police victims of violence, does not alter the fact that there has still been no overall rise in the number of murders committed, and that increases in convictions for crimes of violence have remained constant since the total abolition of capital punishment in 1965.

The increase in violent crime is a world-wide problem, and there is no simple panacea for so complex a social evil. Present arrangements for the licensing and sale of fire-arms certainly require investigation. Nor should we diminish our efforts—by long-term analysis and research—to find the roots of crime and deepen our understanding of the criminal mentality. One thing is certain—we shall not solve this problem if the public is apathetic or the government reluctant to spend the taxpayer's money. If the mounting support for the police leads to a better paid, highly mobile and efficiently equipped constabulary, then we shall be building up a really effective deterrent to the criminal: the certainty that he will be caught.

(a) What items of news, as far as you can tell from reading these comments, prompted these newspaper reactions?

(b) Both these newspapers are imaginary, but of which real newspapers are their attitudes and styles typical? What kind of reader do you think each would be mainly aimed at?

(c) Is there any element of self-advertisement in either or both of these newspapers' pieces?

(d) Generally, one newspaper piece is in favour of restoring hanging and the other against it. Why doesn't each editor state his position more definitely?

(e) If the "Views of the World" printed, alongside this piece, a ballot-form on which readers could vote for or against restoring the death penalty, what would you expect the result of such a poll to be?

(f) The terms "hanging", "death penalty", "the rope" and "capital punishment" all mean the same. In what ways are these terms *emotionally toned*, (i.e. emotive descriptions) and how and why do the pieces differ in their use of the various terms?

(g) Contrast the language of the two passages whenever either mentions criminals or violence.

(h) What features of style (paragraphing, vocabulary, sentence structure) and layout (headlines, order of statements, different type or underlining) make the first piece easier to read than the second? Which is more thoughtful and more thought-provoking, in your opinion?

(i) How does each piece indicate that the number of crimes of violence is increasing? To what extent is each of them misleading about this?

(*j*) Richard Hoggart wrote in "The Uses of Literacy", about popular culture: " . . . the world is divided into 'Them' and 'Us'. 'They' are 'the people at the top', 'the higher-ups', the people who give you your dole, call you up, tell you to go to war, fine you . . . "
How does the "Views of the World" piece imply a similar contrast between a governing minority and the popular opinions of the majority? Whose side is the paper on, and how does it indicate its attitude to 'Us' and 'Them'?

2. *Colloquial Writing.* Pick out all the colloquial words and phrases in this chapter's extract. Are any of them unfamiliar to you? Are any of them confined to a particular region of the country, i.e., are there idioms or dialect words in this passage?

Which of the colloquialisms would you class as slang? How many words would you define as swear words? Why did Alan Sillitoe include these expressions? What was your reaction to them? Would the story lose any of its impact if these words were removed? If you had to edit this passage, which expressions would you use to replace those which might cause offence? Do you think stories should be altered in this way?

Do you think the story would have seemed more authentic still if the author had tried to reproduce in writing the accent of the narrator?

Alan Sillitoe has included a number of original similes in this description, e.g. "loudspeakers set around the field like elephants' ears". Pick out others. How effective are they, and how well do they blend in with the colloquial tone of the piece? Would someone like the narrator be likely to invent and use such striking comparisons? Can you quote any lively and original similes that you have heard used in conversation?

3. *Legal Jargon.* Lawyers have to be very careful to express themselves so that their legal documents cannot be misinterpreted in any way. Legal language on forms, agreements and lists of rules therefore, is often complicated. The meaning, however, can usually be put more clearly and briefly.

e.g. This policy shall be null and void if it shall have been obtained through any fraudulent or wilful misrepresentation or concealment or through any knowingly untrue statement.

This means:
This policy will be invalid if it was obtained by giving false information.
Can you see how the second, briefer statement could be "twisted" by a lawyer if a dispute arose?

Make up clear, brief explanations of the following statements, eliminating all legal jargon.

(a) No claim in respect of injury or loss to the goods transmitted arising from theft, fire, accidental damage or the negligence of the Company's servants, or from any cause whatsoever, can be entertained by the Company.

(b) The Licensee shall pay to the Authority a sum not exceeding that which he paid heretofore, provided always that the terms of his license have not been altered by the Schedule attached hereto.

(c) Notwithstanding anything herein contained to the contrary, it is hereby declared and agreed that the Company shall only be liable for the excess of £10 for each and every claim made.

(d) Poems by deceased writers are eligible under the conditions of entry for the Society's poetry competition only within twelve months from the date of the writer's decease.

(e) It is further agreed that should the vehicle not be repairable owing to parts being unobtainable the liability of the Company shall be limited to an amount which is equivalent to the estimated cost of the repairs rendered necessary by the accident not exceeding the Insured's estimated value as stated in the Policy.

Correct English, and Vocabulary

4. *Misuse of like/as, owing to/due to.* Consider this quotation.

"I'd stick them up against a wall and let them have it, *like* they'd have done with blokes like us years ago, . . ." (Incorrect)

"As" should be substituted for "like".

I'd stick them up against a wall and let them have it, *as* they'd have done with blokes like us years ago. (Correct)

Alan Sillitoe made this error deliberately, of course, because it is the sort of mistake that his narrator would have made. Can you find any other examples of this error in the extract?

Another common error is to confuse "owing to" with "due to".

He died due to his own stupidity. (Incorrect)

He died owing to his own stupidity. (Correct)

As a general rule, the simplest way to avoid this confusion is to remember that:

Like should precede a noun or pronoun (i.e. it is used to compare things or people). *As* is used for introducing a group of words containing a verb (i.e. it is used to compare actions).

Things are *due to*. Actions are *owing to*.

Correct mistakes of this kind in the following sentences.

(*a*) Don't think you can catch me like you did my father.

(*b*) You should always tell the truth like George Washington did.

(*c*) The police are unable to search the moor due to a shortage of staff.

(*d*) Due to his home background, he became a criminal at an early age.

(*e*) His capture was entirely owing to his own carelessness.

5. *Quotation Marks.* (i) State for what purposes quotation marks are used, and then comment on the difference between the sentences in each of these pairs.

(*a*) Of course, the constable said, "I must take your name and address."
"Of course," the constable said, "I must take your name and address."

(*b*) Have you found Oliver Twist yet?
Have you found "Oliver Twist" yet?

(*c*) I shall never forget my uncle's advice: crime does not pay.
I shall never forget my uncle's advice: "Crime does not pay".

How would you use quotation marks if the whole of the last sentence was direct speech, i.e. if it began: He said, "I shall never forget . . .

Quotation marks are also used to show that a word means just the word and not what it stands for. They are used for this purpose in the instructions for Exercise 4. (Sometimes italics can be used as an alternative, as they are in Exercise 4.)

Examine the use of quotation marks in the passage.

Explain the difference between these sentences.

(*a*) Can you spell correctly?
Can you spell "correctly"?

(*b*) It will make all the difference if you delete theirs.
It will make all the difference if you delete "theirs".

(*c*) "I shall write now,", she said.
"I shall write 'now' " she said.

(*d*) "Your handwriting is appalling. This 'b' looks like 'u', said the teacher, pointing to the book.
"Your handwriting is appalling. This 'bee' looks like 'you'," said the teacher, pointing to the book.
"Your handwriting is appalling. This bee looks like you," said the teacher, pointing to the book.

(ii) Insert the necessary quotation marks in the following sentences.

(*a*) If the word narrative means a tale and extinguish means to put out, can you take a dog by the narrative and extinguish him?

(*b*) The teacher asked John for a sentence beginning with I.

I is . . ., began John.

You should never say I is. You must always say I am, she told him firmly.

All right, he said. I am the ninth letter of the alphabet.

(*c*) If I write n, e, w, asked the teacher, what does it spell?

New, replied a boy at the front.

And if I write k in front of it? she continued.

Canoe, laughed the boy.

TOPICS FOR WRITTEN WORK

1. Write a poem entitled "Prisoner".

Hints

You may either describe a prisoner, or imagine that you, yourself, are imprisoned. Describe the surroundings, the atmosphere, the attitude of any guards, and the thoughts and feelings of the prisoner.

2. Study the information below, which is taken from the book "Hanged by the Neck" by Arthur Koestler and C. H. Rolph. (*a*) Then use the material in an essay arguing against capital punishment. (*b*) Or, if you are against the abolition of capital punishment, take each of the points and try to show its weaknesses.

(*a*) The following quotations are taken from letters or comments of close relatives of murdered people:

When I heard that my daughter's murderer was not to be executed my first reaction was immense relief from an additional torment. We are delighted (at his reprieve). I know we have suffered, but hanging him would not bring my baby back to life.

I feel now more convinced than ever that capital punishment is an evil and unnecessary thing.

(*b*) Most victims are people known to the murderer; about two-thirds of them are women who have had a close relationship with the murderer.

(*c*) In 1810, in the House of Lords, a vehement speech was made against a Bill to remove the death penalty for shop-lifting to the value of five-shillings and over, on the grounds that if the death penalty was removed for this offence, no-one would dare leave his house, for fear of finding it burgled when he returned.

(*d*) It was found by the Royal Commission on Capital Punishment in 1949, that over the previous thirty years, in Belgium, Denmark, The Netherlands, Norway, Sweden and Switzerland, where there was no death penalty, altogether six convicted murderers committed crimes of violence after their release.

200

Hints

Put the contents of your essay in a logical order. If you use emotionally toned words and phrases, choose them with care. Avoid jargon and colloquialisms.

3. Imagine that you witness a road accident. Write the statement that you would give to the police.

Hints

Set the accident in an area that you know well, so that you can give the names of all the relevant streets, and refer to landmarks and directions. State exactly where you were positioned at the time of the accident. Describe the cars and people involved, estimate the speed of the vehicles, and say what has happened after the accident had occurred.

Pupils' Work
This Prison

These four walls,
These four blank walls.
That black iron-fingered door.
These cold flagstones,
And that damned stool.

Squatting round
And prim and low in the corner
(I hate that stool more than anything else).
Placed beside it, the utility table,
On which there stands

A bowl of water,
A piece of yellow soap,
A coarse oblong towel,
Which I must always keep
Neatly folded, and in its proper place.

There is the same smell
Of disinfectant every day
Sweet and sickly, and mixed
With the same smell of sweat, and there is
The same ache in the air every day.

Man-made prison,
Man-made objects,
Man-made atmospheres,
And to make it complete:
Me—a man.

C. Pepper

Condemned
The man in his cell,
Waiting, waiting,
Slowly the minutes slipped by.
Sweat of fear trickling down his face,
As he waited.
He started to cry:
Tears dropped to the darkening floor.
He tried to sleep,
But lay awake,
Thinking.

R. K. Warwick

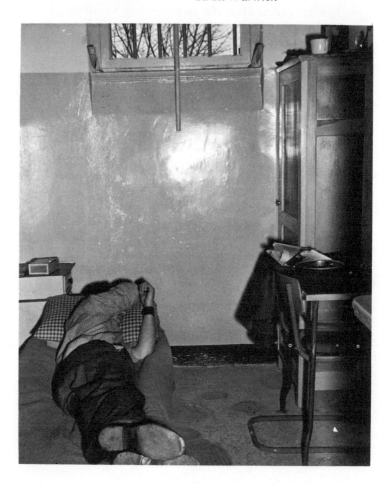

202

ORAL WORK

1. Discuss all or some of the following provocative remarks and quotations on the subject of crime and punishment:

   (a) "All punishment is mischief: all punishment in itself is evil." (Jeremy Boutham, 1748-1832).

   (b) Punishment should be designed to fit the criminal, not the crime.

   (c) "I and all the people I know would prefer the cat to a long sentence any time. After three days it doesn't hurt any more, and the scars soon heal, except those on your mind. What you feel is anger, resentment, and, most of all, a determination somehow to get your own back. But being deterred? The idea never gets a look in." (R. Allerton, a hardened criminal, as recorded by T. Parker in "The Courage of his Convictions").

   (d) "Criminals are the butts on to whom the rest of us can discharge our own angry feelings . . . To discharge them upon our friends and neighbours is not permissible . . . (The criminal) has given us plenty of excuse. We can hate him and punish him with a positive sense of virtue." ("Crime in a Changing Society" by Howard Jones.)

   (e) "The main thing it (punishment in a detention centre) does, I think, is to reinforce your attitude towards authority: . . . it's always "Them" and "Us", you know, like in *Loneliness of the Long Distance Runner*, and you're just you running your own separate race, and you don't care what anybody does. The first thing you want to do is to get out and live your own life, but you come up feeling they're all bastards, they hate me." (From a B.B.C. interview with a young offender.)

   (f) Criminals are made, not born.

   (g) "Crime can in fact be regarded as essentially an expression of immaturity, a continuation into adult life of modes of feeling and patterns of behaviour that are characteristic of a childish stage of development." ("The English Penal System" by Winifred Elkin.)

   (h) When there is such widespread dishonesty, petty theft, cheating over taxes, fiddling of public money, and a general resort to violence, both in entertainment and in international affairs, who can blame criminals for looking after themselves?

   (i) We shall never get anywhere in the fight against crime until we can make informers completely acceptable, and get rid of the idea that the only mistake a criminal makes is to be found out.

   (j) "Through tatter'd clothes small vices do appear;
   Robes and furr'd gowns hide all. Plate sin with gold,
   And the strong lance of justice hurtless breaks;
   Arm it in rags, a pigmy's straw does pierce it.
   None does offend none, I say, none."
                    (the mad King Lear in Shakespeare's play)

2. What conclusions can you draw from the graphs below?

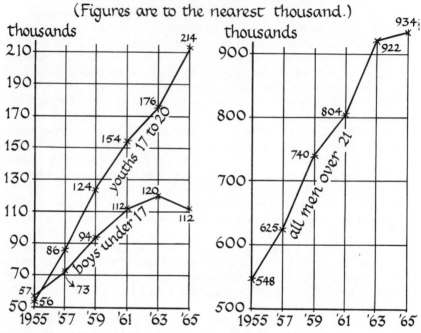

MEN AND BOYS FOUND GUILTY OF OFFENCES
IN ENGLAND AND WALES
(Figures are to the nearest thousand.)

3. Read the following passage; discuss the point that it makes; and say how you would like to see various traffic offences, e.g., drunken driving, dealt with. You will have a more fruitful discussion if you find out what the present penalties are.

At least half the criminal convictions each year are for motoring offences and many of these are for serious crimes endangering lives; indeed there are almost as many of these latter convictions as there are for burglary. And even though such crimes are frequently more disastrous than theft, the motorist is neither condemned as a criminal, nor punished heavily. One can argue, of course, that organised crime, such as burglary, is intentional. and that a road accident is not. But surely we should consider the result as well as the intent? Probably the real reason for the discrepency in treatment stems from a misguided sense of self-protection: we are all more likely to commit a motoring offence than any other sort of crime.

204

4. Imagine that you are the Home Secretary's personal assistant and that he has just asked you to tell him what attitudes the "Views of the World" and the "National Independent" (Exercise 1) are adopting towards the shootings in Battersea and Soho, and the question of capital punishment? He also asks you how much influence you think the arguments of these two papers should have on any decisions he makes. Give your reply.

HUMILIATION futility
DEFEAT despair

ACTIVITIES AND RESEARCH

1. See if you can borrow the "Annual Abstract of Statistics" from the reference section of your library and bring up to date the graph on page 204, which was based on figures given in this publication. Then study the other figures given. For example, consider the statistics for female offenders; look at the number of prisoners serving a second, third or further term in jail. See what other relevant figures, such as the strength of the Police Force, are given.
2. Find out the answers to the following questions.

What were: the Poor Law, the Workhouse, and the Debtor's Prisons?

What offences were punishable by hanging in the 18th century?

What kinds of punishment were: transportation, ducking, the pillory, the stocks, the treadmill, the cat-o'-nine tails, the rack?

Can you be prosecuted just for being on private land? If you see a path marked on an ordnance survey map, can you claim the right to follow that route?

What happens if a person of your age is charged by the police?

What is meant by: "the bench, a juvenile court, a probation officer, Petty Sessions and Quarter Sessions?

What is the difference between a judge, a stipendiary magistrate, and an ordinary magistrate, or J.P.?

Does a cyclist have to observe traffic regulations and signals when he is wheeling his bicycle? Is a cyclist allowed (*a*) to park his cycle where there are "No Waiting" restrictions (*b*) to carry a passenger (*c*) to ride without brakes?

How are parking meters used? What is a ticket fine?

3. Find out all you can about crime and the treatment of criminals in other countries. Which countries have capital punishment? Is there any difference in the murder rate between these countries and those without capital punishment? Compare our traffic regulations, and our investigation and sentencing of drunken drivers, with the systems used in other countries. Is it generally true that countries with rising standards of living also have rising crime rates?

FURTHER READING

The Loneliness of the Long Distance Runner by Alan Sillitoe (W. H. Allen; Pan; Longmans).

The edited version printed in this chapter is much shorter than the original story, which is the title piece of a remarkably good collection. The other stories are on more or less related themes, all of them evoking very vividly the atmosphere of poverty and rebellion. Particularly recommended are *Uncle Ernest* (which is about a lonely, middle-aged man who finds friendship, only to have it torn away by the hand of authority) and *On Saturday Afternoon* (which is told by a young boy who watches a man trying to hang himself).

Saturday Night and Sunday Morning (W. H. Allen; Pan; Longmans).

To Arthur Seaton, who works on a lathe in a Nottingham factory, life is one long battle with authority. When he has finished work, Arthur goes off to the pubs, raring for adventure. His slogan is "If it's going, it's for me"; his aim is to cheat the world before it can cheat him.

Key to the Door (Macmillan; Pan).

This is the story of the author's own generation (he was born in Nottingham in 1928) as revealed through the experiences in Nottingham and Malaya of a young boy.

The Ragman's Daughter (W. H. Allen).

Although perhaps not as good a collection as *The Loneliness of the Long Distance Runner*, this volume of short stories is still of a very high standard.

CHAPTER 14   **All The Same**

*In this short story we are projected into the future, when
to deviate from the universally accepted pattern of
leisure time behaviour is to invite more than curiosity.*

TO enter out into that silence that was the city at eight o'clock of a
misty evening in November, to put your feet upon that buckling
concrete walk, to step over grassy seams and make your way,
hands in pockets, through the silences, that was what Mr. Leonard
Mead most dearly loved to do. He would stand upon the corner of an
intersection and peer down the long moonlit avenues of sidewalk in four
directions, deciding which way to go, but it really made no difference; he
was alone in this world of A.D. 2052, or as good as alone, and with a
final decision made, a path selected, he would stride off, sending patterns
of frosty air before him like the smoke of a cigar . . . .

On this particular evening he began his journey in a westerly direction,
toward the hidden sea. There was a good crystal frost in the air; it cut
the nose and made the lungs blaze like a Christmas tree inside; you could
feel the cold light going on and off, all the branches filled with invisible
snow. He listened to the faint push of his soft shoes through autumn
leaves with satisfaction, and whistled a cold quiet whistle between his
teeth, occasionally picking up a leaf as he passed, examining its skeletal
pattern in the infrequent lamplights as he went on, smelling its rusty
smell.

"Hello, in there," he whispered to every house on every side as he
moved. "What's up to-night on Channel 4, Channel 7, Channel 9?
Where are the cowboys rushing, and do I see the United States Cavalry
over the next hill to the rescue?" . . .

"What is it now?" he asked the houses, noticing his wrist watch.
"Eight-thirty p.m.? Time for a dozen assorted murders? A quiz? A
revue? A comedian falling off the stage?" . . .

He came to a cloverleaf intersection which stood silent where two
main highways crossed the town. During the day it was a thunderous
surge of cars, the gas station open, a great insect rustling and a ceaseless

jockeying for position as the scarab-beetles, a faint incense puttering from their exhausts, skimmed homeward to the far directions. But now these highways, too, were like streams in a dry season, all stone and bed and moon radiance.

He turned back on a side street, circling around toward his home. He was within a block of his destination when the lone car turned a corner quite suddenly and flashed a fierce white cone of light upon him. He stood entranced, not unlike a night moth, stunned by the illumination, and then drawn toward it.

A metallic voice called to him:

"Stand still. Stay where you are! Don't move!

He halted.

"Put up your hands!"

"But—" he said.

"Your hands up! Or we'll shoot!"

The police, of course, but what a rare, incredible thing; in a city of three million, there was only one police car left, wasn't that correct? Ever since a year ago, 2052, the election year, the force had been cut down from three cars to one. Crime was ebbing; there was no need now for the police, save for this one lone car wandering and wandering the empty streets.

"Your name?" said the police car in a metallic whisper. He couldn't see the men in it for the bright light in his eyes.

"Leonard Mead," he said.

"Speak up!"

"Leonard Mead!"

"Business or profession?"

"I guess you'd call me a writer."

"No profession," said the police car, as if talking to itself. The light held him fixed, like a museum specimen, needle thrust through chest.

"You might say that," said Mr. Mead. He hadn't written in years. Magazines and books didn't sell any more. Everything went on in the tomblike houses at night now, he thought, continuing his fancy. The tombs, ill-lit by television light, where the people sat like the dead, the grey or multicoloured lights touching their faces, but never really touching them.

"No profession," said the phonograph voice, hissing. "What are you doing out?"

"Walking," said Leonard Mead.

"Walking!"

"Just walking," he said simply, but his face felt cold.

"Walking, just walking, walking?"

"Yes, sir".

"Walking where? For what?"

"Walking for air. Walking to see."

"Your address!"

"Eleven South Saint James Street."

"And there is air in your house, you have an air *conditioner*, Mr. Mead?"

"Yes."

"And you have a viewing screen in your house to see with?"

"No."

"No?" There was a crackling quiet that in itself was an accusation.

"Are you married, Mr. Mead?"

"No."

"Not married," said the police voice behind the fiery beam. The moon was high and clear among the stars and the houses were grey and silent.

"Nobody wanted me," said Leonard Mead with a smile.

"Don't speak unless you're spoken to!"

Leonard Mead waited in the cold night.

"Just walking, Mr. Mead?"

"Yes."

"But you haven't explained for what purpose."

"I explained; for air, and to see, and just to walk."

"Have you done this often?"

"Every night for years."

The police car sat in the centre of the street with its radio throat faintly humming.

"Well, Mr. Mead," it said.

"Is that all?" he asked politely.

"Yes," said the voice. "Here." There was a sigh, a pop. The back door of the police car sprang wide. "Get in."

"Wait a minute, I haven't done anything!"

"Get in."

"I protest!"

"Mr. Mead."

He walked like a man suddenly drunk. As he passed the front window of the car he looked in. As he had expected, there was no one in the front seat, no one in the car at all.

"Get in."

He put his hand to the door and peered into the back seat, which was a little cell, a little black jail with bars. It smelled of riveted steel. It smelled of harsh antiseptic; it smelled too clean and hard and metallic. There was nothing soft there.

"Now if you had a wife to give you an alibi," said the iron voice. "But—"

"Where are you taking me?"

The car hesitated, or rather gave a faint whirring click, as if information, somewhere, was dripping card by punch-slotted card under electric eyes. "To the Psychiatric Centre for Research on Regressive Tendencies."

He got in. The door shut with a soft thud. The police car rolled through the night avenues, flashing its dim lights ahead.

They passed one house on one street a moment later, one house in an entire city of houses that were dark, but this one particular house had all of its electric lights brightly lit, every window a loud yellow illumination, square and warm in the cool darkness.

"That's my house," said Leonard Mead.

No one answered him.

The car moved down the empty river-bed streets and off away, leaving the empty streets with the empty sidewalks, and no sound and no motion all the rest of the chill November night.

(from *The Pedestrian,* a short story by Ray Bradbury)

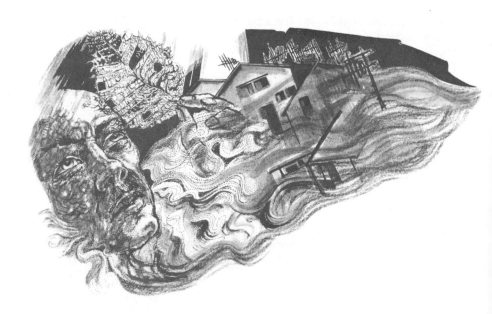

APPRECIATION AND DISCUSSION

1. What *information* does Ray Bradbury include in the first paragraph to set the scene for the story? What descriptive details does he include to create *atmosphere*?

2. What were the other inhabitants of the city doing while Leonard Mead was out walking?

3. Why was the light from the police car shaped like a cone? Why was it "fierce"? In what respects was Leonard "not unlike a night moth" in his reaction to the light?

4. Can you suggest why, at the time of this incident, "crime was ebbing", so that there was no need for a police force?

5. Why was being a writer at this time the same as having no profession?

6. The light from their television sets touched the faces of the people watching, but never really touched "*them*". What does Ray Bradbury mean by this?
   Refer to the other italicised words in this story. What effect do the italics have when the sentences are read aloud?

7. That there was nobody in the police car is hinted at earlier in the story. Which words and phrases suggest this? Is the fact that the car is operated by remote control an important point?

8. What are "regressive tendencies"?

9. What was it about the society in which he lived that was repulsive to Leonard Mead? Do you think such dangers are real? Do people, even now, rely on and become addicted to "canned" entertainment to such an extent that they would feel lost without it? Consider, for example, the widespread use of transistor radios.

10. Leonard Mead was regarded with suspicion because he did not conform—he did not sit at home and watch television as everybody else did. What sorts of non-conformity (e.g. in dress) are regarded with suspicion in present-day society?

11. For what reasons do some people refuse to accept conventional forms of dress, behaviour, etc? Are there any occasions when a refusal to conform could be dangerous?

12. How do you feel about "outsiders", who refuse to conform? Why are the majority of people suspicious of them? Is such suspicion usually justified?

Little Boxes

Little boxes on the hillside,
Little boxes made of ticky tacky,
Little boxes, little boxes, little boxes all the same.
There's a green one and a pink one
    and a blue one and a yellow one,
And they're all made out of ticky tacky
And they all look just the same.

And the people in the houses all go to the university,
And they all get put in boxes, little boxes all the same.
And there's doctors and there's lawyers
    and business executives,
And they're all made out of ticky tacky
And they all look just the same.

And they all play on the golf course
And drink their martini dry,
And they all have pretty children
    and the children go to school,
And the children go to summer camp
    and then to the university,
And they all get put in boxes
And they all come out the same.

And the boys go into business
    and marry and raise a family,
And they all get put in boxes, little boxes all the same.
There's a green one and a pink
    one and a blue one and a yellow one,
And they're all made out of ticky tacky,
And they all look just the same.

Malvina Reynolds

DISCUSSING THE POEM

1. Is this poem (which was originally a song lyric) gently poking fun at people who follow a very conventional pattern of life, or is it viciously attacking them?
2. List the ways in which these people are "all the same".
3. Obviously these comments do not apply to everybody in society, but just one section of it. At which social class, at what sort of people, are the comments directed?

212

4. The poem is referring to one section of American society. To what extent does it apply to the corresponding section of society in Britain? Which comments would have to be changed or replaced to make it completely applicable?
5. Do you consider it is necessarily a bad thing that these people are "all the same"?
6. The expression "ticky tacky" is applied to both the people and their houses. What does this description suggest about them?

TECHNIQUES

The Use of Language, and Style

1. *Similes and Metaphors.* To create striking similes we need to use unlike objects and show how they are comparable in particular respects. For instance, how is a helicopter like a dragonfly? They are similar in shape, if not in size. Both hover and move in a similar way. The position and the speed of the helicopter's blades are similar to those of the dragonfly's wings; and the wheels or skids of the helicopter are comparable to the insect's legs.

Explain the points of comparison in these four similes from the passage.
(*a*) ". . . he would stride off, sending patterns of frosty air before him like the smoke of a cigar."
(*b*) "There was a good crystal frost; it cut the nose and made the lungs blaze like a Christmas tree inside;"
(*c*) "But now these highways, too, were like streams in a dry season."
(*d*) "The light held him fixed, like a museum specimen,"
Ray Bradbury has also used several interesting metaphors.
   e.g. The cars were referred to as "scarab-beetles", the houses as "tombs".
Explain the points of comparison in the two metaphors mentioned above, and the two given below.
   (a train) The great iron horse, its white mane flying in the wind, thundered down the track.
   (a crane) The monster, stretched above us, picked up the rubble in its steel claw.
There are, too, a number of single adjectives and verbs that have been used metaphorically.
   e.g. "a *cold* quiet whistle"
        "information, somewhere, *was dripping* card by punch-slotted card"

213

Find other unusual and vivid words in the passage; then make up original and striking descriptions of the following, using similes and metaphors.

(a) a waterfall in sunshine
(b) a noisy piece of machinery
(c) the lights of a fairground
(d) autumn leaves
(e) heavy rain
(f) an exploding petrol tank

2. *Symbols.* By emphasising it and contrasting it with other factors in his story, a writer can make something quite ordinary into an important symbol. In "The Pedestrian", for example, Leonard Mead's house, with "all its electric lights brightly lit, every window a loud yellow illumination", was to him a symbol of his beliefs and his defiance.

Decide what each of the following might symbolise, and outline the situation in which such a symbol could effectively occur.

e.g. a small ray of light

This could symbolise hope for a man trapped underground.

(a) two trees with their branches intertwined
(b) ivy clinging to the trunk of a tree
(c) thunder and lightning
(d) a deluge of rain
(e) a rock, worn away by the steady dripping of water
(f) a single flower growing out of a concrete wall
(g) a deep, dark cave
(h) a beautifully designed silver dagger
(i) a hypodermic needle

3. *Emotive Language.* You have seen already that many words are emotionally toned, and suggest particular feelings and attitudes. Consider, for example, Ray Bradbury's choice of the word "incense" for the exhaust fumes of the cars:

"the scarab-beetles, a faint incense puttering from their exhausts, skimmed homeward".

What do we normally associate with the burning of incense? What sort of smell does incense have? What attitude to the cars is suggested by the word and its associations?

Now consider some other words for a smell:

perfume   fragrance   scent   aroma   odour   fume   stink   stench.

Notice how these words range in meaning from something delicate and delightful to something repellent and disgusting. Try using each of the words in place of "incense" in the quotation above, and consider the effect that each one creates.

Compile a list of nouns for: (a) a light, e.g. a glimmer, a flicker, a glare (b) a noise, e.g., a tinkle.

Compile a list of adjectives, ranging from complimentary to insulting, to describe (a) a thin person (b) a fat person.

Rewrite Ray Bradbury's description of:

(a) Leonard Mead's walk in the frosty autumn evening (paragraph 2)— making it seem an unpleasant experience

(b) people watching television ("Everything went on in the tomb-like houses . . ." etc.)—making this seem a desirable activity

(c) the inside of the police car ("He put his hand to the door . . ." etc.) —making it seem clean and comfortable.

4. *Comprehension Practice.* Read the following extract carefully and then, in one or two sentences, answer each of the questions below it.

The judge moved in and sat down slowly. He was a heavy man and not young . . . .

A solicitor got up: "Might I mention to your Honour," he began.

"No, not yet," said the judge irritably.

The solicitor sat down with a sigh . . . .

"Mrs. Turner," called the clerk, and a small woman went into the witness box. She was making an application for some money to be paid out to her from a fund in Court. She was a widow whose husband had been killed some years before in an accident and the Court controlled her use of the damages she had been awarded.

"Well," said the judge, after glancing at the papers in front of him, "what do you want £10 for?"

He asked her as though she were a beggar at the back door when she was, in fact, the owner of the fund in Court. It was her money, but the Court had the paternal duty of seeing that she did not expend it too foolishly. The judge's manner was not in the least paternal.

"Please, your Worship," the woman began—

"She's had it," whispered a solicitor, "calling him your worship."

"It's a first payment for a television set."

The judge's eyes gleamed. His remarks about television and other abominations of the modern age had frequently been reported in the Press.

"A television set," he growled. "What on earth d'you want with one of those things? Read a good book and get it from the library. Cost you nothing."

"Please, your Worship, I can't read, not really."

"What on earth have we been paying taxes for all these years? It's disgraceful."

"Please, your Worship, I'm nearly blind."

"Oh, I'm sorry," said the judge. He thought for a moment and then added in a more kindly tone: "But is a television set much use to you then? Why not have a wireless instead?"

"Oh, I have a wireless, your Worship."

"I see."

The judge hesitated.

"You think you'll get some pleasure out of a television set, do you?"

"Oh, yes, your Worship. Mrs. Crane across the road has one and she can't see a thing."

"Perhaps it's an advantage then," said the judge. "Yes, very well, Mrs. Turner. You shall have your television set. Ten pounds I think you want. Very well. Can you pay the instalments all right? Good. They'll give you your money in the office. I hope your sight improves."

"Might I now mention to your Honour," began the solicitor who had tried before, hoping that the shock which the judge had just received might have put him in a more receptive mood.

"Certainly not," said the judge just as fiercely as before, but not quite for the same reason. He was visualizing Mrs. Turner's life without her husband and without much sight. "And probably she hasn't much to think with either," he was pondering, "though p'raps it's just as well," when the solicitor had interrupted.

(from *Brothers in Law* by Henry Cecil)

(*a*) Why did the judge snap at the solicitor who spoke to him before the case began?

(*b*) How did Mrs. Turner come to own the money for which she was applying?

(*c*) Why did she need to have the judge's permission before she could spend it?

(*d*) What was the judge's attitude towards Mrs. Turner when the case began?

(*e*) Why did the solicitor think that Mrs. Turner had "had it" when she addressed the judge as "Your Worship"?

(*f*) Why did the judge's eyes gleam when Mrs. Turner explained why whe wanted the money?

(*g*) What did the judge mean by his remark about taxes?

(*h*) Why did he at first try to bully Mrs. Turner into not getting a television? Why did he hesitate before later granting her request?

(*i*) Why did he finally agree to let her have the money?

(*j*) What was the shock that the judge received?

(k) Why did he come to the conclusion that Mrs. Turner probably hadn't "much to think with"?

(l) Why did he consider that this was perhaps just as well?

(m) Why did he snap at the solicitor who again tried to speak to him when Mrs. Turner had left?

Correct English, and Vocabulary

5. *Apostrophes.* Write out the following passage, inserting all the possessive apostrophes that are required.

Ten minutes walk from the towns centre, on ones way to the police station, is Cloverleaf Park. The Parks Committees plan for this, the boroughs main park, included the Parks Superintendents ideas and his senior deputys suggestion for a hotel with a television room for both residents and visitors enjoyment. After a months argument the superintendent and Mr. Bliss, his deputy, were openly insulting each others proposals, and the superintendent referred to the project as "Blisss Folly".

6. *Definitions.* Consider this definition of a television set.

A television set is something that shows pictures.

It is an inadequate definition because it is not precise enough. A film projector could also be defined in the same vague terms, and yet the two devices are quite different. The following definitions are more accurate.

A television set is a device for receiving electrical impulses and converting them into pictures and sounds.

A film projector is a machine that throws images from a moving length of film on to a screen; it can also reproduce sound from the sound track.

Criticise the following definitions, and point out other objects or people to which they could apply.

(a) A window is part of a house that you can see out of.

(b) A table is something made of wood, and has four legs.

(c) A boxer is someone who likes boxing.

(d) A church is a building with stained glass windows.

(e) A tyrant is someone who punishes you.

Now define each of the following objects in one or two sentences, making sure that there is no confusion between them.

(a) a telephone (b) a radio (c) garden shears (d) scissors

(e) a nail (f) a screw (g) an overcoat (h) a cardigan

(i) a wheelbarrow (j) a trolley

217

TOPICS FOR WRITTEN WORK

1. Write a short story set in a future society where everybody is required to be the same as far as athletic ability is concerned.

Hints

Imagine what it would be like if nobody was allowed to be better or worse than anybody else at football, hockey, running, jumping, weight-lifting and so on, between the ages of fifteen and fifty. You would probably need to have inspectors whose job it was to handicap those people who had greater physical ability than average. What sort of devices might they use to handicap these people? How would those people below average be dealt with? What would happen to cripples? As your central character, you could have someone who rebels against this idea of enforced conformity (as Leonard Mead did in Ray Bradbury's story).

2. Write a poem entitled "All the Same".

Hints

You may take "Little Boxes" as a model, if you wish, rewriting it so that it applies to one section of English society. For instance, if you decide to write about the ordinary Englishman you might begin:

> Terraced castles in the suburbs,
> Terraced castles made of candifloss.

Or, if you write about "pop" musicians:

> 'Lectric guitars round their kneecaps,
> 'Lectric guitars making tiny twangs.

Alternatively, you may use the photograph on page 219 as a starting point, writing whatever it suggests to you.

218

3. Refer to the extract from "Brothers in Law" on page 215 and then write these three different versions of what happened in court: (a) an extract in the judge's diary (b) a letter to a friend, written by the solicitor who interrupted the judge (c) the account given by Mrs. Turner when talking to a neighbour.

Hints

Each of these versions will portray the events in a different way; none of the individuals concerned will remember what happened in the same light. The styles of the three versions will also differ: the judge's record could be rather pompous; the solicitor's letter would be chatty, and might contain such phrases as "old boy", "absolutely terrific"; Mrs. Turner's account would be very colloquial and even slangy. (Make sure you punctuate the direct speech correctly.)

Pupils' Work
Days all the Same

Your continuous thought of the day,
And the day is over, and the day is wasted.
The night comes, you go to bed to try and forget it.
And the next day comes, and it goes, and it's wasted.
But you live on, hoping the next day will bring something new,
But it doesn't.
Yet you're surrounded by people,
Masses in a blur,
A jumble of noises. Shouting. Incomprehensible.
And you. The clear centre. Alone. Still. Silent.
But something will break you into the blur,
Into a new world.
And your lonely thoughts disappear
and you forget.

Alan Hart

"All the Fun of the Fair?"

But what about
The people not having fun?
The Boxer challenging
Man after man?
The same act
Put on
Time after time?
Does he ever get tired?
The man in the ticket box,
Behind his smile
The same old smile
Does he tire?
The fortune teller,
Dressed in the same clothes,
The gypsy clothes,
Time after time
Telling
Fortune after fortune.
Does he run out of fortunes?

The maintenance man,
Mending
Bulb after bulb
And
Machine after machine,
Stubborn horse after horse.
When hooligans venture
Through the gate
For some "fun",
Does he get tired of
"All the fun"?
The happy clown,
Yes even on the fairground,
The happy clown,
Transformed behind his mask
Of greasepaint,
What does he feel?
The man with lover lost,
Come to lose his thoughts
And money,
And even himself,
He is not really part of it
Yet he wishes he was,
Seeing the gaiety.
Does he know?
Know that there are
Unhappy ones,
Like himself,
Who work for pay
More than enjoyment?
Does the man with lover lost
Does he know?
And does he still wish?

Janet Hughes.

CONFORMITY

1.(*a*) Imagine that Leonard Mead, the character in "The Pedestrian", is to be tried in a court of law after being picked up by the police car. Arrange for this trial to be held. (See Book 3, Chapter 13, page 150 for a list of some of the people who will be involved in a mock trial.) What charges might be brought against him? What arguments, accusations and evidence would the prosecuting counsel put forward? What would be the best approach for the defence to take? What sentence could be passed if Mead was to be found guilty?

(*b*) Imagine that Mrs. Turner's application had to be resolved in a court of law (extract from "Brothers in Law", Exercise 4) and that there was a lawyer to speak on her behalf, and a lawyer opposing her application. Work out and perform the speeches of the two lawyers.

2. Dramatise "The Pedestrian" as a short play for radio. Add dialogue where necessary, incorporating information given in the narrative; do *not* have a narrator to read these parts. Some of the information could be included in Leonard Mead's opening soliloquy; other details could be added to the dialogue between him and the police car; further points might be conveyed through sound effects, e.g. a clock chiming to show that it was eight o'clock when he started his walk.

3. Define and discuss the difference between "active" and "passive" pastimes. Give examples of leisure pursuits that are active, and pursuits that are normally thought of as passive. Are reading, and watching television passive pastimes? Is an active pastime necessarily better than a passive one? What percentage of your leisure time is spent passively, and how much of it is spent in an active way? How did you acquire your various leisure time interests? Which do you enjoy the most? Is it active or passive in nature?

ACTIVITIES AND RESEARCH

1. Ray Bradbury described very exactly the way in which Leonard Mead walked

    e.g. "he would stride off"

    "He walked like a man suddenly drunk".

    (Can you find one exact verb to describe the way in which somebody who suddenly felt drunk would walk?)

    Each person can choose three exact verbs for ways of walking, e.g., totter, stumble, gallop, and can then mime these before the other members of the class, who have to guess which actions he is performing.

    Verbs were also used imaginatively or metaphorically, i.e. taken out of their normal context and applied to something different.

    e.g. cars "*skimmed* homeward"

    "The police car *rolled* through the night avenues"

    The class can suggest, say, twenty unusual, imaginative verbs for ways of walking, which can be written on the blackboard. People can then demonstrate what, in their opinion, these actions would look like. For instance, how would you demonstrate "hiccuping along"?

    Bradbury has not, however, invented any words. But you can try making up some new verbs for ways of walking, e.g. to smooze, to frimp, and then demonstrate them to the rest of the class.

2. Find out how experts expect the world to develop over the next thirty years. What are their predictions about population, housing, transport, the possibility of a nuclear war, the amount of leisure time we shall have, and so on?

3. Refer to science fiction stories written in the first half of the century, (those of H. G. Wells would be very suitable) and see how many of their predictions have already come true and how many will obviously never materialise. Find a science fiction story, written within the last ten years, containing a prediction which you think is very likely to come true. Bring the story to school and compare its ideas with those in the stories brought by other members of the class.

4. The best known version of "Little Boxes" is sung by Pete Seeger. See if you can obtain a copy of his record to play to the class.

FURTHER READING

The Pedestrian from *The Golden Apples of the Sun* by Ray Bradbury (Rupert Hart-Davis).

To describe this collection of short stories as science fiction is rather misleading. It is true that there are a number of stories which, like *The Pedestrian*, are set in worlds of the future and which pass comment on the social conditions and attitudes to be found there. But there are also many tales of fantasy, and others, such as *The Garbage Collector*, dealing with incidents which take place in the present. This chapter's extract provides a fair example of Bradbury's style, which is sometimes rather sentimental, but always poetic.

The October Country (Hart-Davis; Four Square)

There are no science fiction stories in this collection; the tales here, perhaps best described as "Horror and Imagination", deal with the "fears and wickedness of the human heart". Their eerie mood is very well caught by the illustrations of Joe Mugnaini.

Fahrenheit 451 (Hart-Davis; Corgi)

In this science fiction novel, firemen are people who do not put out fires but set fire to every habitation which still contains books. Against this world, where private thought or action is criminal, the hero, Montag, rebels. He hides a book. The account of his rebellion and pursuit is not only exciting but thought-provoking, warning us, as many of Bradbury's stories do, against the continual assaults that are made upon the world of our imaginations.

Other books by the same author are:

The Illustrated Man
The Day it Rained Forever
The Silver Locusts

CHAPTER 15

Advertising

Modern advertising can no longer claim to have as its main function the passing on of information to the consumer. Nowadays manufacturers use it primarily to stimulate and persuade people to buy their products.

This urgently felt need to "stimulate" people brought new power, glory, and prosperity to the professional stimulators or persuaders of American industry . . . .

For each man, woman and child in America in 1955 roughly $53 was spent to persuade him or her to buy products of industry. Some cosmetic firms began spending a fourth of all their income from sales on advertising and promotion . . . .

One big and intimidating obstacle confronting the stimulators was the fact that most Americans already possessed perfectly usable stoves, cars, TV sets, clothes, etc. Waiting for these products to wear out or become physically obsolete before urging replacements upon the owner was intolerable. More and more, ad men began talking of the desirability of creating "psychological obsolescence" . . . .

By the mid-fifties merchandisers of many different products were being urged by psychological counsellors to become "merchants of discontent". One ad executive exclaimed with fervour: "What makes this country great is the creation of wants and desires, the creation of dissatisfaction with the old and outmoded!"

Another major dilemma that was forcing marketers to search for more powerful tools of persuasion was the growing sameness of their products, with increased standardization. Too many people were complacently saying that the gasoline brands were 'all the same' and equally good . . . .

Ad agency president David Ogilvy commented on this problem by stating:

"I am astonished to find how many advertising men, even among the new generation, believe that women can be persuaded by logic and argument to buy one brand in preference to another, even when the two brands concerned are technically identical . . . . The greater the similarity between products, the less part reason really plays in brand selection.

There really isn't any significant difference between the various brands of whisky or the various cigarettes or the various brands of beer. They are all about the same, and so are the cake mixes and the detergents and the automobiles . . . ."

It was soon widely realised that to attempt to persuade people to buy by appealing to their reason was ineffective. It was to people's subconscious and often irrational feelings that pressure had to be applied. As a result, advertising agencies instigated investigations by psychiatrists and social scientists to help in planning their campaigns, and became what Packard calls "depth merchandisers".

In searching for extra psychological values that they could add to products to give them a more potent appeal, the depth merchandisers came upon many gratifying clues by studying our subconscious needs, yearnings, and cravings . . . .

The Weiss and Geller advertising agency became suspicious of the conventional reasons people gave for buying home freezers. In many cases it found that economically, the freezers didn't make sense when you added up the initial cost, the monthly cost added on the electric bill, and the amount of frozen left-overs in the box that eventually would be thrown out. When all factors were added, the food that was consumed from the freezer often became very costly indeed.

Its curiosity aroused, the agency made a psychiatric pilot study. The probers found significance in the fact that the home freezer first came into widespread popularity after the Second World War when many families were filled with inner anxieties because of uncertainties involving not only food but just about everything else in their lives. These people began thinking fondly of former periods of safety and security, which subconsciously took them back to childhood where there was the mother who never disappointed and love was closely related with the giving of food. The probers concluded: "The freezer represents to many the assurance that there is always food in the house, and food in the home represents security, warmth, and safety." People who feel insecure, they found, need more food around than they can eat. The agency decided that the merchandising of freezers should take this squirrel factor into account in shaping campaigns . . . .

Other motivations analysts pointed out that snob appeal was the basic motivation governing the purchase of sterling silver flatwear. Women talk at length about its fine durability and craftsmanship but actually want it for prestige and show-off value . . . .

One way merchandisers found they could sell us their products as

226

status symbols was through the price tag. By seemingly inverse logic, many discovered they could increase their sales by raising their price tag, in the topsy-turvy merchandising battle of the mid-fifties.

This battle for the Biggest Price Tag was waged with particular vehemence in the car field where, "Tide" magazine observed, "the almost insane drive by the consumer for a social prestige car has kept auto makers racing to produce the most luxurious vehicle." As Ford Motor Company prepared to unveil its Continental with an up to $10,000 price tag insiders explained that the real goal was, for prestige purposes, to get a higher, price car in the Ford line than General Motors had in the Cadillac . . . .

An interesting success story among the toothpastes is that of Gleem, which on the surface had nothing spectacular to offer in the way of killing the dragons in our mouth. It had an ingredient called GL-70 that was apparently a competent bacteria-killer, but as "Fortune" pointed out GL-70 seemed pretty puny as a peg for ad copy when compared to the more spectacular cleansers that had been ballyhooed. Gleem, however, had discovered a secret weapon. Investigators had uncovered the fact that many people—as a result of being subjected for years to the alarums of toothpaste makers—felt vaguely guilty because they didn't brush their teeth after each meal. Gleem began promising tooth salvation to these guilt-ridden people by saying it was designed for people who "can't brush their teeth after every meal." (This, of course, includes most of the population.) Two years after it was introduced Gleem was outselling all but one rival dentifrice . . . .

These motivational analysts, in working with the symbol manipulators, are adding depth to the selling of ideas and products. They are learning, for example, to offer us considerably more than the actual item involved. A Milwaukee advertising executive commented to colleagues in print on the fact that women will pay two dollars and a half for skin cream but no more than twenty-five cents for a cake of soap. Why? Soap, he explained, only promises to make them clean. The cream promises to make them beautiful. (Soaps have now started promising beauty as well as cleanness.) This executive added, "The women are buying a promise." Then he went on to say: "The cosmetic manufacturers are not selling lanolin, they are selling hope . . . . We no longer buy oranges we buy vitality. We do not buy just auto, we buy prestige" . . . .

The depth investigators also found that people's subconscious reasons for rejecting certain products were as illogical as those which led to buying— as in the case of the unfortunate prune.

The merchandisers of prunes had become exceedingly discouraged in their efforts to persuade Americans to eat prunes, even in the quantities consumed in former years. With something akin to desperation the California Prune Advisory Board turned to the Institute for Motivation Research for counsel. Dr. Dicher, perhaps naturally, suspected that subconscious resistances were working against the prune. (A non-subconscious factor might be the problem of coping with pips while eating prunes.) The variety of hidden meanings the prune held to Americans, however, astonished even his case workers. The prune's image was ridden with meanings, all unfortunate.

When word-association tests were tried on people, the first thoughts that came to the surface of their minds in reference to prunes were such thoughts as "old maid", "dried up". In his studies of the place the word prune had in the English language he came upon such phrases as "old prune face" and "dried up old prune". When his investigators conducted their depth interviews they found that prunes were thought of as a symbol of decrepitude and devitalization. Others thought of prunes in terms of parental authority. They remembered that as children they were often directed to eat prunes because they "ought to", or because "prunes are good for you". Prunes were associated with boarding-houses where they were served by parsimonious landladies, with stingy, ungiving people, with joyless puritans. The black murky colour of prunes as commonly served was commented upon unpleasantly. The colour black was considered somehow symbolically sinister, and in at least one case the poor prune was associated with witches.

Pervading all of these associations and dominating the image of prunes was still another meaning. The prune was thought of primarily as a laxative. In word-association when people were asked to write in the first word they thought of in connection with prunes, many wrote "constipation". Now this laxative image was not entirely unfortunate. In fact the prune people had once prospered when the prune's laxative powers first became common knowledge. By the mid fifties, however, the laxative market was crowded, and the prune's laxative connotations were felt by Dr. Dichter to be a mixed blessing even though the prune people were still stressing the laxative aspect of their advertising . . . .

Dr. Dichter felt that what was needed was a top-to-bottom surgery job on the public's image of the prune so that the public could "rediscover" it as a brand-new fruit. The prune, he decided, would be the new "wonder fruit". The whole concept of the prune as a dried-out fruit for people in need of a laxative was recast into a more "dynamic" image under his guidance by the California prune people. The aim in stressing "new

228

wonder fruit" was to reassure housewives that it was now perfectly acceptable to serve people prunes.

Overnight the prune became a delightful, sweet fruit, almost a candy, if you were to believe the ads. The new imagery showed prunes in a setting as far away as you could get from the dark, murky, old-maidish look of old in which four black prunes were shown floating in a dark fluid. In the new ads, gay, bright colours were used, and childish figures were shown playing. Later the image figures of "youth" gradually changed from children to pretty girls figure-skating or playing tennis. And where prunes were shown they were in bright, gay-coloured dishes or shown against white cottage cheese. With the pictures were jingles saying "Put Wings on Your Feet" and "Get that Top of The World Feeling". One ad said, "Prunes help bring colour to your blood and a glow to your face." In its public image the prune became a true-life Cinderella!

As for the laxative angle it was now mentioned in passing near the bottom of the message. One ad showing the cute figure skater concluded with these words: "—and, a gentle aid to regularity. When you feel good, good things happen to you. So start eating prunes today till you have energy to spare."

The rediscovered prune soon was enjoying a spurt in sales.

(from *The Hidden Persuaders* by Vance Packard)

APPRECIATION AND DISCUSSION

1. Give one reason why it was difficult to persuade people to buy new stoves, cars, TV sets, etc. What tactics were used to overcome this obstacle?

2. What difficulty was there in persuading people to buy one brand of a product rather than another brand? What tactics were most effective in overcoming this difficulty?

3. Explain, in your own words, the findings of the Weiss and Geller investigation into the reasons that people bought refrigerators. Do you think that this explanation is a likely one, or do you consider it too far-fetched?

4. Why did American car manufacturers compete so fiercely to produce very expensive cars? Can you draw any comparisons with the British market? Which cars in Britain have the greatest snob appeal, the greatest social prestige value? Are they also the most expensive?

5. What other techniques, in addition to a high price-tag, can be used to give a product snob appeal?

6. What emotion did the advertisers of Gleem play upon in order to sell their toothpaste? What had caused this feeling to arise in the first place?

   Other depth investigations revealed that the desire to protect their teeth was not the primary motive that many people had for cleaning them. Can you deduce, from toothpaste advertisements you have seen, what other reasons people might have for cleaning their teeth? How are these motives capitalised upon by toothpaste advertisements?

7. "Soaps have now started promising beauty as well as cleanliness." Is this true of soap advertisements in Britain today? What other things are promised in the soap advertisements? Are these promises made directly, or by implication? Quote examples.

8. "The cosmetic manufacturers are not selling lanolin, they are selling hope." What "hope" are they selling and to whom?

   "We no longer buy oranges, we buy vitality." Can you quote any advertisements for oranges (or other fruits) that associate the product with vitality and health? What other products adopt this approach?

9. Can you complete the following statements in a similar fashion to those quoted above?

   Detergents now promise not only cleanliness, but ———.

   Chocolate and malt drinks not only promise sound sleep, they also promise ———.

10. In a word-association test a person is asked to give the first words or phrases that come into his head after being presented with a reference to the subject under investigation. The resulting list of words, given without consciously working out his response, is supposed to indicate the person's subconscious attitude to the subject, which may well be different from what he would say if allowed time to think about it.

    Write down the first words and phrases that come into your head in connection with the word "PRUNE". Why, however, might these words no longer give a true indication of your subconscious attitude? Carry out word association tests to try and discover how members of the class feel about other objects and ideas.

230

11. What techniques were used to give the prune a new image? Can you think of any other approaches which could have been used to promote it as "the new wonder fruit"?

12. From a consumer's point of view, do you consider it right that so much money should be spent on advertising, and that techniques such as those described in this extract should be used to make people buy? Do you consider that advertisements which employ these techniques are at all unfair or dishonest? Do they distort the truth? Is it wrong to persuade people to buy products they do not really need?

Lather as You Go
Beneath this slab
John Brown is stowed.
He watched the ads
And not the road.
Ogden Nash

DISCUSSING THE POEM

1. At what sort of advertisements would John Brown probably have been looking?
2. Do you think that some advertisements provide a serious distraction to drivers and pedestrians?
3. Many of the highways in America are lined on both sides with advertisement hoardings. Would you object to this happening here?
4. In what sort of places in towns should hoardings be (a) prohibited (b) allowed? Refer to places in your own town, and give reasons to support your views.
5. Can you make up a short, four line verse, similar to "Lather as You Go", which makes some comment about advertising?

The Use of Language, and Style

1. *Advertisement Analysis.* Ideally, the purpose of advertisements is to draw the attention of the consumer to "desirable merchandise". To do this, an advertisement should supply a certain amount of information for the consumer to consider.

    What information should an advertisement contain?

    But, as you know, simply supplying information rarely increases sales, and it is to increase sales that manufacturers advertise. People do not buy a product because of what they are told about it; they buy it because of the way they feel about it. So, advertisements are designed to play upon people's feelings.

    What style of language is most suitable for conveying facts?

    What style of language is most suitable for appealing to emotions?

    What style of language is generally used in advertisements?

    Explain what feelings the following advertisements appeal to.

    (a)

If you died tomorrow this could happen to **YOUR** family

Let **FLEECE-U INSURANCE** take care of them

(b) Stand out in a crowd with a CRUMBLETON PIPE.

(c) You know you're safe with PEELOFF PAINT.

    More people use PEELOFF than any other brand of paint.

(d) To get to the top nowadays, you need qualifications! Study with the SWOT CORRESPONDENCE COLLEGE and start climbing the ladder of success now!

(*e*)

The ROGUE ROADSTER

Just look at the new SLEEK lines

2. *Advertisement Presentation.* It is little use composing an advertisement, however persuasively it may play upon people's feelings, unless you can get people to look at it or listen to it, and then remember it. There are a number of techniques that are used to present advertisements so that they are noticed and remembered.

Techniques to make people Notice Advertisements:

(i) *in Newspapers and on Posters:*

(*a*) large print

(*b*) colour

(*c*) striking photographs and pictures

(*d*) unusual design and layout

(ii) *on Television and Radio:*

(*e*) evocative photography
(*f*) trick photographic effects
(*g*) music and noises.

Techniques to make people Remember Advertisements:

(*h*) repetition of advertisements
(*i*) repetition of key words within advertisement
(*j*) slogans and jingles which use—
      alliteration   rhyme   puns

Now complete the following sentences giving details of actual advertisements which use the presentation techniques listed above; you will, of course, have to carry out research (perhaps for homework) in order to complete them accurately.

(*a*) An advertisement for (*name of product*) which appeared in (*name and date of newspaper*) had print (*how many?*) inches high.

(*b*) A very colourful poster advertisement is the one for (*name of product*)

(*c*) The advertisement for (*name of product*) which appeared in (*name and date of newspaper*) used a very striking photograph.

(*d*) The design and layout of the (*name of product*) advertisement which I saw (*date and place where seen*) is very unusual.

(*e*) A recent television advertisement which uses evocative photography is the (*name of product*) advertisement.

(*f*) A recent television advertisement which uses trick photographic effects is the one for (*name of product*).

(*g*) The (*radio or television?*) advertisement for (*name of product*) uses loud (*music or noises?*) to attract attention.

(*h*) The advertisement for (*name of product*) appeared on television at least (*how many?*) times on (*date*).

(*i*) In the (*television, radio, or newspaper?*) advertisement for (*name of product*) the name of the product is repeated at least (*how many?*) times.

(*j*) This slogan for (*name of product*) uses alliteration: "(*quote slogan*)"

(*k*) This (*slogan or jingle*)? for (*name of product*) uses rhyme: "(*quote slogan or jingle*)".

(*l*) This slogan for (*name of product*) contains a pun: "(*quote slogan*)".

(*m*) I think this jingle for (*name of product*) is very catchy: "(*quote jingle*)".

235

3. *Comprehensive Practice; Advertisement Analysis.* Study the advertisement on page 235 and then answer, in complete sentences, the following questions.

  (*a*) The advertisement is designed to catch a reader's eye by appealing to his or her vanity. Explain exactly how it does this. Is there any connection between this and the actual contents of the advertisement? Do you consider such a technique dishonest in any way?

  (*b*) Quote a phrase which plays upon fear.

  (*c*) Where does the advertisement use scientific jargon? Why does it do this?

  (*d*) Where does the advertisement flatter the reader?

  (*e*) How does the advertisement play upon our faith in experts?

  (*f*) Pick out an illogical contradiction that occurs in the advertisement.

  (*g*) Pick out evocative phrases and comment on the figures of speech that they contain.

  (*h*) Pick out a catchy sentence that would be suitable for a radio or television jingle. What figure of speech is used in this sentence?

  (*i*) How does the wording of the advertisement help to give the reader the idea that he or she is tired and listless?

  (*j*) Is this advertisement aimed at men, or at women, or at both? How can you tell?

  (*k*) To what sort of people would it particularly appeal? If you were to ask a random selection of 100 normal adults whether they had been feeling "a little tired and listless lately", how many, do you think, would reply "yes"? Would you expect these people to be persuaded to buy Gunge as a result of reading the advertisement?

  (*l*) Do you think an average person who had never studied the techniques of advertising would realise how this advertisement was attempting to play upon his or her feelings?

  (*m*) In what sort of newspapers and magazines would you expect to find this advertisement? For what sort of newspapers and magazines is it unsuitable, and why?

  (*n*) What is the purpose of the illustrations?

  (*o*) What information is *not* given in this advertisement that you would want to know before buying the product?

4. *Making Up Advertisements; Symbols.* (i) Here is a real test of your ability to write persuasively. Imagine that you are responsible for advertising:

    (*a*) slow cars, incapable of going faster than 20 m.p.h.
    (*b*) old-fashioned mangles
    (*c*) either refrigerators or suntan lotion—to Eskimos
    (*d*) blunt razor blades
    (*e*) packets of weed seeds.

Make up advertisements for the above products. You may incorporate illustrations into your advertisements.

(ii) Imagine that you are responsible for advertising three brands of a certain product. Although all three brands are basically the same, each one is to be advertised in a different way, to attract consumers with different requirements. Take detergents, for example. Some housewives will consider cleaning power the most important factor, others will want a detergent which is gentle to their hands, others a powder which leaves the clothes smelling fresh and sweet. To help differentiate between the three brands, each one could be associated with an appropriate symbol. You might choose a picture of a wave smashing against a cliff for the first detergent, a dove for the second, and a rose for the third.

Consider the products listed below. Decide on three different qualities that people look for in each of the products, and then choose appropriate symbols for each of the three brands. Explain why you have chosen these symbols.

    (*a*) cigarettes (*b*) petrol (*c*) pain relievers (*d*) toothpaste (*e*) instant coffee
    (*f*) disinfectant (*g*) men's hair lotion, or women's hair lacquer
    (*h*) margarine

Correct English, and Vocabulary

5. *Ambiguity.* (i) "The Hidden Persuaders" is a book with a fundamentally serious purpose—to make the average person aware of the manipulation techniques employed by "depth persuaders". The author, Vance Packard, is a journalist, and some people have criticised the book because of its journalistic style and approach.

One of the most common faults of journalistic work is hasty composition, which often leads to ambiguity.

Consider these four sentences quoted from the passage and compare each one with the two possible meanings given below it. Explain the difference in meaning between the two versions and state which meaning Vance Packard intended to convey.

(*a*) "Some cosmetics firms began spending a fourth of all their income from sales on advertising and promotion."

Some cosmetics firms began spending, on advertising and promotion, a fourth of all their income from sales.

Some cosmetics firms began spending a fourth of all their income from sales based on advertising and promotion.

(*b*) " . . . economically, the freezers didn't make sense when you added up the initial cost, the monthly cost added on the electric bill, and the amount of frozen left-overs in the box that would eventually be thrown out."

Economically, the freezers didn't make sense when you added up the initial cost, the monthly cost added on the electric bill, and, in the box that would eventually be thrown out, the amount of frozen left-overs.

Economically, the freezers didn't make sense when you added up the initial cost, the monthly cost added on the electric bill, and the amount of frozen left-overs that would eventually be thrown out of the box.

(*c*) "A Milwaukee advertising executive commented to colleagues in print on the fact that women will pay two dollars and a half for skin cream. . ."

To colleagues who were in print, a Milwaukee advertising executive commented on the fact that women will pay two dollars and a half for skin cream.

To his colleagues, a Milwaukee advertising executive commented in print, on the fact that women will pay two dollars and a half for skin cream.

(*d*) "Now this laxative image was not entirely unfortunate."

At the present time this laxative image was not entirely unfortunate.

Now, this laxative image was not entirely unfortunate.

(N.B. When punctuated as above, "now" has much the same meaning as "however".)

How serious do you consider the above ambiguities to be? Are readers likely to be misled by them?

(ii) Ambiguity frequently arises when the word "only" is incorrectly positioned in a sentence. Explain how the following sentence, quoted from the passage, differs in meaning from the one below it.

(a) "Soap, he explained, only promises to make them clean.
   Soap, he explained, promises only to make them clean.
   Which meaning did Vance Packard intend?
   Now explain the difference in meaning between these sentences.
(b) Only soap, he explained, promises to make them clean.
(c) Soap, he explained, promises to make only them clean.
(d) Soap, only he explained, promises to make them clean.
6. *Vocabulary*. Give the meaning of each of the following words as it
   is used in the extract.

intimidating	durability	devitalization
obsolete	vehemence	parsimonious
standardization	dentifrice	connotations
potent	decrepitude	concept

Explain in simpler English, the following expressions. How many of
them would you class as advertising jargon?

psychological obsolescence	a peg for ad copy
basic motivation	motivational analysts
seemingly inverse logic	symbol manipulators
prestige purposes	dynamic image

TOPICS FOR WRITTEN WORK

1. Write an essay giving your opinions about advertising.
Hints
   You could start by saying whether you think the techniques employed
in modern advertising are in any way unfair. Do they, in your opinion,
succeed in making people spend money on products that they do not
really need or want? Can you quote any advertisements that give a
misleading impression of the products concerned? Is too much money
spent on advertising? Would you like to see stricter regulations about
advertising? For example, should it be compulsory for an advertisement
to include the price of the product, the name of the manufacturer, etc?
Would you go even further and ban all persuasive techniques, i.e. make it
illegal for advertisements to contain anything but purely factual material?
Could such regulations be enforced? Comment on the issues raised by
the preceding questions, and on any other points that you have definite
views about. The discussion points in "Oral Work" No. 1 may provide
you with more material for this essay.

2. Comment on the facts given about portable tape-recorders (fictitious) in the table below.

Make	Price	Dimensions w × h × d (cm)	Weight (kg)	No. of hrs. per 1p given by batteries	Sound quality	Recording quality	No. of faults developed during testing
Essex	£17·20	19 × 7 × 10	1·8	7	Poor	Fair	1
Supreme	£31·75	16 × 9 × 9	1·1	3	Fair	Very Good	0
Fab	£5·45	30 × 12 × 15	2·4	8	Fair	Poor	5
Royal	£11·35	21 × 10 × 15	2·2	5	Fair	Poor	2*
Classic	£17·60	20 × 7 × 12	2·2	9	Fair	Fairly Good	1
Tudor	£19·95	25 × 11 × 12	2·7	9	Fairly Good	Fair	3
Majestic	£25·25	21 × 6 × 10	1·8	10	Fair	Fair	1

* Potentially dangerous fault

Hints

Do not simply reproduce in writing all the information given in the table; draw conclusions from it. The following questions suggest the sort of comments you should make. Which tape-recorder do you consider is the "best buy" for the average consumer? Which recorders would you select as your second and third choices? What advantages does your best buy have over these? In what respects are they superior to your best buy? Are there any machines that you would advise people *not* to buy? For what types of consumer might you recommend (*a*) the Supreme (*b*) the Fab? Can you see any relationship between quality and price? (Support your answer by referring to data given in the table). How does the information given in this table differ from that given in an advertising brochure? How useful would a table such as this be for someone wishing to buy a portable tape-recorder? What else would you want to know about the machines before buying one?

3. Compose a scenario for a short television advertisement.
Hints

Study the example of an actual television advertisement given on page 241. Follow its construction, in terms of layout and the amount of detail provided, when writing your own scenario. Use at least some of the presentation techniques discussed in Exercise 2 of this chapter to ensure that your advertisement would be noticed and remembered if it were shown on television. You may either invent a brand name for the product you are advertising, or use an existing, well known brand name.

TV/FILM SCRIPT

Client	
Product	
Job No.	
Time Length	
Total Word Count	
Transmission Date	
Comm. No.	
Title	
Revision No.	
Date typed	

SCRIPT
AS
RECORDED

Signed

....

Date...................

Signature for Client Approval..

FRAME	VISION	SOUND
1.	Open up on C.U. plate of beans on toast.	1½ seconds silence
2.	Mother puts plate in front of boy of about 8. Evidence of Dad eating his breakfast can be seen right of frame.	Mother: These are the last beans you'll have for a fortnight. We don't get any in that continental hotel.
3.	Boy stares after Mother aghast ...	
4.	... and begins to eat his beans rapidly.	A million housewives every day, Pick up a tin of beans and say ...
5.	Cut to super: BEANZ MEANZ HEINZ	... BEANZ MEANZ HEINZ
6.	Cut to Mother in hall with suitcase and holiday equipment. Outside Dad is packing cases into the car.	Mother: Hurry, Colin, we're ready to go.
7.	Camera pans round to boy who is staggering under the weight of a large hold-all.	
8.	Camera tracks in as Mother thrusts her hands into hold-all.	Mother: What on earth do you have in here?
9.	Mother pulls out one of many tins of beans ...	Colin: We couldn't go without beans for two weeks, Mum!
10.	... and camera follows tin up to C.U. of Mother reacting as jingle begins.	A million housewives every day ...
11.	Cut to tin of beans in limbo. Hand comes in and takes it out of frame.	... Pick up a tin of beans and say ...
12.	Super: BEANZ MEANZ HEINZ	... BEANZ MEANZ HEINZ.

1. The following are some of the rules from the 1st edition of "The Independent Television Code of Advertising Standards and Practice." Discuss the usefulness of these rules, saying why you think they were made and whether, in fact, they are adhered to by advertisers. (See "Activities and Research" No. 1)

(a) "Audible matter in advertisements must not be excessively noisy or strident."

(b) "Advertisements must not without justifiable reason play on fear."

(c) (i) "No advertisement which encourages children to enter strange places or to converse with strangers in an effort to collect coupons, wrappers, labels, etc., is allowed."

(ii) "No advertisement for a commercial product or service is allowed if it contains any appeal to children which suggests in any way that unless the children themselves buy or encourage other people to buy the product or service they will be failing some duty or lacking in loyalty towards some person or organisation . . . "

(iii) "No advertisement is allowed which leads children to believe that if they do not own the product advertised they will be inferior in some way to other children or that they are liable to be held in contempt or ridicule for not owning it."

(iv) "While it is recognised that children are not the direct purchasers of many products over which they are allowed to exercise preference, care should be taken that they are not encouraged to make themselves a nuisance to other people in the interests of any particular product or service. In an advertisement offering a free gift, a premium or a competition for children, the main emphasis of the advertisement must be on the product with which the offer is associated."

(v) "To help in the fair portrayal of gifts for children, an advertisement should, where necessary, make it easy to see the true size of the gift by showing it in relation to some common object against which its scale can be judged."

(d) "Advertisements for products or services coming within the recognised character of, or specifically concerned with, the following are not acceptable:
(i) products or treatments for bust development . . .
(ii) contraceptives

(*iii*) smoking cures

(*iv*) products for the treatment of alcoholism

(*v*) contact or corneal lenses

(*vi*) clinics for the treatment of scalp and hair

(*vii*) products for the treatment of haemorrhoids."

(*e*) "In advertisements for medicines, treatments and products which are claimed to promote health or to be beneficial in illness, the following are not allowable:

(*i*) visual presentation of doctors, dentists, pharmaceutical chemists, nurses, midwives, etc., which give the impression of professional advice or recommendation, and

(*ii*) statements giving the impression of professional advice or recommendation made by persons who appear in the advertisement and who are presented, either directly or by implication as being qualified to give such advice or recommendation."

(*f*) "No advertisement should state or imply that good health is likely to be endangered solely because people do not supplement their diets with vitamins."

2. The Consumer's Association is a non-profit-making organisation that carries out independent and very stringent tests on a wide variety of goods and services. The results of these tests, which give accurate, factual information, are published in their magazine "Which?" This magazine is sent to all members of the Association, who pay an annual subscription. "Which?" is obtainable from the reference section of most public libraries, and a number of school libraries also take it. If your teacher can bring an index of all the products and services that have been tested, each member of the class can choose an item in which he is particularly interested, obtain the appropriate issue of "Which?", and report back to the rest of the class, in his own words, the results of the Association's tests.

3. A persuasive and unscrupulous door-to-door salesman at work: use this as the basis for a series of impromptu sketches. The people on whom he will call can decide beforehand what sort of characters they are going to be, but the salesman should not be told this. He must adapt his sales talk to suit the characters, as he meets them.

4. Hold a debate or a discussion on the following motion:
"Without advertising, trade would stagnate, and the world would be a poorer and much duller place."

ACTIVITIES AND RESEARCH

1. Make a detailed survey of television advertisements appearing over a period of, say, three weeks. See if you can find any that break or nearly break one or more of the rules listed in "Oral Work" No. 1. The class could arrange a rota for this survey so that as many advertisements as possible are examined.

2. If you and a number of others in your class find the magazine "Which?" interesting and useful, you may each like to pay a small amount towards a year's subscription, so that you can receive the next twelve issues.

3. You could test a number of brands of a certain product in the same way that the Consumers' Association does. The product that you choose to investigate will have to be one that does not require complicated equipment for testing, and is relatively inexpensive, e.g. ballpoint pens costing less than fifteen newpence. Each brand must be given exactly the same test, which must not rely on subjective impressions. Only facts should be given, and, on the basis of these you should recommend a "best buy". With a cheap ballpoint pen, for example, you could give: (a) the make, and the shop at which it was purchased (b) the price (c) details of its construction, e.g. whether it has a clip, whether the point is retractable (d) the price of refills, if these are available (e) the amount of writing that can be done before the ink runs out; this could be tested objectively by seeing how many lines, of a fixed length, can be drawn with the pen (f) the ease with which the pen writes, whether it blots, etc.; this can be judged from the lines drawn with the pen (g) the results of simple tests to see how sturdy the pen is, e.g. it could be dropped from a height of, say, thirty feet.

4. Cut out advertisements in magazines and newspapers and mount them on the wall of your classroom. Underneath each one put a brief explanation of the techniques it uses to make its appeal.

5. Much of this chapter has been concerned with advertising which employs "unfair" techniques. But there are a great many advertisements which do not fall into this category, which give ample information, and which are very clever and well designed. Collect examples of, or make notes about, advertisements which you think are of a high standard and which present their products attractively and effectively without using unfair pressures to promote sales.

244

FURTHER READING

The Hidden Persuaders by Vance Packard (Longmans; Penguin).

This account of the techniques developed and applied by American, "mental-depth" advertisers has been described as both alarming and entertaining. Although most of the material is American, the author points out in a short foreword that we, in Britain, "have little ground for complacency" and that "no-one anywhere can be sure nowadays that he is not being worked upon by the depth persuaders". It is a book which is interesting, informative, and easy to read; it will cause you to look at advertisements more closely, and with more understanding and concern than before.

The Status Seekers (Longmans; Penguin).

In this study, Vance Packard examines the classes into which American society is being divided. He looks at the behaviour, the cars, the clothes, etc., that Americans use in order to maintain and improve their status in society. As with *The Hidden Persuaders*, the book's findings can be applied very easily to Great Britain and other European countries.

The Waste Makers (Longmans; Penguin).

This is a useful follow-up to *The Hidden Persuaders*; it develops in much greater detail one of the points to be found in the first section of this chapter's extract—"the creation of wants and desires" in order to ensure that consumption keeps up with production. It examines the argument that "if consumers exercise their option not to buy a large share of what is produced, a great depression is not far behind", and paints a vivid picture of America "stampeded into the stores by a hurricane of advertising" that is so much a part of this age of over-production.

The Pyramid Climbers (Longmans; Penguin).

Although the subject may not seem of such immediate interest as some of the author's other studies, this look at the top men in the American business world is still very readable. The typical American executive emerges as a "male, six foot, humourless, college-trained, white Anglo-Saxon Protestant", who is devoted to his work and has little time for other aspects of life, such as reading, or his wife.

CHAPTER 16

The World of Work

The action of the play takes place in the kitchen of the Tivoli restaurant.

CAST:

Raymond	}	Pastrycooks
Paul		
Max	Butcher	
Magi	Night Porter	
Dimitri	Kitchen Porter	
Anne	Dessert and Coffee	
Bertha	Vegetable Cook	
Daphne	}	Waitresses
Gwen		
Cynthia		

CHARACTERS MENTIONED

Peter	German Cook
Gaston	Cypriot Cook
Monique	Waitress
Mr. Marango	Proprietor

ANNE: Hey, Raymond, tell me, what happened to Peter in the end, you know, last night?

RAYMOND: Now he's a silly boy, eh? Don't you think so? I don't even know what it was all about anyway. You know, Paul?

PAUL: All I know is he had a fight with Gaston. Why? I don't know. Over a ladle I think, or maybe a . . .

MAX: He's a bloody German, a fool, that's what he is. He is always quarrelling, always. There's no one he hasn't quarrelled with, am I right? No one! That's some scheme that is, exchanging cooks! What do we want to exchange cooks for? Three years he's been here, three years! (*Exits to get more beer*).

ANNE: Ah, the boy's in love.

RAYMOND: What love! You ever see him? When Monique does a turn as hostess by the stairs he watches her through that mirror there. (*Points to glass partition.*)

ANNE: Rubbish.

RAYMOND: And he walks round the kitchen and looks to see if she's talking or flirting with any of the customers.

ANNE: I don't believe it.

BERTHA: Never.

RAYMOND: You don't believe me?

PAUL: And they quarrel in front of everybody as well. They shout at each other. Shout! You know, sometimes she doesn't even look at him, and waits for her orders with her back turned.

ANNE: The poor boy. He's no parents you know. But what happened last night? I want to know.

(*MAGI re-enters.*)

MAX: Ask Magi.

MAGI: Any coffee, Anne?

ANNE: Sure dear. (*Pours.*) Help yourself.

RAYMOND: Hey Magi, what happened with Peter last night, uh?

MAGI (*unconcerned*): They nearly killed him.

ANNE: Oh God.

RAYMOND (*gesticulating*): But what was it all about, tell me? I don't know nothing, me.

MAGI: Well *you* should know that—I wasn't here.

PAUL: All we know is that they suddenly started shouting at each other. And you know, Peter always shouts more than the other and you can always hear Peter—well, so then it stopped, and then a few seconds later they were fighting, and I saw Gaston raise a boning knife and Peter knock it out of his hand, and then . . .

RAYMOND: And then he lifted him and nearly sat him on the stove and . . .

PAUL: And then the Chef came along and . . .

ANNE: Well I saw the Chef separate them and I heard Gaston say "I haven't finished yet, it's not over yet," but I still don't know what it was all about.

PAUL: Who cares? I say good-morning to Peter but never good-night.

MAGI: Well I came in at nine last night. The boys were changing and suddenly Peter comes and Gaston follows him. Gaston says Peter called him a lousy Cypro and the boys make circle round him and want to murder him! All of them . . . but Peter says "No, everyone for me is the same—it makes no difference race, you misunderstand . . ." They all wanted to hit him! And he was scared! I never seen him so white.

ANNE: But what was it about to begin with?

247

MAX: A ladle, I tell you.

PAUL: Who knows? There's always fights, who knows how they begin?

MAGI (*laying down cup*): Well, I'm going.

PAUL: Have a good kip, old son.

ANNE: And I must get started too. (*Looks round empty kitchen.*) You wouldn't think this place will become a madhouse in two hours, would you now. (*Moves off with MAGI.*)

> (*RAYMOND, PAUL and MAX continue to work in silence. Enter DAPHNE, GWEN and CYNTHIA, waitresses, to dining-room.*)

DAPHNE: So if he doesn't come home tonight I'm going to leave.

CYNTHIA: Well he does have to work in the afternoon.

GWEN: That's right.

MAX: Any luck on the pools, Ray?

RAYMOND: Huh!

MAX: Norwich and Leyton let me down. Twenty points. Twenty points!

> (*Enter HETTIE from dining-room for a coffee. Pause.*)

HETTIE: Morning, Annie love.

PAUL: Read about the man in the mental home who won thirty-five thousand pounds?

RAYMOND: And his wife turned up after eighteen years?

> (*Enter DAPHNE from dining-room for a coffee.*)

PAUL: Eighteen years!

> (*Pause. DIMITRI enters. A Cypriot kitchen porter, young, good-looking and intelligent. He is carrying in his hand a home-made portable radio. He is happy as he takes it to PAUL. He speaks with an accent.*
> *Enter MOLLY, JACKIE, waitresses, to dining-room.*)

DIMITRI: I make it Paul, I make it. There! (*Lays it on table near by.*) She does not look handsome. I'm sorry for that.

PAUL: Ah you good boy, Dimitri. Can we play it? (*He looks round to see if authority is in sight. Only DAPHNE and HETTIE approach. One has a bucket in her hand and her hair is tied up with a scarf. The other one is similarly attired and carries a feather duster.*) Anyone around?

HETTIE: (*pointing to portable*): What is it, Paul?

PAUL: Is Marango around yet?

DAPHNE: Not yet. Whose is it?

PAUL: It's mine. Dimitri here made it.

RAYMOND: You made it on your own? All those little wires and plugs? Tell me, what are you doing here? Why you waste your time with dishes in this place? You can't get a job in a factory?

DIMITRI: A factory? You think I find happiness in a factory? What I make there? Uh? This little wire, you see it? This I would make, or that . . . what you call it?

PAUL: Knob.

DIMITRI: Knob. That perhaps I could put in. All day I would screw in knobs. I tell you, in a factory a man makes a little piece till he becomes a little piece, you know what I mean?

HETTIE: It's true, he's right, you know.

DIMITRI: Sure I know, my brother, he works there. I know all right.

RAYMOND: Hey Dimitri, *you* know what happened to Peter last night?

DIMITRI: They nearly kill him. Why?

DAPHNE: Oh my Gawd.

DIMITRI: But you think it was all Peter's fault? They all wanted to fight. Listen, you put a man in the plate-room all day, he's got dishes to make clean, and stinking bins to take away, and floors to sweep, what else there is for him to do—he wants to fight. He got to show he is a man some way. So—blame him!

(*DIMITRI turns on the radio, which plays a loud rock 'n' roll tune.*)

(from *The Kitchen* by Arnold Wesker)

APPRECIATION AND DISCUSSION

1. Using the comments of his fellow workers as a guide, try to describe Peter's personality. Was he generally well-liked?

2. What is Peter's attitude to Monique? What sort of relationship do they seem to have? Do you know any people with a similar relationship?

3. What sort of person does Max appear to be? Quote from the extract to support your assessment.

4. Can you deduce anything about Anne's character from her comments?

5. What did Paul mean when he said, "I say good-morning to Peter but never good-night"?

6. Why was the restaurant due to become a "madhouse" in two hours?

7. ". . . in a factory a man makes a little piece till he becomes a little piece." Can you explain this statement of Dimitri's more fully? Do you agree with his philosophy?

8. "There's always fights, who knows how they begin?" What was Dimitri's explanation for the fight? How does this fit in with his philosophy about working in a factory?

9. Do you think the conversation in this extract is realistic? What sort of topics do people talk about while they are at work? What does your conversation normally centre around (a) at school (b) at home (c) in your leisure time with your friends?

10. What career are you hoping to follow when you leave school? Would you prefer an outdoor job or an indoor job? Would you rather work with a crowd of people, or on your own?

11. Discuss the relative importance of the following factors when choosing a job (a) on leaving school (b) after getting married (c) if you had a family to support.
(i) high, but variable wages, no security (ii) moderate wages, with considerable security, e.g. sickness pay, pension (iii) moderate wage, with a short working week and long holidays (iv) low starting wage but chances of promotion (v) moderate wage, with varied and interesting work (vi) dull, routine work, with high wages.

12. "All workers should be compelled to join a union because those people who opt out, and do not pay union dues or join in strikes for higher pay and better working conditions, benefit from the efforts of union members without making any effort themselves." Discuss this statement.

Toads

Why should I let the toad WORK
　　Squat on my life?
Can't I use my wit as a pitchfork
　　And drive the brute off?

Six days of the week it soils
　　With its sickening poison—
Just for paying a few bills!
　　That's out of proportion.

Lots of folk live on their wits:
　　Lecturers, lispers,
Losels, loblolly-men, louts—
　　They don't end up as paupers.

Lots of folk live up lanes
　　With a fire in a bucket;
Eat windfalls and tinned sardines—
　　They seem to like it.

Their nippers have got bare feet,
　　Their unspeakable wives
Are skinny as whippets—and yet
　　No one actually *starves*.

Ah, were I courageous enough
　　To shout "Stuff your pension!"
But I know, all too well, that's the stuff
　　That dreams are made on:

For something sufficiently toad-like
　　Squats in me too;
Its hunkers are heavy as hard luck
　　And cold as snow.

And will never allow me to blarney
　　My way to getting
The fame and the girl and the money
　　All at one sitting.

I don't say, one bodies the other
　　One's spiritual truth;
But I do say it's hard to lose either,
　　When you have both.

Philip Larkin

DISCUSSING THE POEM

1. What does the poet mean by calling work "a toad"?
2. Do most of the people that you know work "just to pay a few bills", or do they also get some satisfaction from their jobs?
3. What kinds of people who don't work are mentioned in the poem? Does the writer envy them?
4. Why does he want to shout: "Stuff your pension!"?
5. What daydreams does the poet have—what would he like to be able to do? What prevents him from making these daydreams come true?
6. Do you feel the same way about school or about a part-time job as the author of this poem feels about work?

TECHNIQUES

The Use of Language, and Style

1. *Diagramatic Explanation.* Once you begin work and start earning a regular income, you will soon find yourself faced with a bewildering array of regulations and instructions, which often seem very complex. There will be forms about Income Tax, Sickness, Benefit, Pensions, and Savings Schemes, to name but a few; in addition, you will probably take out hire purchase agreements and private insurances, for which there are often complicated contracts.

According to two psychologists, Dr. Peter Wilson and Dr. Sheila Jones, the English language does not lend itself easily to explaining complex regulations. They give the following example from regulations about retirement pensions for married women. Which do you find easier to understand—(*a*) or (*b*)?

(a) 'The earliest age at which a woman can draw a retirement pension is 60. On her own insurance she can get a pension when she reaches that age, if she has then retired from regular employment. Otherwise she has to wait until she retires or reaches age 65. At age 65 pensions can be paid irrespective of retirement. On her husband's insurance, however, she cannot get a pension, even though she is over 60, until he has reached age 65 and retired from regular employment, or until he is 70 if he does not retire before reaching that age'.

MARRIED WOMAN'S (flat rate) RETIREMENT PENSION

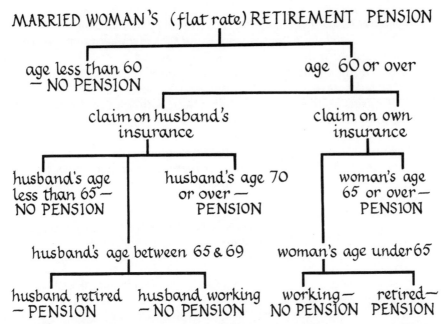

Try to express the information given above in the form of continuous prose, so that it can be easily understood without the help of the diagram.

Given below are the regulations, to be found at the back of a Post Office Savings Book, for withdrawal of money from the Post Office Savings Bank. They are not unduly complex, but see if you can set them out any more clearly as a simple diagram. Afterwards, try re-writing them in your own words, re-arranging the order in which the information is presented here, if you feel this would be an improvement. Would a more frequent use of the active voice bring about any improvement?

WITHDRAWALS.—Up to £20 is payable on demand at a Savings Bank Post Office, but the paying officer retains the book for examination at the Chief Office when more than one withdrawal on demand over £5 is made in any period of seven days. Not more than one withdrawal on demand is permitted in any one day. Larger amounts can be withdrawn by notice to the Chief Office on a form of application obtainable at a Post Office. Withdrawals may also be made by telegraph. Four days (cash deposits) or eight days (cheque deposits) must elapse before a deposit is withdrawn. These days exclude Sundays, Public Holidays and the days of deposit and withdrawal.

2. *Comprehensive Practice; Press Styles and Emotive Language.*

> " 'The Kitchen' achieves something that few playwrights have ever attempted: it dramatises work." *Observer*
>
> "Flashing, illuminating, moving, funny, passionate, authentic." *Daily Express*
>
> "Charged with emotion, with rhythm, with scale and with a certain grandeur." *Sunday Times*
>
> "A brilliant and original piece." *New Statesman*

The above are snippets from four Press reviews of "The Kitchen", all praising the play. Critics are rarely so unanimous in their views, however. Study the following two reviews and then write answers to the questions below them.

> 1. Here at last. An honest, down-to-earth play about ordinary folk. A real slice of life served up with a spicy sauce of humour to help you forget your troubles—that's "If His Lordship Pleases" at the Crofton Empire this week. His Lordship: none other than Tony Smithson, fresh from his success as "Our Tone" on TV.
>
> Fans rocked with laughter from first scene to tenth curtain-call last night. The impossible scrapes he gets into turn mum and dad grey with despair. And when girl-friend one (Betty Buding) faces girl-friend two (Sonia Harvey) in the Hansons' front parlour . . !
>
> This is the Tony we have all learned to love, now proving that he goes over just as big in the live theatre. More, please.
>
> 2. The superficial domestic comedy "If His Lordship Pleases" (Crofton Empire) serves as further proof that television material is unsuited to the legitimate theatre. In the ITV series, Tony Smithson's role of the inadvertantly disruptive adolescent is amusing enough for a twenty-minute sketch; two hours of this unrealistic nonsense is simply tedious, and the actors themselves showed signs of the strain. Betty Buding and Sonia Harvey are accomplished young actresses in their own right—it is painful to see them as mere foils for Mr. Smithson's formula comedy. No doubt the star's devoted following will ensure this production a long West End run, but it can never be more than a light television show repeated *ad nauseam*.

(*a*) Comparing both these reviews, what can you conclude about the plot and setting of this play?

(*b*) What did the first reviewer think of other plays that had been recently produced, in contrast to this one? How does he imply this?

(*c*) How does each reviewer inform his readers that this play presents Tony Smithson in a similar role to his television one? Quote the relevant phrases.

(d) What was the theatre audience's reaction to this play? How does each reviewer inform us of this?

(e) Which reviewer does more justice to the supporting cast? What reason might there be for the difference in emphasis between the two reviews?

(f) What are the second reviewer's objections to this play?

(g) What does the second reviewer mean by the following?
domestic comedy — the legitimate theatre — the inadvertantly disruptive adolescent — unrealistic nonsense — mere foils — formula comedy — a long West End run — repeated *ad nauseam*

(h) Which of these two reviews is more likely to appear in a popular newspaper? How do the reviewers appeal to or flatter their respective audiences?

(i) The publicity for a play (in posters, newspapers, handbills, etc.) often quotes a few words or phrases from different reviews. What short quotations do you think a publicity manager (especially one who is not scrupulously honest) could take from these reviews?

(j) Study the sentence and paragraph structure of these pieces and comment on them. Why, for example, does the first reviewer use incomplete sentences? Which style do you prefer?

(k) Would you want to see this play after reading these reviews? Give reasons for your decision.

3. *Definitions.* Bearing in mind the advice given in Exercise 6, Chapter 14, write a single sentence definition of each of the people listed below. Then, after your definition, write another three or four sentences describing in more detail the work of each person.
   (a) a school caretaker   (e) a plumber
   (b) a cashier   (f) a nurse
   (c) a draughtsman   (g) a telephonist
   (d) a typist   (h) a bus conductor

Correct English, and Vocabulary

4. *Double Negative; Common Mistakes.* (i) One rule for solving certain problems in Mathematics is that "two minuses make a plus". The same rule applies in English. Two negatives in the same sentence can make it into a positive statement.
   e.g. RAYMOND: . . . I don't know nothing. (Incorrect)
   This means: I know something.
   What Raymond meant to say was:
   I don't know anything. *or* I know nothing.

255

Correct the following sentences, which also contain double negative mistakes.

(*a*) You don't win nothing on the football pools.

(*b*) He never goes nowhere with his girl-friend.

(*c*) She won't marry him, neither now nor tomorrow.

(*d*) He hasn't got nobody to help him.

(*e*) There are a lot of storm clouds overhead, so I shan't be surprised if it doesn't rain in a minute.

Can you find a correct use of the double negative in one of Max's speeches?

(ii) Which three of these five quotations from the play contain the following mistakes: singular verb with a plural noun; different pronouns for the same object; incorrect tense form of the verb?

(*a*) PAUL: All we know is that they suddenly started shouting at each other.

(*b*) MAGI: . . . I never seen him so white.

(*c*) PAUL: . . . There's always fights.

(*d*) MAX: Norwich and Leyton let me down.

(*e*) DIMITRI: . . . I make it. There. She does not look handsome.

Write out the incorrect sentences correctly. Then look through the extract and say what other alterations would be needed to make all the dialogue conform to the rules of formal English.

5. *Punctuation.* Because of the lack of punctuation, the two sentences quoted below are ambiguous. Say which of the possible meanings given beneath them Wesker intended.

Can you convey this meaning by inserting the correct punctuation in the original sentence?

(*a*) ANNE: He's no parents you know.

He has no parents that you know.

You know that he has no parents.

(*b*) DAPHNE: So if he doesn't come home tonight I'm going to leave.

So I'm going to leave tonight if he doesn't come home.

So I'm going to leave if he doesn't come home tonight.

Consider carefully the punctuation of this chapter's extract from "The Kitchen", and discuss how it could be improved; pay particular attention to Wesker's use of commas.

e.g. RAYMOND: But what was it all about, tell me?

Here, two sentences might be more appropriate.

But what was it all about? Tell me.

TOPICS FOR WRITTEN WORK

1. (*a*) Write about the career that you hope to follow when you leave school.

(*b*) If you have not yet made up your mind, write about the jobs you are considering.

Hints

In your first sentence, state what job or what sort of job you wish to take up. What has caused you to choose this job? Have you been influenced by the advice of friends, relatives or teachers? Have you any experience of this sort of work? What qualifications do you need? How long do you intend to continue studying, either at your present school or elsewhere? Does the job involve a period of training or apprenticeship? What is the starting wage? What does it rise to? Are there opportunities for promotion? What further advice and information about the job would you appreciate before you actually start work?

2. As a poem or in prose, write a vivid description of someone at work.

Hints

Use all your senses to collect details of the person and his place of work. Describe not only his appearance, his manner, his surrounding, and his job, but also his attitude towards his work, and the way in which he is regarded by other people. If possible, base your description on someone you know. Make it as precise as possible, so that the character you are describing emerges as a distinct individual.

3. Write a letter applying for a job.

Hints

Set this out as a business letter. Remember that if you are writing to a firm, you will begin your letter: *Dear Sirs*; if you are writing to one particular person in the firm, you will begin: *Dear Sir*. Follow the plan given below, when composing your letter.

Introduction. Give full details of the job that you are applying for, and say how you know about it, e.g. where and when you saw it advertised.

Development. State how old you are, where you have been educated (including dates), what qualifications and training you have, and any other information that may be relevant, e.g. posts of responsibility that you have held at school.

Conclusion. Ask for an application form and say when you will be available for an interview (if, these points have been mentioned in connection with the job). Finish the letter with *Yours faithfully*, and sign your first name and surname.

Pupils' Work

The Blacksmith

The blacksmith working on his anvil
Working, working, working hard,
Making a weather cock for the church steeple,
Fixing a shoe on the old cart horse.

Blacksmith, blacksmith, where have you gone?
The smithy is empty, the fire is out.
Long ago were the days when he stood at his work.
Making cocks for the steeple and shoes for the horse.

Lindsay Flaxman

The Closing of the Forge

As I walked down the street, I found the old stone building of the forge, its old Kentish ragstone walls, the weathered tiles, and the smoke curling out of the top of the chimney. Soon I could hear the hard high metallic ring of the hammer as it smote the red-hot horse-shoe. The ringing stopped, and I heard a sizzle as the shoe was thrust into the water trough. As I came round the corner by the butcher, Mr. Bacon, I saw more smoke coming from the chimney, I guessed the smith was using the big bellows which he had. But when I did see the forge, the smith was leaning over the lower part of the stable-like doors.

"How do!" said he. "Back 'ome again then? How long this time?"

I greeted him and told him that I had a month's holiday.

"Ah," said he, "and longer 'an they used to give us as kids, but I suppose they make you work harder."

I told him that I didn't know about that. He mumbled something about the weather and we said goodbye, then parted.

The last holidays I got off the bus to a village silent of ringing hammers. Mr. Bacon told me that the forge had been closed down and the smith had retired.

I remember the days when I would lean against the doorpost and watch him at his work. He would talk as he worked, and my mind would drift away into the misty summer heat and I would be brought back to life by the ringing of his hammer.

I remembered watching him like a boy watching a train, almost in a trance. The slow, strong movements he made with his hammer were like the starting of the "Flying Scotsman". The hissing sounds of the hot object as it went into the water were like that of a local train letting off steam in the station. Then the smith himself with a body like that of the "Golden Arrow".

From then on whenever I passed the silent forge I felt a lump in my throat. It's like the old craft dying, having to make way for the factories of tomorrow.

Charles Fyson

ORAL WORK

1. Act or tape-record this chapter's extract from "The Kitchen".
2. Arrange a series of interviews between an employer, and people applying for a job. This will provide valuable practice for the time when you have to attend a real interview. The part of the employer could be taken either by your teacher or by a member of your class. Consider beforehand all the questions that you think an employer might ask, and work out answers to them. Be prepared, however, to have to answer unexpected questions. Afterwards, your teacher can tell you what you need to do to improve the impression that you create at an interview. These criticisms can then form the basis for a class discussion, in which other points, such as the sort of clothes that should or should not be worn at interviews, are also dealt with.
3. Each member of the class can read aloud his essay about the career he hopes to follow, putting a few important facts and figures on the blackboard. You should practise reading the essay aloud beforehand.
4. MAX: Any luck on the pools, Ray?
Every week millions of people, like Max and Ray, try their luck on the football pools. Hold a class discussion on this and other forms of gambling. Here are some of the questions you can consider.— Should people be discouraged from gambling? Are some forms of gambling worse than others? Are there any forms of gambling that you think should be made illegal? Should there be a limit on the amount a person can win in one bet? Should winnings be subject to income tax in the same way that earnings are? Is there any difference between money which is inherited or acquired by a stroke of good fortune, and money which is obtained as a result of deliberate gambling? What are the dangers facing someone who suddenly wins a large amount of money? If you were to win £10,000, how would you spend it?

ACTIVITIES AND RESEARCH

1. From encyclopaedias and other reference books, find out all you can about Trade Unions, the organisations to which employers belong, and other important institutions such as the Confederation of British Industries. Also look up the Factory Acts to find out what rights people at work are entitled to.
2. An officer of the Youth Employment Service may already have visited your school to talk about the careers that are open to you. If not, your teacher may be able to arrange for this to be done. You could also invite other people, such as a Trade Union official and a local employer, to talk to you about various aspects of the world of work.
3. Bring to school, copies of some of the official forms that a person at work has to deal with. The local offices of the Inland Revenue, the Ministry of Pensions and National Insurance, the Labour Exchange and the Youth Employment Service may be able to supply you with these documents and provide other information and advice.
4. Arrange class visits to nearby firms, so that you can see for yourselves what is involved in various kinds of jobs.

   Even though the day when you start work may seem to be a long way ahead, remember that you will be engaged in work for most of your life and that time spent now, carefully considering your career, may make all the difference to the attitude that you develop towards your work and the satisfaction you get from it.

FURTHER READING

The Kitchen by Arnold Wesker (Cape).

In the heat and tension of the overcrowded kitchen, the scurrying cooks and waitresses never really have time to understand one another or to develop close relationships. They can only get in one another's way, hit out, or despair. Near the end of the play, there is an unexpected and final burst of violence which emphasises this idea. The author himself worked as a pastry cook for four years.

Chicken Soup with Barley (Cape; Penguin; Longmans).

The centre of the play's action is a middle-aged Jewish woman, Sarah Kahn, and the story, which covers a period of twenty years, deals with the distintegration of Sarah's husband. Although it has a basically tragic theme, the play is full of humour and warmth. It forms part of a triology; the other two plays are *Roots* and *I'm Talking about Jerusalem*.

Roots (Longmans).

Beatie Bryant returns from London to stay with her working class family in Norfolk. She tells them about, and frequently quotes, Ronnie Kahn, the man she hopes to marry, and who has attempted (unsuccessfully, it later emerges) to make her "really aware and alive". Her family, however, resent her "preaching". Then Beatie receives a letter from Ronnie, breaking off their engagement. In her outburst of anger and frustration she finds that she is finally able to think and talk for herself.

Chips With Everything (Cape; Blackie).

The events of this play take place during the eight week period of square-bashing in the R.A.F. But it is no more a play about the R.A.F. than *The Kitchen* is a play about cooking. It is about a young man who rebels against the sort of life he is expected to follow, but who is defeated by being subtly absorbed into the very society against which he is rebelling.

CHAPTER 17

In Love

This short story consists of memories of youth in "the old home town", related in a casual, rather whimsical style.

It was very cold the year I broke a ligament in my right leg and fell in love with soft-eyed brown-haired angel-on-earth Emma Haines and got a job as a messenger boy after school and sent away to New York for a free booklet on how to get the most of out of anything and everything, anybody and everybody.

It was the coldest year in the history of the San Joaquin valley since 1854. The paper said it was, in cold print, and I guess it was. It was cold enough to make me hate to get up in the morning, even after the booklet came from New York and said I should do the things I didn't feel like doing.

The fundamental thing I didn't feel like doing was getting out of bed in the morning. All I wanted to do was sleep. I just didn't feel in the mood to get up and shiver in the cold.

The booklet from New York was severe, though. A constipated man pointed a menacing finger at you and asked, *Are you drifting down-stream? Only fools follow the line of least resistance. Wise men struggle against the forces of the world and finally reach goals of glory, fame and wealth.*

Even so, I thought. What sort of glory could a man struggle with the forces of the world for and get? And what could he be famous *as*?

I busted the ligament in my right leg playing football. It was the cold. If it hadn't been so cold when I had punted, I would have gotten it away very nicely, like on hot days, but instead all I did was snap a ligament and fall down with unholy pain and order my team mates to tackle the man carrying the ball: *Tackle him, I'm dying, don't let him make a touchdown.*

No general ever sank to defeat with greater dignity and irritation.

I didn't want to be a hero. I figured it might kill me and I didn't want to die, because I hadn't seen enough of the world. I hadn't talked to Emma Haines either . . . .

I rubbed a lot of Sloan's Liniment on my leg where it hurt and the liniment burned and my leg got very red, but in the morning I couldn't walk, so I didn't go to school. At nine o'clock the mailman brought me the booklet from the correspondence school in New York. I read it from cover to cover. I didn't know what the idea was, but it seemed to be that it was better to read text-books and learn stuff than to hang around poolrooms and smoke cigarettes. There was a picture of a young man sitting alone in a little room reading a book, and another picture of another young man leaning against the wall of a poolroom, having just spit into a spittoon. The young man who was reading the book was supposed to be the one to admire and imitate, but I didn't know. The other one seemed to be having a much better time. He had just hit the bull's eye and was watching a fellow make a tough shot.

Which of these young men will be a success? the booklet asked.

It didn't say what kind of a success. I could see the young man who was loafing around in poolrooms learning everything he could about billiards and becoming world's champion billiard player, but I couldn't see the young man reading the book being anything but a dope. What he'd probably do, I figured, was study a long time and then get a job as a clerk somewhere and be a success. Well, that was his affair.

I decided not to take the correspondence course . . . .

I'd always wanted to get a job as a messenger and make some money and buy some guns and fishing tackle and maybe a little Ford and spend a lot of time hunting and fishing, but I was always afraid to go in and ask for a job. I wasn't old enough for one thing, and for another I was scared, but when the ligament of my right leg busted and I could barely walk, let alone ride a bicycle, I went into the telegraph office and asked for a job, and got a job . . . .

My working hours were from four in the afternoon until twelve o'clock midnight, and it seemed like those were the coldest hours of the day and night . . . .

I wouldn't get to bed till one in the morning and the alarm clock would ring at seven. That was only six hours of sleep. I needed thirteen. I wouldn't want to get out of bed. It was too cold. But I would always get out of bed and have breakfast and jump on to my wheel and race to school because I knew I'd see Emma Haines. I'd be very sleepy all day. Emma Haines would be nearby, across the aisle, and I'd be very tired and pretty soon I'd start to sleep with my eyes wide open and our teacher, Mrs. Hagerty, would call my name and ask me a question and I'd be dead to the world.

I'd be dreaming about Emma Haines, who was across the aisle all the time . . . .

One day when I woke up and was yawning I noticed she was looking at me.

After school I saw her walking down the corridor with another girl whose Papa was rich. Emma Haine's Papa was just about the richest man in town. I don't know why I had to fall in love with her, but I did. I guess maybe it was because she was so well-fed-looking and smelled so good. I could smell her a block away, I guess. I went down the corridor, figuring I'd talk to Emma. I hadn't ever said anything to her. I caught up with her and the other rich girl, and they stopped, waiting for me to talk, but when I tried to open my mouth I found I had lock-jaw. The two girls got very sore, especially Emma, and they went away in a huff, passing remarks about certain fellows at school, including me.

It was mighty cold that night, and the streets were darker than ever. It was agony having telegrams to deliver to people in little houses on dark streets, in winter, and everybody with any sense inside, by a warm fire. I felt terrible. And Emma Haines taking an attitude like that. That was the worst of it. I thought it would kill me if Emma Haines didn't understand what sort of a guy I was, riding a bicycle all hours of the night through the dark streets, in the awful dark world, mad dogs chasing me, houses hidden, and everything cold. I'd just die if Emma Haines didn't know me and give me some of the well-fed glow that she had. I'd just go to sleep some night and never wake up again if that was the attitude she wanted to take.

I began to look at her more often at school, but her attitude went from bad to worse. She wouldn't even look at me. One day I put a little love letter on her desk. It said:

Emma, I love you, Dewey.

She handed the note to Mrs. Hagerty and Mrs. Hagerty said, Young man, did you write this appalling message?

Yes, ma'am, I said.

Go to the office, she said.

I went.

Mr. Bowler, the principal, was practically a giant. He said, Is this true, boy? Did you write this note?

Yes, sir, I said.

Don't you realize who Emma Haines is? he said.

Or do you? he added.

Well, I said, I know her father owns a lot of buildings and stores in town and a lot of farms in the country. I know he's rich.

265

And you wrote the note anyway? he said.

Yes, sir, I said.

It's one of the most touching love letters of our age, he said. I must punish you just the same. For the rest of the day you will act as my orderly. I'm too tired to give you a strapping.

I acted as Mr. Bowler's orderly for the rest of the day. He sent me six blocks to Pabst's for two hams on rye and two bottles of strawberry pop, and he made me eat one of the sandwiches and drink one of the bottles of pop.

One thing, though, he said, I think I must accept the obligation to tell you. Stop being in love with Emma Haines.

Why? I said.

It's no good, he said, She's a rich man's daughter. You're a poor man's son. It won't work.

It was terrible, but I guessed Mr. Bowler was right.

Maybe she loves me and don't know it, I said.

Not a chance, said Mr. Bowler. Just forget her. You'll get into a heap of trouble. What made you write that brief love letter?

I love her, I said.

Well, he said, it is well-written.

The winter was long and the paper said it was the coldest winter since the year 1854. I didn't get over being in love with Emma Haines until I don't know when. I saw her riding around in classy automobiles with boys whose fathers were rich and I figured maybe I'd die of grief.

It was like my lame leg, though. Sloan's Liniment couldn't cure love, but *something* could; the original of Sloan's Liniment, I guess.

One day in the spring when the sun was shining and everything was warm in the world I found out I was healed. I was riding my bicycle through town. All of a sudden I saw Emma Haines sitting in a slick green Buick roadster with the biggest sissy in the world, Everett Rhodes.

It was a marvellous opportunity for me to put Emma Haines in her place, not loving a guy like me when I told her I loved her, going around with a sissy like Everett Rhodes. I caught up with them and made a very loud noise with my tongue and lips that people heard a block away, and then I rode on down the street, acrobatically, as it were.

I guessed I didn't need to take any lousy correspondence course on anything. My leg healed all right. The coldest winter since 1854 ended. And I got over Emma Haines.

I did some mighty ornamental riding, celebrating the great victories.

(from *The Coldest Winter Since* 1854 by William Saroyan)

266

APPRECIATION AND DISCUSSION

1. What emotive words does the author use to prejudice the reader against "the booklet from New York"?
2. Do you sympathise at all with the narrator's reaction to the ideas contained in the booklet, and with his own philosophy of life?
3. Why was this an unsuitable time for him to get a job as a messenger boy? Can you suggest why he might, nevertheless, have chosen to get a job at this time?
4. Why did he still go to school every morning, even though he was extremely tired?

5. What do you think of the reasons that Dewey, the narrator, gives for falling in love with Emma Haines? Was he trying to be funny or was he, in fact, genuinely attracted by these apparently trivial points? Was he really in love with Emma, or was it what she stood for that attracted him?

6. What sort of person was Mr. Bowler, the principal? Was he being sarcastic when he described Dewey's note as "one of the most touching love letters of our age"? Did he really punish Dewey?

7. "She's a rich man's daughter. You're a poor man's son. It won't work." Do you think that this is generally true? What do you consider are the things a boy and his girl-friend should have in common if their relationship is to be successful? What differences in background and personality are most difficult to overcome?

8. What caused Dewey to stop being in love with Emma Haines? How might somebody else have reacted to the incident that "cured" him of his love?

9. William Saroyan has described the way in which he writes as a "jump in the river and start to swim immediately" style. Can you explain this comment more fully, and apply it to "The coldest Winter Since 1854"? Are there any similarities between the style of this passage and that of "A Piece of Pie" by Damon Runyon?

10. A boy falling in love with a girl who is unattainable, being rebuffed, but still remaining in love with her until something happens to change his attitude, is a situation that can be written about in many different ways. It can, for example, be portrayed in a deeply personal, perhaps bitter way; or it can be treated in a quite superficial way, with a sentimental or even comic air. What sort of approach has William Saroyan used? How has he achieved his effect? Quote other examples of "love stories" that you have read and compare them with this story. Which sort of treatment do you prefer?

11. If you were in love, would you be prepared to reveal your feelings in an open, sincere way, either to the person with whom you were in love or to one of your close friends? Or would you talk about it in a casual, off-hand way? Or would you keep your feelings to yourself? Is there any difference between boys and girls in this respect? Why are some people reluctant to disclose their feelings?

12. When the subject of love is discussed, the following words and phrases are often used. What do you understand by them?

| calf love | infatuation | platonic love |
| a "crush" | physical attraction | a love-hate relationship |

The Picnic

It is the picnic with Ruth in the spring.
Ruth was third on my list of seven girls
But the first two were gone (Betty) or else
Had someone (Ellen has accepted Doug).
Indian Gully the last day of school;
Girls make the lunches for the boys too.
I wrote a note to Ruth in algebra class
Day before the test. She smiled, and nodded.
We left the cars and walked through the young corn
The shoots green as paint and the leaves like tongues
Trembling. Beyond the fence where we stood
Some wild strawberry flowered by an elm tree
And Jack-in-the-pulpit was olive ripe.
A blackbird fled as I crossed, and showed
A spot of gold or red under its quick wing.
I held the wire for Ruth and watched the whip
Of her long, striped skirt as she followed.
Three freckles blossomed on her thin, white back
Underneath the loop where the blouse buttoned.
We went for our lunch away from the rest,
Stretched in the new grass, our heads close
Over unknown things wrapped up in wax papers.
Ruth tried for the same, I forget what it was,
And our hands were together. She laughed,
And a breeze caught the edge of her little
Collar and the edge of her brown, loose hair
That touched my cheek. I turned my face into
The gentle fall. I saw how sweet it smelled.
She didn't move her head or take her hand.
I felt a soft caving in my stomach
As at the top of the highest slide
When I had been a child, but was not afraid,
And did not know why my eyes moved with wet
As I brushed her cheek with my lips and brushed
Her lips with my own lips. She said to me

Jack, Jack, different than I had ever heard,
Because she wasn't calling me, I think,
Or telling me. She used my name to
Talk in another way I wanted to know.
She laughed again and then she took her hand;
I gave her what we both had touched—can't
Remember what it was, and we ate the lunch.
Afterward we walked in the small, cool creek
Our shoes off, skirt hitched, and she smiling,
My pants rolled, and then we climbed up the high
Side of Indian Gully and looked
Where we had been, our hands together again.
It was then some bright thing came in my eyes,
Starting at the back of them and flowing
Suddenly through my head and down my arms
And stomach and my bare legs that seemed not
To stop in feet, not to feel the red earth
Of the Gully, as though we hung in a
Touch of birds. There was a word in my throat
With the feeling and I knew the first time
What it meant and I said, it's beautiful.
Yes, she said, and I felt the sound and word
In my hand join the sound and word in hers
As in one name said, or in one cupped hand.
We put back on our shoes and socks and we
Sat in the grass awhile, crosslegged, under
A blowing tree, not saying anything.
And Ruth played with shells she found in the creek,
As I watched. Her small wrist which was so sweet
To me turned by her breast and the shells dropped
Green, white, blue, easily into her lap,
Passing light through themselves. She gave the pale
Shells to me, and got up and touched her hips
With her light hands, and we walked down slowly
To play the school games with the others.

John Logan

DISCUSSING THE POEM

1. What were the names of the first two girls on Jack's list? Why did he no longer go out with them?
2. When did the picnic take place? Where was it held? When did Jack ask Ruth if she would go with him on the picnic?
3. Say how old you think these young people were, and describe Ruth as fully as possible.
4. Can you name, or describe in your own words, the emotions which Jack experienced, and which he described in the parts of the poem beginning:

    "I felt a soft caving in my stomach"

    and

    It was then some bright thing came in my eyes"?

    Have you ever felt like this and, if so, on what occasions?

5. " . . . she wasn't calling me, I think,
   Or telling me. She used my name to
   Talk in another way I wanted to know."
   What, do you think, was Ruth trying to say?
6. How does the poet suggest that Jack felt more mature in some way after the picnic with Ruth?
7. Relate in your own words the story of the picnic, and say how Ruth and Jack were affected.
8. Did you enjoy this poem or did you think it was "soppy"? Give reasons to support your answer.

TECHNIQUES

The Use of Language, and Style

1. *Logical Thinking.*

   Facts: Dewey is a poor man's son. Emma is a rich man's daughter.
   Question: Are they suitable for one another?

   Mr. Bowler said most emphatically that they were not suitable for one another—"It won't work". Solely on the basis of the information given above, however, a definite answer cannot be given to this question. What other facts would you want to know before you felt that you could give a conclusive reply?

   Which of the questions below can be answered conclusively on the basis of the facts given? Explain how you arrive at each of these conclusions. Where a definite answer cannot be given, explain why this is so, and say what additional information would be required.

   (a) *Facts:* Emma's brother was born in 1957. He is two years and one month older than Emma.
   Question: In what year was Emma born?

   (b) *Facts:* This is the coldest winter since 1854.
   Question: Has there ever been a colder winter?

   (c) *Facts:* To be a success you must study hard. This young man studies hard.
   Question: Will he be a success?

   (d) *Facts:* Mr. Bowler's brother-in-law is not married.
   Question: Is Mr. Bowler married?

272

(e) *Facts:* Mr. and Mrs. Haggerty have one son and one daughter. One of them is called Pat. Pat's brother-in-law, who has no brothers, is unmarried.

Question: Is Pat the son or the daughter?

2. *Figurative Language.* Can you explain how the following examples of figurative language, to be found in the passage and the poem, achieve their effect? Using these techniques, compose similar statements. There are starting points suggested in brackets, but you may ignore them if you wish.

(a) " ... when I tried to open my mouth I found out I had lock-jaw."
(When I tried to run away, I found ———.)

(b) " ... I didn't want to die, because I hadn't seen enough of the world. I hadn't talked to Emma Haines either."
(I don't want to die, because I haven't achieved any of my ambitions. I haven't ——— either.)

(c) "No general ever sank to defeat with such dignity and irritation."
(No-one else has ever written love letters that are so romantic and so ———.)

(d) "The shoots green as grass and the leaves like tongues trembling."
(Her eyes were as blue as ——— and her hair fell to her shoulders like ———.)

(e) "I held the wire for Ruth and watched the whip
Of her long, striped skirt"
(The wind whistled, ——— through the dark streets.)

3. *Sentence Structure.* William Saroyan's sentence structures provide interesting contrasts. Sometimes many statements are contained in one sentence, the statements being joined together very simply, often by "and" and "but". Consider, for example, the sentence that makes up the first paragraph. This cumulative style is also widely used in the Bible. Look up the word "cumulative" in your dictionary. Find a passage in the Bible where this technique is used.

In contract to this there is often a series of short, jerky sentences; e.g., "That was only six hours of sleep. I needed thirteen. I wouldn't want to get out of bed. It was too cold." Can you name any other books in which this abrupt style is used.?

Search through the passage and find other examples of long, cumulative sentences and short, abrupt sentences. Then say how you would alter them to make them into conventionally "well-constructed" sentences. What effect do these alterations have upon the tone of the passage? Do they improve it, or do they, in fact, destroy some of the story's quality?

4. *Direct Speech.* William Saroyan has not used quotation marks to enclose the direct speech which occurs in this story. Did you find this at all confusing? How would you punctuate and paragraph the direct speech to make it conform to the rules that you have been given? Each member of the class could take a short section and write it out with quotation marks inserted.

5. *Vocabulary.* Here is a word game to test your vocabulary. See if you can remember, and spell correctly, words beginning with WIN that fit the following clues.

e.g. This WIN is the fourth season=WINTER
This WIN is a reaction to pain.
This WIN is a device for hauling.
This WIN is an unexpected benefit.
This WIN is a machine for grinding.
This WIN is a hole for admitting light.
This WIN is a passage in the throat.
This WIN is a liquid made from grapes.
This WIN is the limb of a bird.
This WIN is a movement of the eyelid.
This WIN is the one who succeeds.

Here is another list to test your vocabulary.
This COL is a lack of heat.
This COL is a pain in the stomach.
This COL is a band worn round the neck.
This COL is a partner.
This COL is a place of education.
This COL is a dog.
This COL is a coal mine.
This COL is a striking together.
This COL is an expression used only in conversation.
This COL is a punctuation mark.
This COL is an officer.
This COL is a body of settlers.
This COL is an American State.
This COL is a young horse.
This COL is a cylindrical pillar.

TOPICS FOR WRITTEN WORK

1. Write an account of a time when you were in some way disappointed in love.

Hints

   Try writing this in the casual, off-hand style employed by both William Saroyan, in "The Coldest Winter Since 1854", and John Wilson, in "My Eighth Heaven". Do not be afraid of revealing how you felt at the time, but make your account light-hearted and flippant. Use colloquial expressions where they are appropriate, as Saroyan and John have done, e.g. "a dope,", "crummy", and techniques such as exaggeration and anti-climax to create a semi-comic effect.

2. Write a poem about a time when you were either very happy or very sad because you were in love with someone.

Hints

   In this piece of work, do *not* try to create an atmosphere of flippancy. Instead, attempt to capture honestly how you felt at the time, and express this in such a way that anyone reading your poem will be able to understand and share these feelings. You may change some details, such as the name of the person with whom you were in love, but be as accurate and as sincere as possible when describing important points. Notice how both John Logan and Robert Baker have included apparently insignificant details to make their poems very personal in nature and to enable a reader to imagine the situations very clearly.

3. Write a letter to a girl-friend (or boy-friend), explaining why you no longer wish to go out with her (or him).

Hints

   Your letter should make it quite clear why you wish to finish the relationship, but you should do this as tactfully as possible. Remember that the person receiving your letter may be hurt and surprised by it, particularly if he or she has done nothing to make you take such a step; (you may, for example, have met someone else, whom you find more attractive). Even if the person has made you feel bitter and jealous, do not let these emotions cause you to be vicious. Explain how you feel, perhaps criticise the way the person has behaved, but do not make spiteful and unnecessary comments. (Can you see any point in doing so?)

275

My Eighth Heaven or An Adolescent Paradise

It's surprising how many people walk along the street and never really see what's in front of them. It never registers, you know? But me, I never do that. I always try to analyse everything. I don't know why because everything seems basically the same these days. Take, for example, the time I was walking down Putney Hill. I suddenly got the idea that everything I could see was made up of little bits of the lives of thousands of people, all trying to scrape the money to keep their wives or what-have-you alive. "Mosaic of Life" you could call it, except it looked more like Death from where I was. Still I hadn't come to think about a load of cods like that. I'd come to meet a girl.

Of course, she was late, but when she did come . . . boy, I mean, it had been worth waiting. She was dressed up in this tartan thing, with a black belt and a white cardigan. But what really took me was the way she'd done her hair. It was all curled round in front with a fringe, so that it made almost a frame for her face. What could I say? I just couldn't get angry.

Anyway, it was time to get to Richmond to get to The Beat Club. You've seen it all on T.V. This was all the same. You know. A big auditorium. The walls smothered in coloured paper and pictures of gummy birds. A delving grey-yellow half-light. An earthquake of florid kids possessed by some devil making them writhe. The place stank of sweat. The row was something to run you nutty. A dull hum, someone plucking a rubber band and the guitars clashing and grating. I wanted to get out or, at least, just stand and wonder, but she was there all the time yelling at me to "get dancing". God! I felt like throwing up at her. If only I'd known she'd turn out like this.

But I stayed till they closed up. After a while that row just lost itself. Everything was lost except for her in front, swaying, curving like a wind-raked sapling. A sapling with dry-rot I thought later.

We went for some coffee after. Trust me to find the worst hovel in Richmond. The sort of place that has oak benches with curses and pin-cushion hearts scratched in under three coats of varnish, and crumby formica-topped tables. The girl serving looked real dim. Sort of cold crushing gloom instead of a face. You know what I mean? Anyway, as soon as she'd brought the coffee over, she played this French record on the juke box. She started jiving to it on her own. She couldn't move in those pink overalls. And you know what these French records are. Tenor sax belches, a bloke going "bum-de-bum-bum" off key in a real deep voice, and a lead "singer" getting fit to crack his larynx.

Needless to say, we cut out and how. We went to sit by the river instead. God it was cold. But to complete a lovely evening, it was low tide and we sat above a sewage outlet. By the time we found this out, tho', it was time to take her home. Boy, I did that quick, too. I don't think I ever lost affection for someone as quick as I lost it for her.

Also, she would have to live in a really crummy area. Her house hadn't even got a porch to it, so when we kissed goodbye, every creep in the road saw. Not that it really mattered; it was more like an animated lie than a kiss. I never wanted to see her again. That was the best New-Year's Eve ever! I mean!

John Wilson

Guts

She lived just opposite me.
  At eight o'clock she goes to school
And I, late as I may be,
  Watch her from my bedroom window.
At night I lie awake,
  Trying to get up enough courage,
Like a recharging battery,
  To ask her out.
My friends laugh at me.
  And I laugh with them,
As again my courage fails me.
  (How many people have to laugh at themselves?)
On other occasions
I blame my parents for spoiling me,
  When again my courage fails me
But I know really I haven't enough guts,
The next time, I tell myself, I shall stand up to my doubts,
  And laugh at them genuinely.
That is unless my courage doesn't desert me again.

Robert Baker

ORAL WORK

1. Discuss the point of view that young people today spend too much of their time and energy earning money while they are still at school, that the amounts they earn are too large and that, in any case, the money is usually wasted.

   For this discussion to be balanced, you must make an honest attempt to see the situation from the point of view of an adult who, when young, had little pocket money, and could earn only low wages when he first went to work full-time, let alone earn good money from a part-time job. What is he likely to feel about the younger generation today? Would he have good reasons for his views?

2. Discuss the following statement.

Boys and girls who attend mixed schools, where they are not segregated, are usually much more mature and relaxed in their attitude to one another than are boys and girls who attend single-sex schools.

3. Practise reading aloud both the passage and the poem. How should they be read in order to bring out their different tones?

ACTIVITIES AND RESEARCH

1. An interested group could make a survey of pocket money, part-time jobs and money earned, the way in which this is spent, and the number of young people still at school who have regular girl-friends or boy-friends. The survey could be carried out on your own class, the whole school, or possibly two or more schools. The table of figures on this page might suggest some basic questions. It is important to plan questions in such a way that the answers can be quickly analysed and turned into percentages. It will be more interesting, of course, if the same series of questions can be answered by different groups—girls as opposed to boys, sixth formers as opposed to first formers, and so on.

	Age	Average earned income	Average total income	% of pupils contributing to clothes or keep	% of pupils with a regular boy-friend or girl-friend	Average amount of money spent on a hobby	Average amount of money spent on or with girl/boy friend
BOYS	12	12½p	30p	2%	15%	—	—
	14	40p	75p	6%	30%	—	—
	16	80p	£1·25	25%	55%	—	—
	18	£1·35	£2·00	55%	72%	—	—
GIRLS	12	12½p	30p	0%	25%	—	—
	14	25p	65p	6%	50%	—	—
	16	75p	£1·00	25%	70%	—	—
	18	95p	£1·50	60%	80%	—	—

278

2. Given below are the names of twelve well-known pairs of lovers, but the names are not paired off correctly. Match them up and then find out all you can about each pair—what they were, whether they were real or fictitious characters, when they existed, and so on.

Anthony	Guinivere
Dante	Juliet
Orpheus	Josephine
Lord Nelson	Helen
Lancelot	Iseult
Tristram	Cleopatra
Romeo	Beatrix
Leander	Lady Hamilton
Paris	Penelope
Napoleon	Cressida
Ulysses	Hero
Troilus	Eurydice.

FURTHER READING

The Coldest Winter Since 1854 by William Saroyan (Faber).

The above short story is a typical example of this Californian author's work. His ability to use what he calls the "jump in the river start to swim immediately" style of writing give his stories a quite distinctive flavour. They deal with all sorts of people, ranging from Armenian-American workers to middle class business men, and include all sorts of whimsical and sentimental incidents. The stories themselves are too numerous, and the volumes in which they appear, too wide in range, to allow separate details to be given; but if you enjoyed *The Coldest Winter* try:

The Daring Young Man on the Flying Trapeze
My Name is Aram
The Whole Voyald
Little Children
Laughing Matter
The Adventures of Wesley Jackson

There is also a representative collection of his stories entitled *Best Stories* (Faber).

INDEX